John Henry Overton

The Evangelical Revival in the Eighteenth Century

John Henry Overton

The Evangelical Revival in the Eighteenth Century

ISBN/EAN: 9783744660518

Printed in Europe, USA, Canada, Australia, Japan

Cover: Foto ©Lupo / pixelio.de

More available books at **www.hansebooks.com**

THE

EVANGELICAL REVIVAL

IN THE

EIGHTEENTH CENTURY

BY

JOHN HENRY OVERTON, D.D.

CANON OF LINCOLN

NEW IMPRESSION

LONGMANS, GREEN, AND CO.

39 PATERNOSTER ROW, LONDON

NEW YORK AND BOMBAY

1900

PREFACE.

THE object of the following sketch is to give a general idea of a most important movement in the English Church in the last century. Those who desire to fill up its details, and to trace its connexion with the general history of the Church and Nation, may be referred to Canon Perry's 'History of the Church of England,' to Dr. Stoughton's 'Ecclesiastical History of England,' to Mr. W. E. H. Lecky's 'History of England in the Eighteenth Century,' to Mr. Leslie Stephen's 'History of English Thought in the Eighteenth Century,' to Abbey and Overton's 'English Church in the Eighteenth Century,' to Sir James Stephen's 'Essays on Ecclesiastical Biography,' to Bishop Ryle's 'Christian Leaders in the Last Century,' and to the many lives of, and essays about, John Wesley, which it would be impossible to enumerate, and invidious to select from, in this short Preface. While the present writer gratefully acknowledges his obligations to these works, and to others written in the nineteenth century, he must add that he has studied much more carefully those written in the eighteenth century, especially the works of the Revivalists themselves; from these he has endeavoured to form an independent judgment. While he has not shrunk from dealing fearlessly with burning questions, he trusts that he has not been guilty of any conscious unfairness, or of any breach of Christian charity.

J. H. O.

EPWORTH RECTORY:
Festival of SS. Philip and James, 1886.

CONTENTS.

CHAPTER I.

INTRODUCTION.

CHAPTER II.

JOHN WESLEY.

CHAPTER III.

GEORGE WHITEFIELD AND OTHERS.

CHAPTER IV.

METHODISM AND EVANGELICALISM.

CHAPTER V.

THE EVANGELICAL CLERGY.

CHAPTER VI.

THE EVANGELICAL LAITY.

CHAPTER VII.

LITERATURE OF THE REVIVAL.

CHAPTER VIII.

RESULTS OF THE REVIVAL.

CHAPTER IX.

OPPOSITION TO THE REVIVAL.

CHAPTER X.

THE DOCTRINES OF THE REVIVAL.

CHAPTER XI.

THE EVANGELICAL REVIVAL COMPARED WITH OTHER MOVEMENTS.

THE EVANGELICAL REVIVAL

IN THE

EIGHTEENTH CENTURY.

——◆◆◆——

CHAPTER I.

INTRODUCTION.

THE religious apathy which set in with the accession of the Hanoverian dynasty in England is one of the most

1700–1714. remarkable phenomena in the history of reli-
a period of religious activity gion. It is a popular but grievous error to suppose that the *whole* of the eighteenth century was, from a religious point of view, a period of inertness apart from the Evangelical Revival. On the contrary, it would be difficult to find a period of greater activity than the first fourteen years of that century. And it is peculiarly ungrateful of us to ignore that activity, because we are reaping the benefits of it up to the present day. Then it was that our two oldest Church societies for spreading Christian knowledge at home and abroad were floated. It is true that the earlier society was founded before the seventeenth century closed, but it was not till the eighteenth century

C. H. B

that it began to make its influence generally felt. Then
it was that the first scheme on any great scale for pro-
viding a religious education for the poor was established
in the shape of the charity schools. Then it was that a
real effort was made for relieving the crying poverty of
the great mass of the clergy through the influence
brought to bear upon the bountiful Queen Anne. Then
it was that the largest and most English, and, we may
now add, one of the most practically useful, of our
national temples—St. Paul's, London—was completed.
Then it was that a scheme was projected for keeping
pace with the growing wants of the metropolis in the
provision of means of grace; and in the time of which
we are speaking as much progress was made in the
carrying out of that scheme as could reasonably be
expected. Then church bells rang for divine service
almost as frequently as they do in our own active day.
Then the religious societies for young men, and the
societies for the reformation of manners (a more questionable scheme), which were founded in the preceding
century, were most flourishing. Then the Church had
so strong a hold upon the people that her bitterest foes
were obliged to veil their real meaning, or to adopt an
apologetic tone and profess that they were writing in her
interests, in order to obtain a hearing at all.

But with the advent of the first George all these
symptoms of activity gradually began to droop, and in a
short time faded quite away; and it was not till more
Apathy set
in with the
Georgian era   than another century had elapsed that they re-
appeared in a similar form. Detailed proofs
of this relapse are easily forthcoming. Though the
Society for Promoting Christian Knowledge certainly

remained alive during the Georgian era, it as certainly
did not keep up the promise of growth and expansion
which it gave in the reign of Queen Anne. The same
may be said of its earliest offshoot, the Society for the
Propagation of the Gospel in Foreign Parts. A glaring
proof of the stagnation of the latter society may be
found in the fact that it at once let slip the project,
which, before the death of the queen, was all but accomplished, of establishing a colonial episcopate—surely an
essential feature of any missionary effort which was
professedly conducted on the lines of the Church of
England. The charity schools became suspected of
political propagandism, and fell into bad odour. No
such munificent gift to the clergy as that of Queen
Anne's Bounty was repeated. The scheme for building
fifty-two new churches in London and the suburbs was
quietly allowed to drop, after only twelve had been
built and a few more repaired. The number of church
services grew small by degrees and beautifully less. A
most painful contrast will be found between a published
record of the services held in London in 1714,[1] and
another published in 1824;[2] and a similar falling off
would have been discovered in the country at large, if
statistics had been · taken. The religious societies
lingered on long enough to give a sort of framework to
the societies of the Methodists, and then died a natural
death; the societies for the reformation of manners
died out with them. The Church continued to be a
name to conjure with, but her whole tone was per-
ceptibly lowered; and other religious bodies shared the
same plight.

[1] Paterson's *Pietas Londinensis*.　[2] *London Parishes, &c.*, 1824.

It is not difficult to trace the causes of this collapse. The seeds had been sown in the preceding period.

Causes of the collapse The morbid dread of falling either into the Scylla of Romanism on the one hand or the Charybdis of Puritanism on the other, tended to make men value unduly the virtues of caution and quiet. The reaction against the reign of the Saints had by no means spent its force; while Romanism was still a present danger, with a Romish king over the water ready to take possession of England at the first favourable opportunity. Sometimes these two utterly opposite causes of alarm oddly enough combined to raise a prejudice against the same man or cause. John Wesley was at least as often charged with encouraging Romanism as with encouraging Puritanism. To avoid danger on either side a somewhat colourless style of teaching, after the Tillotsonian type, became fashionable. What is intended to offend nobody is apt also to affect nobody. In studying to maintain 'moderation' and avoid 'enthusiasm,' the prevailing theology lost much of its vivifying power; preaching too much degenerated into the mere moral essay. Men's spiritual consciousness could hardly be awakened by discourses, however sound, on 'the reasonableness of Christianity.'

The political situation greatly tended, in more ways than one, to paralyse the spiritual life. In the first Political situation place, the contrast between Queen Anne and the two first Georges in relation to religious matters was very marked. The queen may not have been a strong-minded woman, nor a high type of Christian, but all her public influence was thrown into the scale of religious earnestness, while that of her two cynical successors was certainly thrown into the opposite scale. Then again, the vast majority of the clergy submitted with a very bad grace to the new *régime*. Many of them had to eat their own words, or to explain them away in a non-natural sense, which was demoralising to their characters and detrimental to their influence. The bishops, on the other hand, were, almost to a man, Whigs. The Bangorian controversy, culminating in the suspension of Convocation, was a type of the differences which existed everywhere between the mass of the Church and her appointed rulers. Such conditions of antagonism between the rulers and the ruled are obviously not conducive to the success of religious effort. The bishops carried the day. Hoadly's biographer exultingly records that the bishop lived long enough to see all the opposition which had been raised against him die out. He did, but it was by no means to the advantage of the Church or of religious life generally. How can a work go on without any definite system? How can an institution prosper without any common ground on which to meet? and now that Convocation entirely ceased to meet, where was the common ground?

But it really is not too much to say that the influence of one man contributed more than all the other causes combined to the religious apathy of the early Georgian era. That man was, of course, the all-powerful minister Sir Robert Walpole. His policy from the beginning to the end of his career was, systematically and avowedly, to put a stop to all religious activity. His conduct in the matter of the missionary enterprise of one of the greatest and best

Sir Robert Walpole

men of the age, Dean (afterwards Bishop) Berkeley, is
only a specimen of his general method of dealing with
Church questions. That good man was allowed to sacrifice all his worldly prospects to the cause of Christian
missions with the distinct promise of public support,
was put off, tampered with, and at last completely let
down. At the same time, Sir Robert Walpole's peace
policy, tending as it did to the increase of material
prosperity, and consequently to the increase of large
centres of industry, rendered Church activity all the
more necessary, in order to overtake the masses of the
people who had quite outgrown the old parochial
machinery.

Another cause must be noted, which brought out
both the strength and the weakness of the Christianity
Preva'ence of the period, viz. the prevalence of religious
of contro-
versy   controversy on the most fundamental points.
A great part of the energy of preachers, writers, and
workers generally, was expended upon the defence of
revealed truth, and was consequently diverted from
questions of directly practical import. But this energy
was not wasted. Never were the Christian champions
more active and more successful than they were at this
time ; they measured swords with opponents from all
quarters and were triumphant over all. This was owing
partly to the inherent strength of their case, partly to
their own intellectual superiority. The strength of their
case, as against Arians, Socinians, and Deists, was that
all these really endeavoured to stand upon a descending
scale. Having gone so far out of the road of orthodoxy,
they were bound logically to go farther. This was pressed
home upon them with irresistible force by their antago-

nists, and gave the latter the advantage, even when in intellectual power there was not much to choose between the combatants. Thus, in intellectual power, Samuel Clarke and Daniel Waterland were perhaps pretty fairly matched; but Waterland was victor all along the line, because Clarke's position of semi-Arianism was in itself untenable. But in other cases the champions were absurdly unequal. If one compares the works, e.g. of Toland, Tindal, Collins and Chubb, with those of Butler, Berkeley, Law, and Warburton, the intellectual inequality becomes at once apparent. 'They (the Deists) are,' writes Mr. Leslie Stephen, 'but a ragged regiment, whose whole ammunition of learning was a trifle when compared with the abundant stores of a single light of orthodoxy; whilst in speculative ability they were children by the side of some of their antagonists.' The result was that Christianity in England at the commencement of the Revival was in this strange position. It had been irrefragably proved, as against its then opponents; it was established speculatively on the firmest of firm bases; but speculation was not carried into practice. The doctrine was accepted, but the life was not lived. Such a state of things could not last; if the actual promoters of a revival had not existed, others must have arisen.

Thus the train was laid, and it only required a spark to kindle the fire. That spark was, oddly enough, thrown out by one who had no sympathy with the course which the fire took when it was lighted. It is not surprising that there should have been some reluctance in owning the share which William Law took in originating the Evangelical Revival. For in the two

Law's 'Serious Call'

practical treatises which, alone of his writings, were
directly concerned with the Revival, there is little of
what is popularly understood by Evangelical teaching;
while, in his controversial works, and still more in his
later mystical works, he is quite at variance with that
teaching.   Nevertheless, the connexion of Law with the
movement is undoubted. The testimony of the eighteenth
century is clear upon the point.   Dr. Coke, who was
Wesley's right hand man, after describing the deplorable
state of religion when Wesley's societies were formed,
adds: 'The great Mr. Law was an exception indeed. . . .
Though a non-juror, and deprived on that account of the
exercise of his public ministry, he enforced by his excellent pen that essential doctrine of the Gospel, the
necessity of the inspiration of the Holy Ghost. . . .
This considerable writer was the great fore-runner of the
Revival which followed, and did more to promote it than
any other individual whatsoever ; yea, more perhaps than
the rest of the nation collectively taken.'   John Wesley
himself owns as much ; and he and his brother Charles,
George Whitefield, Thomas Scott, Henry Venn, John
Newton, Thomas Adam, and many other Evangelical
leaders all express their personal obligations to Law.   In
one respect, indeed, Law is rather a connecting link
between the Caroline divines and the Oxford school of
Pusey and Newman.   In another he is a connecting
link between the evidence writers who unconsciously
prepared the way for the Revival, and the Revivalists
themselves.   In intellectual power, he will bear comparison with Butler and Waterland; in devotedness of
life, with Wesley and Whitefield.   His direct connexion
with the Revival was briefly this:—the truths of Chris-

tianity being proved triumphantly against all the assailants of that day, what was most needed was an appeal which would stir men's hearts and set them aglow. The 'Christian Perfection' and the 'Serious Call' were such appeals, and they had the desired effect. But here Law's connexion with the movement ends; he stood quite aloof from its course; and in later times it was not the Evangelicals, but the old-fashioned, pious, High-Churchmen (of whom there were always many specimens) who took the 'Serious Call' as their devotional manual. Hence Law's place belongs simply to this introductory chapter; he was rather the precursor than actor in the Revival, and so we may pass on to consider who were the real actors therein.

CHAPTER II.

JOHN WESLEY.

JOHN WESLEY was by far the most conspicuous character connected with the Revival, and requires and deserves a chapter to himself. No adequate idea can be conceived of John Wesley without taking into full account his early training. The spot on which these lines are written influenced his character and career far more than either Charterhouse or Christ Church did. Born at Epworth in 1703, he received his early training almost exclusively from his mother, whose influence over him extended to the last hour of her life. It was at Epworth that he first learnt to undervalue the parochial system; for he saw there a

Epworth rectory

good-parish priest labouring for nearly forty years and reaping apparently very little fruit from his labours; and, on the other hand, it was at Epworth that he imbibed that deep attachment to the Church of England which he néver lost, for his father and mother were Church-people to the backbone. It was at Epworth that he was first impressed with that strong conviction of the special intervention of a particular Providence in the commonest events of life which is brought out so markedly in his journal; for his providential rescue, as a brand snatched from the burning, in the famous fire at Epworth rectory in 1709, left an indelible impression upon his mind. It was at Epworth that that vein of credulity and superstition which certainly tinged his character to the day of his death was first formed: 'Old Jeffrey,' the famous Epworth ghost, in the supernatural character of whom he never ceased to believe, had a considerable share in moulding some of the phases, both of Methodism and its founder. It was at Epworth that he formed, from his mother's example and teaching, those habits of order and discipline which rendered the name of 'Methodist' so singularly appropriate to him. It was at Epworth, with the sight of a highly educated father, mother, and elder brother before him, that he learned to appreciate the advantages of education; and so never joined in that silly depreciation of 'human learning' which exasperates sensible men in the writings of some who were connected with the Revival.

There is a singular absence of any traces of the influence which either his school days at Charterhouse or his undergraduate days at Christ Church left upon him.

It was not till he became Fellow of Lincoln that Oxford began to make its real impress upon him. But Lincoln College, Oxford the period which he spent as resident Fellow was a marked epoch in his life. For some time he was 'moderator of the classes' which were held every day in the college hall 'for exercises and disputations;' and his work in this office developed that logical acumen which stood him in stead on many occasions in his unwilling disputes with adversaries from various quarters. His position as a college don was an excellent training for that almost royal attitude which he maintained to the end among his 'helpers' and followers. And the atmosphere of Oxford generally tended to give him larger views of life than one ✓ who had passed less time at that noble university, with its time-honoured traditions and its roll of great men in all departments, could probably have held.

His residence at Oxford had been interrupted for two years, during which he acted as his father's curate Oxford Methodism at Epworth and Wroot. It was during that interval that the nucleus of Methodism was formed. On his return to Oxford he found a little society formed under the auspices of his younger brother, Charles (then a student of Christ Church), for the purpose of the mutual improvement, both in mind and soul, of its members. The little band at once placed themselves under the direction of John, who, from his age and high character for learning and piety, was their natural leader. There seems to have been absolutely nothing remarkable to our views in the conduct of this little band. They simply strove to live holier lives and obey more strictly the rules of the Church of their baptism, than was usual in those lax days. And nothing shows more clearly the need there was of some spiritual movement than the way in which they were treated. It seems difficult to realise the fact that, in a place especially devoted to Christian education, the mere sight of a few young men going quietly to receive the Holy Communion every Sunday at St. Mary's, their own university church, should have attracted a crowd of ridiculing spectators ; or that the effort to observe strictly the plain rules of the Church should have branded them with what were intended to be opprobrious nicknames, but which were in reality most honourable titles—the Holy Club, the Godly Club, the Reformers, the Sacramentarians, and, finally, the Methodists. To read the classics and the Greek Testament together, to visit the poor in the city and the prisoners in the gaol, to fast when the Church plainly told them to fast, and to attend diligently to all the appointed means of grace, —this was thought eccentric in a little body of men, the leader of whom was an ordained clergyman, and all of whom were intending to take holy orders ! How far Mr. Law was their spiritual director it is difficult to ascertain ; but there is no doubt that of all living writers he was the one who attracted John Wesley most, and that his personal influence over the two brothers was very con-siderable. They used to make pilgrimages on foot (to save the money for the poor) to Putney, where Mr. Law then resided, to ask his counsel. 'It is true,' wrote John Wesley in his journal, 'that Mr. Law, whom I love and reverence now (1760), was once a kind of oracle to me.'

The oracle was consulted when John was invited

by the benevolent General Oglethorpe to accompany him to Georgia, partly as a parochial clergyman to the new English colony there, and partly as a mis-

Georgia

sionary to the Indians. This was immediately after the death of the elder Mr. Wesley, and when the oldest brother, Samuel, was obviously failing. The noble self-sacrifice of the widowed mother, who not only consented, but urged her two sons, John and Charles, to set forth, is very characteristic. 'Had I twenty sons I should rejoice that they were all so employed though I should never see them more.'

The experience of John Wesley in Georgia, disastrous though it was, was a most important factor in

Important factor in his career

moulding his future career. It first brought him into contact with the Moravians—in itself a crucial event. But this was not all. The failure of the attempt was probably, to a very great extent, responsible for the irregularities with which he was subsequently charged. Hot from the influence of William Law, John Wesley attempted to carry out to the very letter all the rules of the Church in an infant colony, the very last place in the world which was likely to submit to such rigour. He insisted upon baptizing by immersion, and would admit none but communicants as sponsors. He refused the Holy Communion to Dissenters unless they would consent to be rebaptized; he would not read the burial service over Dissenters; and finally, as a climax, he repelled from the Holy Table the wife of one of the principal men in the colony, who had before this all but become the wife of Wesley himself, and when remonstrated with he assumed a statuesque attitude and replied in language which Law himself might have used : 'When Mrs. Williamson openly declares herself to have repented I will administer to her the mysteries of God.' In short he attempted, not only to present the full system of the Church but to enforce its discipline, and that even in doubtful points, among a people who were totally unfit to receive it. They could not understand what he was aiming at. 'They say,' he was told, 'they are Protestants, but as for you they cannot tell what religion you are of; they never heard of such a religion before.' They were not very well acquainted with Church history, otherwise they would have certainly 'heard of such a religion before.' They would have heard of its having flourished in their own mother-country only a generation before their own time, for it was assuredly the religion of all the great Caroline divines. But we may admit that Wesley attempted to draw the reins too tight, and we may also fairly presume that his painful experience in Georgia as a parochial clergyman (the missionary work was hardly attempted) may have combined with his experience of Epworth to make him hold so cheaply as he did the value of parochial work.

There is no trace of pique in Wesley's account of the dismal failure of his experiment; he was not well treated, but he lays all the blame on himself. 'I went to America,' he says, 'to convert the Indians, but I was not converted myself.' It is a relief to find that in his old age he added a note: 'I am not sure of this;' and that instead of maintaining the sweeping assertion that in these early days he was utterly devoid of faith, he distinguished between the faith of a servant and the faith of a son, owning that he had the former but not the latter, until the memorable day now to be described.

On his voyage both ways, and after his return home, Wesley fell under the influence of the Moravians, especially of a very remarkable man, Peter Böhler. It was at one of their meetings that his 'conversion' was completed. 'In the evening [of May 24, 1738] I went very unwillingly to a society in Aldersgate Street, where one was reading Luther's Preface to the Epistle to the Romans. ⊦About a quarter before nine, while he was describing the change which God works in the heart through faith in Christ, I felt my heart strangely warmed. I felt I did trust in Christ, Christ alone, for salvation, and an assurance was given me " that He had taken away my sins, even mine, and saved me from the law of sin and death."' It was quite right that he should be thankful for the blessing, but there was no need for him to turn upon his old teacher and upbraid him for not having given him the light. However, Law was well able to take care of himself; in intellectual power he was more than a match for far stronger antagonists than John Wesley. Those who read the correspondence now will not be at a loss to decide who had the worst of it. But it is a credit to Wesley that though he must have had sense enough to see that he had been completely overmastered in argument, he never ceased to regard Law with the utmost reverence and love, and bore frequent and warm testimony to the extraordinary power and usefulness of his old mentor's practical writings, and the loftiness of his Christian character. This fact is too often forgotten by those who lay great stress upon the influence which the

(margin note: Moravian influence — Conversion)

Moravians exercised over Wesley, nor do they seem duly to weigh the fact that Wesley afterwards differed from the Moravians at least as widely as he did from Law.

But Wesley was now launched upon a course in which he was quite out of sympathy with Law's views and tastes. He commenced that career of exhaustless labour which he continued for more than half a century. It is not as the founder of a sect (which he never desired to be), but simply as a reformer that he must come before us in these pages, and that only in general outline, not in details. That his designs from beginning to end were purely unselfish, must surely be manifest to all unprejudiced persons who will study him in that wonderfully life-like portrait of himself which he has given us in his own Journal, instead of being content to look at him through the spectacles of others. If ever a man poured forth the whole secrets of his soul, surely Wesley did in his Journal. It is, on the face of it, a real, not a conventional, account of his thoughts and doings, and deserves to be studied at first-hand.

The Journal

But apart from this the known facts of his life utterly fail to bear out some of the charges which have been laid against him. It has been said that he was an ambitious, self-seeking man; self-willed, fond of power, brooking no contradiction, inclined to be quarrelsome. His ablest biographer, Dr. Southey, has given the weight of his great name to some of these charges. But let us see how the facts stand. Now it is a remarkable fact that of scarcely any of the plans and designs which are specially con-

Purity of Wesley's motives

nected with John Wesley's name was John Wesley
himself the originator. They were either suggested by
others or were actually set about against his will, and
carried on because he submitted his own judgment to
that of others. We have seen that the first nucleus of
Methodism at Oxford was formed, not by John, but by
Charles Wesley, and that John merely took up what his
younger brother had started. His societies were simply
a carrying on of the idea of the religious societies
which had been established more than half-a-century
before. Field-preaching, which was the very backbone
of Methodism, was not only not begun by John Wesley,
but was regarded by him with great repugnance; a
repugnance which he had the greatest difficulty in over-
coming, and, in fact, never altogether overcame. The
employment of lay-preachers was equally offensive to
him, and his dislike was only overruled by the advice
of one whose counsels he never neglected—his mother.
The class-meetings were not his idea, but the idea of an
unknown follower at Bristol, who suggested the plan
simply to meet a temporary financial exigency. So far
was Wesley from being obstinately wedded to his own
opinions that he laid himself fairly open to the charge
of inconsistency by so frequently modifying them. And,
finally, he was overpersuaded by others to do that which
a Churchman must ever hold to be one of the greatest
errors of his life, when he usurped, in utter defiance of
his obligations as a clergyman, the office of a bishop—
that is, if he really *did* mean to take upon himself the
office of a bishop, but, after all, that is rather doubtful.
He set apart Dr. Coke to be 'a superintendent,' but is
that quite the same thing as 'consecrating' him to be 'a

'bishop'? It is one of those questions in which the meaning of words should be carefully weighed. This, at any rate, is certain—that Wesley, by reading two very inadequate authorities, viz. Stillingfleet's juvenile work, the 'Irenicon,' which that great man in his maturer years recanted, and Mr. (afterwards Lord Chancellor) King's juvenile work on the constitution of the Christian Church, which *he* also virtually recanted in his later years, was convinced that bishops and priests were but one order; in other words, he did not raise himself to the bishop's level, but reduced the bishop to his own level.

That he should adopt a lordly tone with his 'helpers' was an inevitable result of their relative positions; moreover, the tone was, one may almost say,
His defects
hereditary in all the Wesley family; there is an abruptness, a peremptoriness, in their correspondence one with another which might sometimes almost pass for rudeness did we not know the affectionate relations which subsisted between them. At the same time it is admitted that some of Wesley's utterances were very exasperating, and that they naturally tended to widen the breaches which existed between him and many with whom in the main he agreed, as well as those who disagreed both with his principles and his practices. There is often too contemptuous a tone in his correspondence with Whitefield, and the sneering way in which he sometimes alluded to 'the genteel Methodists' was not becoming; nor can he be at all justified in the open defiance which, in the earlier period of the Revival, he showed to the rulers of the Church to whom, as an ordained clergyman, he had solemnly promised canonical

obedience. His sole quarrel, he said, was with sin and Satan, but it is not surprising that his deeds and words often provoked others to quarrel with him. A weakness, too, which was near akin to a virtue, often led him into error. His constant recourse to the foolish and objectionable practice of the ' Sortes Biblicæ ' frequently misled him. His brother Charles thought ' bodily symptoms no sign of grace,' and Whitefield considered· them as ' doubtful indications, and not to be encouraged ; ' but John Wesley undoubtedly encouraged them, and thus led to many wild extravagances which he was the first to deplore. In short, that which, viewed from its strong side may be called guilelessness, from its weak side credulousness, was a dangerous quality for a man in his position to possess. May we not see symptoms of this same guilelessness or credulousness, call it which we will, in his fond belief that his followers would adhere to the Church ? That his wish for them to do so was sincere is unquestionable. He had a positive dislike to Dissenters,[1] and an ever-increasing love for the Church, its services, its ritual, its ministers, and its doctrines. But if we did not take into account his extreme simplicity (in more than one sense of the term) we could hardly believe it possible that he could seriously suppose that his followers shared that love. They went to church because he insisted upon their doing so, and his will was law ; but their heart was with their own societies.

---

[1] So late as 1780 he writes in his Journal: 'Trowbridge. As most of the hearers were Dissenters I did not expect to do much good.' In 1777 : ' Peel-town, Isle of Man. A more loving, simple-hearted people than this I never saw ; and no wonder, for they have but six Papists, *and no Dissenters*, in the island.'

John Berridge saw that they would drift away, so did
Charles Wesley, but John Wesley did not. It is but
bare justice to the many with whom John Wesley was
brought into collision to admit all this. Surely it could
hardly be expected that the clergy would regard with
a favourable eye one who, without in the least intending
to do so, was really leading their flocks away from them.
From no quarter do we hear more complaints of this
than from the Evangelical clergy; and surely, from their
point of view, the complaint was not unreasonable.
But Wesley's faults were all errors of judgment, not of
heart; his was a fine, noble, Christian character, and
his very errors were akin to virtues.

And now we may turn to the more pleasing task of
tracing out his self-denying labours. The first point
His self-   that strikes us is his extraordinary activity.
denying
labours   It is said in the Preface to his Journal with
perfect truth that ' he published more books, travelled
more miles, and preached more sermons, than any
minister of his age.' It is perfectly bewildering to
follow the course of his travels. The whole length and
breadth of England were traversed by him over and over
again; he made frequent journeys into Scotland and
Ireland; and at every town and village where he stayed
he was ready, in season and out of season, to preach
the everlasting Gospel. This went on for more than
half-a-century, and the mere physical labour must have
been enormous. Only a constitution of iron, a temperament of extraordinary buoyancy, and at the same
time one which was never ruffled, a strict abstemious-
ness of life, and, above all, an intense belief in an over-
ruling Providence to which he might always commit

himself, could have enabled him to endure it. He was perfectly fearless of danger, and would face an angry mob with the calm courage of a hero, or rather of a martyr. The readers of a short sketch like the present will hardly expect to find here an account of his work in detail; it must suffice to give a general outline.

John Wesley himself dates the beginning of the Revival, of which he was the heart and soul, from the Date of Revival, 1738 spring of 1738.[1] 'Then,' he says, 'it pleased God to kindle a fire which I trust shall never be extinguished.' The human instrument, he declares, was Peter Böhler. 'Oh! what a work hath God wrought since his coming to England! Such an one as shall never come to an end till heaven and earth shall pass away.' He also credits Peter Böhler with the particular form which Methodism took. 'On May 1, 1738, our little society at Fetter-lane began. Our rules in obedience to God and by the advice of Peter Böhler were——' and then he proceeds to specify them. There is nothing in this inconsistent with the fact that Wesley's societies were intended to be a continuation or reproduction of the religious societies of 1678, whose Church tone was most strongly marked. As a matter of fact it may be perfectly true that 'the religious societies supplied a body to Methodism, the Moravians a soul;' but it is evident that to Wesley's mind no idea of this sharp-drawn distinction occurred. Moravian influence touched him deeply at the beginning

[1] But in another passage he makes 1729 the date of the commencement of the Revival. There is no discrepancy between the two statements—1729 would be the date of the commencement of Methodism in any form, 1738 of the permanent form which it took.

of his career as a reformer; and, if it had continued, it must have materially affected his Church principles. But, while it lasted, it did not do so; indeed, the time when Moravian influence was most fresh and strong upon him was the very time when he was endeavouring to carry out his Church principles most rigorously.

And now began that course of itinerancy which produced such startling and wide-spread effects. Field-preaching became a necessity, and, having been begun first by Whitefield, was adopted most reluctantly by Wesley. On March 31, 1739, he records: 'I reached Bristol and met Mr. Whitefield. I could scarce reconcile myself at first to this strange way of preaching in the fields, of which he set me an example on Sunday; having been all my life (till very lately) so tenacious of every point relating to decency and order that I should have thought the saving of souls almost a sin if it had not been done in a church.' And on the following day: 'At four in the afternoon I submitted to be more vile, and proclaimed in the high-ways the glad tidings of salvation, speaking from a little eminence in a ground adjoining to the city to about three thousand people.' The reformers were breaking no law of the Church by out-door preaching; and it is hard to see how the masses could have been reached without it. For, supposing all the churches had been thrown open to them, it would have been im-possible to crowd into them a tithe of the seething multi-tude, and probably not a tithe of that tithe would ever have been persuaded to enter the doors. But, as a rule, the churches were closed to the new preachers; and much as we may regret the fact, it is hardly fair to

Field-preaching

blame the clergy indiscriminately for refusing to admit them. For the reproach implies that every ordained clergyman has a perfect right to preach in whatever church he pleases. Of course this is not the case, and it would be very undesirable if it were so. If a perfect stranger were to come and ask a clergyman for the use of his pulpit, that clergyman would be more than justified in refusing him; and the case would be still stronger if he had heard nothing of the stranger but to his disparagement. Now it is probable that the clergy who refused their pulpits had either no knowledge of Wesley at all, or had heard of him as a man full of irregularities and extravagances. They did not know, as we do, what he really was. So far from being persecuted at the beginning of his career as a reformer by the dignitaries of the Church, Wesley was treated by them with the utmost courtesy and forbearance. Let us hear the two brothers' own account of their reception by the Primate (Potter) in 1738. 'He showed us,' writes Charles, 'great affection, and cautioned us to give no more umbrage than was necessary for our own defence, to forbear exceptionable phrases, and to keep to the doctrines of the Church.' John calls him 'a great and good man,' and then tells us the advice he gave him: 'If you desire to be extensively useful, do not spend your time and strength in contending for or against things of a disputable nature, but in testifying against open, notorious vice, and in promoting real, essential holiness.' This was the motto of all John Wesley's future career. The Bishop of London (Gibson) 'warned them against Antinomianism and dismissed them kindly;' and as for the Bishop of Gloucester

(Benson), he was almost too kind to their fellow-helper, Whitefield, admitting him to holy orders when he was under the right age, and certainly not above his age in learning and experience. But these pleasant relations between John Wesley and his spiritual superiors did not last long. They were revived in his old age,[1] but in his mid-career they were interrupted; the course which he took was too contrary to the spirit of the Georgian era to admit of their continuance. He became suspected of encouraging that bugbear of the eighteenth century—enthusiasm. In 1739 Bishop Gibson wrote a pastoral letter to the clergy of his diocese, 'by way of caution against lukewarmness on the one hand and enthusiasm on the other;' and he defined enthusiasm as a 'strong persuasion on the mind that they are guided by the immediate impulses of the Spirit of God.' John Wesley himself was equally averse from what he considered enthusiasm; only he would have defined it in rather a different way from what the bishop did. He preached a sermon in which he distinguished between what was called enthusiasm and what he held to be such. He was 'surprised and grieved at a genuine instance of enthusiasm,' the instance being that of a man whom God had told that he should be a king. One would have been inclined to call such a man not an enthusiast but a madman.

The true key-note to John Wesley's whole career is to be found in the advice of Archbishop Potter, already quoted. Everything else was made subservient to his

[1] John Wesley says in December 1789: 'So are the tables turned that I have now more invitations to preach in churches than I can accept of.'

desire of doing practical good. It was with this view that he laid so much stress upon his favourite doctrine of 'Christian Perfection'—a doctrine which gave deep offence to many of his co-religionists, but is surely a very noble and a very true doctrine when defined and guarded as Wesley defined and guarded it. 'Loving God,' he writes in his old age, 'with all our hearts, and our neighbour as ourselves, is the perfection I have taught these forty years. I pin down all its opposers to this definition of it. No evasion! No shifting the question! Where is the delusion of this?' He felt that it was only by taking a high aim, and by feeling that it was possible to attain that aim, that man could ever be elevated and restored to the image of God. The restoration of the image of God in the soul of man was another definition, not contrary to, but explanatory of, the one given above, of Wesley's 'Christian Perfection.'

It was with the same practical end in view that he set so firm a face against Calvinism—again to the deep offence of many of his co-religionists; for he felt that there was a practical danger of Calvinism leading to Antinomianism, as in some instances it undoubtedly did. The same cause led him to oppose the mystic 'stillness' of the Moravians, for he felt that the Christian's duty was to work and not to wait, or rather to wait in working. The same cause brought him into antagonism with the far more refined and intellectual mysticism which fascinated his quondam friend and oracle, William Law. The same desire of doing practical good led him to waive clerical etiquette, and intrude even into the parishes of Evangelical clergymen. The same cause

Key-note to Wesley's whole career

will in part account for his almost morbid dislike of controversy; for he felt that when controversy comes in practical work is apt to go out. With the same view he avoided—thorough gentleman though he was—the congregations of the gentry where he felt he could make little practical impression, and devoted himself almost exclusively to the poor whom he loved. This, too, may be one reason why he did not put so prominently forward as might have been expected, in his sermons and in his intercourse with his people generally, what may be called his Anglican tastes; for he felt that they would not be understood, and that to the one great object of his life all mere personal predilections must be subservient. In fact, he made light—far too light—of mere opinions generally. ‘ Is thy heart right, as my heart is with thy heart ? If so give me thy hand.’ All who would help him in his sole quarrel with sin and Satan he welcomed with open arms, no matter what their opinions might be.[1] This, too, was probably the real cause why he thought it right to rule, not with a rod of iron, but with a benevolent despotism, his constantly increasing body of fellow-labourers; for he knew that he could direct them better than they could direct themselves in that one work which they had to do—the instructing, persuading, and encouraging men to love God with all their hearts and their neighbours as themselves.[2]

[1] ‘ How hard it is,’ he writes, December 11, 1785, ‘ to fix, even on serious hearers, a lasting sense of the nature of true religion ! Let it be right opinions, right modes of worship, or anything, rather than right tempers.’

[2] There is an amusing instance of this in his characteristically abrupt counsel to Mr. Benson, with regard even to the choice of

Perhaps, also, we may attribute to the same cause— viz. the subordination of everything in Wesley's view

to the enforcement of practical religion— that curious contrast between the Methodist movement, or at least the popular idea of it, and the bent of Wesley's own inclinations. Methodism was popularly supposed to be a sort of revival of the old Puritanism of the seventeenth century; and, though the theory is inadequate, and, in many respects, erroneous, there were undoubtedly certain points of resemblance between the two systems. But all Wesley's tastes and sentiments were markedly anti-Puritan. This will be best illustrated by selecting from his Journal some of his opinions on various points. Here, for instance, is an entry on January 30, 1785—'I endeavoured to point out those sins which were the chief cause of that awful transaction we commemorate this day. I believe the chief sin which brought the king to the block was his promoting the real Christians. Hereby he drove them into the hands of designing men, which issued in his own destruction.' Here is an entry which would rather startle ultra-Protestants : February 1786—' Stuart's History of Scotland proves Mary, Queen of Scots not only one of the best princesses then in Europe, but one of the most blameless, yea, the most pious, women.' He rarely took part in politics, but the

books for his own private reading. ' What I recommend I *know* ; if you want more books let *me* recommend more, who best understand my own scheme. Beware you be not swallowed up in books ! an ounce of love is worth a pound of knowledge !' Take again his remarks on the dress of his followers : ' It is true these are little, very little, things, which are not worth defending, therefore give them up, let them drop, throw them away without another word.'

American war stirred him to write strongly in favour of
the Royalist side. His 'Calm Addresses' caused a great
sensation, and raised against him many enemies. But
he felt strongly on the subject of government. 'There
is,' he wrote, 'most liberty of all, civil and religious,
under a limited monarchy, usually less under an aristocracy, and least of all under a democracy.' His
opinion of books is of a similar cast. Of the 'Whole
Duty of Man,' that text-book of Churchmen and Royal-
ists after the Restoration, that abomination of the Evangelicals, he writes, 'I wish none may ever read a worse
book.' He records with delight in January 1784, 'I
spent two hours with that great man, Dr. Johnson.'
He thinks Dr. Horne's 'Commentary on the Psalms'
'the best that ever was wrote.' 'I went on,' he writes
in 1768, 'reading that fine book, Bishop Butler's
"Analogy." But I doubt it is too hard for most of
those for whom it is chiefly intended—Free-thinkers,
so called, are seldom close thinkers.' Bishop Lowth
and Dean Prideaux are also favourite authors with him.
On the other hand it would be difficult, if possible, to
find from him any praise of writers with any Puritan
leaning. Nothing seems to please him more than when
he can record any praise of clergymen, especially of
bishops; and such praise frequently occurs in his
Journal, especially in his later years. 'We had,' he
writes in 1777, 'at Carmarthen a plain, useful sermon
from the Vicar, though some said he did not preach the
Gospel. He preached what these men have great need
to hear, less they seek death in the error of their life.'
He does not conceal his dislike of the Presbyterian
services in Scotland, while nothing can exceed the

enthusiasm with which he speaks of the 'exquisite decency' of the services in the Episcopal churches. He finds Lady Huntingdon's young preachers a great thorn in his side. In short, all his sentiments give one the impression of a man who was the very reverse of an innovator or a demagogue. It is a sad pity that such a man could not have been welcomed as a most valuable aid to the Church, though there were more difficulties in the way than is popularly supposed. Take him for all in all he towers far above all the leaders of the Evangelical Revival, not so much in saintliness, or in intellectual power, or in eloquence, or in sound judgment, or in singleness of purpose, but in general force. If one man had to be picked out as *the* Reviver, that man's name would assuredly be John Wesley.

CHAPTER III.

GEORGE WHITEFIELD—CHARLES WESLEY—JOHN FLETCHER —THE COUNTESS OF HUNTINGDON, AND DR. COKE.

It is a singular fact that, while it may be said that in the eighteenth century John Wesley *was* Methodism, Prominence it is not the name of Wesley that comes of White-field's name before us most frequently and most prominently in the contemporary accounts of the Methodists, but the name of George Whitefield (1714–1770). In the 'Letters of Horace Walpole,' for instance, and literature of that stamp, the name of Wesley rarely occurs, that of Whitefield continually. This may be

accounted for partly by the fact that Wesley scrupulously kept himself aloof from the polite world, 'the
gay, genteel things,' as he called them, from which class
such literature emanated, and for which it was intended,
while Whitefield was constantly among them ; partly
because it was much easier to ridicule Whitefield than
Wesley, who was always, beyond all dispute, a scholar
and a gentleman, as well as a Christian.

A contemporary historian actually calls 'one Whitefield, a young clergyman, *the founder* of an institution of a set of fanatics under the name of Methodists,'[1]
and another puts Whitefield before the two Wesleys
in an equally contemptuous account of the rise of the
Methodists.[2]

But in looking back upon the movement, as it
appears in the dry light of history, we see at once the
very different proportions of the two men.
Whitefield was simply a guileless, self-denying, but ill-trained and very injudicious, enthusiast, in
the nineteenth rather than the eighteenth century's
acceptation of that term. To criticise him would be
like criticising the song of the skylark ; for the one is
hardly more careless than the other of what the world
might say. To preach in every part of the world the
everlasting Gospel in his somewhat narrow view of it,
—this was his work in life. He was not at all likely
to make any permanent mark upon such men as those
who have left what one may call testimonials to his
preaching powers, hard-headed men like David Hume

Whitefield simply a preacher

<hr />

* Continuation of Rapin's *History* by Tindal, vol. v. (of continuation) p. 191.
[2] Smollett's *Continuation of Hume*, vol. v. p. 375.

and Benjamin Franklin, and clever rakes like Lord
Bolingbroke and Lord Chesterfield. But the immediate
effects which he produced were more striking even than
those produced by Wesley. Thousands and tens of
thousands listened to his simple and earnest words, and
were, at least for the time, startled from their security.
And as very many of the uneducated folk who heard
him were really touched and did lead better lives in
consequence, it seems a pity that he should have not
confined himself to them. For how was it reasonable to expect that he could affect people of a more
educated class? Brought up to the menial work of
'drawer' in a Gloucester inn, and thence removed
directly to Oxford in the scarcely less menial capacity of
a servitor at Pembroke College, he had been launched
into the world, through the questionable kindness of
Bishop Benson, as a preacher of the Gospel, at an
even earlier age than youths, not long ago fresh
from school, are usually entrusted with that all-im-
portant message. His fire, his earnestness, his mag-
nificent voice, his dramatic action, his noble person,
took the world by storm. In the wilds of America;
among the colliers of Kingswood, with 'a mount for
his pulpit, and the heavens for his sounding-board' (he
had none of Wesley's repugnance to field-preaching,
he preferred it to any other); amid the hubbub of
St. Bartholomew's fair; in the darkness of midnight in
Hyde Park, when all London was in a panic about an
expected earthquake; in his own great tabernacle in
Tottenham fields, and in Lady Huntingdon's drawing-
room among what he calls 'tiptop nobility;' up and
down in every part of England and Scotland, his voice

had been heard, and had made itself felt, as few had
been felt for many a long year. But it is not surprising
that a reaction set in. He was a preacher and nothing
more; as a preacher he had done a great work for the
Revival, but that work was, in the nature of the case,
ephemeral.¹ He had no system, no method; so that the
term 'Methodist' was singularly inappropriate to him,
though in the estimation of one section of his contemporaries, he was *par excellence* the typical Methodist—
far more even than Wesley. As such he was more
cruelly maligned than any of them. And that, not only
on account of his weak points, which were many, but in
matters in which he was absolutely guiltless. In a
'Comic Romance' of the day entitled 'The Spiritual
Quixote,' he is introduced to the hero, Mr. Geoffrey
Wildgoose, who thought of turning Methodist preacher,
dressed in a purple 'night-gown' (dressing-gown) and
a velvet cap. Instead of a Bible or Prayer-book, as
Wildgoose expected, he had a good basin of chocolate,
and a plate of muffins well-buttered, before him. ' Come
in,' he said, ' come in, my dear friends. I am always at
leisure to receive my Christian brethren. I breakfasted
this morning with some prisoners in Newgate upon
some tea and sea-biscuit, but found my stomach a little
empty, and was refreshing myself with a dish of chocolate.' In short, he is represented as a sleek hypocrite,
who was making a good thing out of his preaching.
The author, the Rev. Richard Graves, had been a
scholar of Pembroke at the very time when Whitefield
was a servitor, and he appears to have been particularly
exasperated because 'a late writer called Mr. Whitefield
a fellow of Pembroke College in Oxford;' but that was

ro reason why he should tell—well, untruths, even
about a servitor. His insinuations are most unjust.
If ever a man had a single eye for God's glory and the
salvation of men it was George Whitefield. He was
ready to spend and be spent in that sacred cause.
And though he

> Stood pilloried on infamy's high stage,
> And bore the pelting scorn of half an age,

yet 'he lov'd the world that hated him,' and only sought
to do it good. His preaching power is too well attested to
be for a moment doubted. If John Wesley's testimony
to ' that torrent of eloquence which frequently bore down
all before it, that astonishing force of persuasion which
the most hardened sinners could not resist,' be suspected as partial, Bishop Warburton is certainly not a
witness biassed in his favour, and he owns that ' of
Whitefield's oratorical powers and their astonishing
influence on the minds of thousands there can be no
doubt.' More evidence from equally unexceptionable
sources might be quoted, but it is needless. George
Whitefield stands forth as emphatically the orator of
the movement.

And equally certain is it that he was an utterly
unselfish, God-fearing man. His faults were all faults
of the head, not of the heart; he was rash and in-
discreet; he frequently violated the rules of good
taste; he was deficient in theological—and, indeed, in
all—learning. It is not altogether surprising that he
raised up many enemies against himself; and still less
surprising that there were many who ridiculed and
spoke contemptuously of him. Men like Dr. Johnson,
for instance, who had a deep respect for Wesley, spoke

very slightingly of Whitefield. But it is also not surprising that his memory survived all the opposition, ill-will, and contempt that he incurred; and that the prophecy of an obituary notice, quoted by John Wesley in his funeral sermon—'The name of George Whitefield will long be remembered with esteem and veneration'—has proved correct.

Far more effective and permanent, though less showy than Whitefield's, was the part which Charles Wesley Charles (1708–1788) took in the Revival. That gift Wesley of sacred song which he possessed in a remarkable, almost an unparalleled, degree, not only gave light and sweetness to the worship of those vast congregations which assembled to hear the 'new lights,' but supplied to a great extent the place of a liturgy and a creed. More people expressed their hopes, their fears, and their beliefs, in the language of Charles Wesley's hymns than in that of John Wesley's sermons. And who can imagine the effect of such hymns on a generation which had previously not dreamed that the praises of God could be sung in any other strain than that of Sternhold and Hopkins, or Tate and Brady? To turn from 'How blest is he who ne'er consents,' to 'Jesu, Lover of my soul,' is almost to turn from the ridiculous to the sublime. Is it conceivable that the devotional feelings of any pious soul should have been elevated by the former? Is it conceivable that they should not have been elevated by the latter? One can well understand the electric shock of sympathy which would thrill through a vast multitude when they lifted up their hearts and voices to join in 'O for a thousand tongues to sing My great Redeemer's praise!' or 'Soldiers of Christ, arise!' John Wesley undoubtedly hit a blot, not in our Church's system, but in her practice, when he contrasted the Psalmody of parish churches with that of his own societies. 'Their solemn addresses to God,' he wrote respecting the latter, 'are not interrupted either by the formal drawl of a parish clerk, the screaming of boys, who bawl out what they neither understand nor feel, or the unreasonable and unmeaning impertinence of a voluntary on the organ. When it is seasonable to sing praise to God they do it with the spirit and the understanding also, not in the miserable, scandalous doggerel of Hopkins and Sternhold, but in psalms and hymns which are both sense and poetry, such as would sooner provoke a critic to turn Christian than a Christian to turn critic.' Of course the hymns were not confined to those of Charles Wesley; John himself contributed some, principally translations from the German ; Watts, Doddridge, Toplady, Olivers, and others were laid under contribution, but Charles Wesley was *par excellence* the sacred poet of the movement. 'The number he wrote,' says Mr. Abbey, ' is something amazing. In more than forty different publications, exclusive of mere selections from former works, he sent out into the world, between 1738 and 1785, 4,100 hymns; and upwards of two thousand more were left at his death in manuscript.' And if he had taken no other part in the Revival than as a hymn-writer he would still have been a factor in it whose importance it would be difficult to exaggerate. But he *did* take a very active part in other ways. He was, before his marriage, almost as active and effective a preacher as John, and on more than one occasion his calmer judgment and

milder temper were of very great service in checking
irregularities and smoothing down asperities in that
great man's conduct. In particular he was the connecting link between John Wesley and Whitefield
when other ties between them were broken; and on
other occasions his office was to pour oil on the troubled
waters. Charles Wesley was, not in intention but in
fact, a far more staunch and consistent Churchman than
his elder brother. He saw more clearly than John the
tendency of Methodism to separate from the Church,
and remonstrated with his brother with the true Wesley
peremptoriness. 'The preachers,' he wrote in 1779,
' do not love the Church of England. When we are
gone a separation is inevitable. Do you not wish to
keep as many good people in the Church as you can ?
Something might be done now to save the remainder if
only you had resolution and would stand by me as
firmly as I will stand by you. Consider what you are
bound to do as a clergyman; and what you do, do
quickly.' He strongly objected to his brother's conduct
in the ordination question, and is said to have written
a *bon mot* which, though it has been often quoted,
deserves to be quoted yet once again :

> How easily are bishops made
> By man or woman's whim !
> Wesley his hands on Coke hath laid
> But who laid hands on him ?

True to his principles to the last he left orders that he
should not be buried in his brother's ground, because it
was not consecrated, but in the churchyard of the
parish in which he died; and his body was carried to
the grave by eight ordained ministers of the Church of

England. But as a rule the two brothers worked most harmoniously together. John Wesley always speaks of their work as joint work. 'My brother and I' is his frequent expression. It is the greatest mistake, however, to regard Charles as John's shadow. He had a very strong will of his own, and knew on occasion how to make it felt. Methodism would have been something very different from what it was had there been no Charles Wesley.

The last of the four leaders of what may be called the Wesley branch of the Evangelical Revival is John Fletcher (1729–1785). He was a Swiss by birth and his name was originally De la Fléchere, but he settled in England and became attracted by the Methodist movement when he was tutor to the sons of Mr. Hill, of Tern Hall (1752). The next year he was admitted into holy orders, and was soon afterwards presented to the living of Madeley. He was one of the few clergymen who thoroughly identified themselves with the Methodist movement, as distinguished from the Evangelical, and yet thoroughly attached themselves to parochial work; indeed, he is generally spoken of in connexion with his parish as 'Fletcher of Madeley.' His indefatigable, and in the end successful, labours for twenty-five years among the rough colliers, as well as the gentry, in this Shropshire village need not be described in detail. All we have to do with him is so far as he affected the general course of the Evangelical Revival. His speciality (if one may use the expression) was to exhibit the Christian model in its highest perfection. If anyone asked, 'Show us an instance of the effects of this system,' he might be referred to Fletcher of Madeley,

Fletcher of Madeley

for his Christian character was undoubtedly the direct product of the system. All his co-religionists seem to have been unanimous in assigning to him, not only a high, but the very highest, place for saintliness among his contemporaries. He was for some time a sort of ' Visitor' at Lady Huntingdon's training college at Trevecca: 'and,' writes Dr. Benson, the first head-master, ' he was received as an angel of God. It is not possible for me to describe the veneration in which we all held him. Like Elijah in the schools of the prophets he was revered, he was loved, he was almost adored. My heart kindles while I write. Here it was that I saw—shall I say an angel in human flesh? I should not far exceed the truth if I said so.' 'Sir,' said Mr. Venn to one who asked him his opinion of Fletcher, ' he was a *luminary*. A luminary, did I say?—he was a sun! I have known all the great men for these fifty years, but none like him?' If John Wesley had wanted a living example of the possibility of attaining to Christian perfection, the best he could have found would have been John Fletcher. And he virtually *did* instance him when he preached after his death on the suggestive words, ' Mark the perfect man, and behold the upright, for the end of that man is peace.' The conclusion of this sermon will be a fitting conclusion to the testimonies, which might be multiplied, if necessary, to the unique saintliness of the man. 'I was,' says the preacher, ' intimately acquainted with him for above thirty years; I conversed with him morning, noon, and night, without the least reserve, during a journey of many hundred miles; and in all that time I never heard him speak one improper word, nor saw him do an improper action. To conclude, many exemplary men have I known, holy in heart and life, within fourscore years, but one equal to him I have not known, one so inwardly and outwardly devoted to God. So unblamable a character in every respect I have not found either in Europe or America, and I scarce expect to find another such on this side eternity.'

Wesley desired that Fletcher should be his successor; but the hale old man survived the younger, who was *Wesley's* always delicate, for several years. And, had *opinion of* *Fletcher* it been otherwise, Fletcher would scarcely have been suited to take Wesley's place. For there was always something of the foreigner about Fletcher, whereas it was one of the secrets of Wesley's influence that he was English to the backbone, and thoroughly understood the mind and ways of Englishmen. Moreover, the vicar of Madeley was not a great admirer of the system of itinerancy, and, much to Wesley's regret, insisted upon wasting his sweetness on the desert air of Madeley; in fact, Wesley not obscurely hints that he killed himself by doing so. 'In the year 1781, with the full approbation of all his friends, he married Miss Bosanquet. By her tender and judicious care, his health was confirmed more and more ; and I am firmly convinced that had he used this health in travelling all over the kingdom, five or six or seven months every year (for which never was man more eminently qualified, no, not Mr. Whitefield himself), he would have done more good than any other man in England. I cannot doubt but this would have been the more excellent way. However, though he did not accept of this honour, he did abundance of good in that narrow sphere of action which he chose; and was a pattern well worthy the imitation of all the parochial ministers in the kingdom.'

It may seem ungallant not to include among the leaders of the Evangelical Revival a lady who gave her Selina Countess of Huntingdon whole heart and soul, her social influence and private fortune, to the work, and who undoubtedly brought within its range many who, but for her, would have stood quite aloof from it. And yet we can scarcely place among its foremost agents Selina Countess of Huntingdon (1707–1791). She devoted herself chiefly to the introduction of the ' New Light ' among her own class of society. And the enumeration of a few among the distinguished individuals whom she persuaded to listen to her favourite preachers will show the extent both of her success and of her failures. The first Earl of Chatham, Lord North, the Earl of Sandwich, Bubb Dodington, George Selwyn, Charles Townshend, Horace Walpole, Lord Camden, the Earl of Bath, Lord Northington, the Earl of Chesterfield, Viscount Bolingbroke, Frederick Prince of Wales, the Duke of Cumberland, John Lord Hervey, the Duke of Bolton, the Duke of Grafton, Sarah Duchess of Marlborough, the Duchess of Buckingham, Lady Townshend were at different times among the hearers. It is marvellous that such personages could have been induced to attend the ministry of Whitefield (who was the chief attraction) at all ; but it would have been still more marvellous if they had really become converts. Truth compels us to own that as a rule they did not. No doubt there were some who listened with good effect. Among the aristocracy who sincerely shared Lady Huntingdon's views were her relatives, the Lady Fanny

Shirley and the Hon. Walter Shirley, the Earl of
Buchan, perhaps the Marquis of Lothian, and others.
Neither is there any reason to doubt that when the
Earl of Bath, Lord Chesterfield, and others spoke with
approbation of what they heard, they spoke what they
really felt at the time. But there is no evidence that
they were permanently affected. Some seem to have
listened with avowed hostility, others with a half-con-
temptuous toleration ; and even the patronising approval
which others condescended to give was hardly less hopeful for any good that the preachers might produce. The
most permanent result of Lady Huntingdon's exertions
was the ' Connexion ' which she formed, the nucleus of
which was the theological college at Trevecca in Wales,
which she founded and supported. John Wesley gives
a very unsatisfactory account of the rawness of some of
the preachers who were sent forth from this seminary ;
but on such a point we must accept his testimony *cum
grano*. Personally Lady Huntingdon's character commands the deepest respect. The moral courage which
enabled a lady, brought up among all the traditions of
an aristocracy such as the aristocracy was in the reigns
of George II. and George III., to cast aside all the
prejudices of her order, and brave all the contempt and
ridicule of those with whom she would naturally be
most brought into contact, and cast in her lot openly
and without reserve with the despised Methodists, is
admirable. If she seems at times to adopt a somewhat
imperious air towards her *protégés*, we must remember
that a countess *was* a countess in those days, and that
she was certainly encouraged in the line she took by
the extravagant homage paid to her by Whitefield and

others. John Wesley, indeed, was never dazzled by her grandeur; on the contrary, he took upon him more than once to rebuke the imperiousness of 'that valuable woman;' Berridge of Everton rebelled laughingly (*more suo*) against her authority; and there is not the slightest trace of undue subserviency in the clergy, like Romaine and Henry Venn and others, who acted *with* rather than *under* her. But the majority of those who were connected with her could not fail to be dazzled by the honour of the connexion; and not only submitted to, but courted, the authority which she was not slack in assuming over them.

The only other person identified with the Methodists whose position and circumstances enabled him to make anything like the same worldly sacrifices as Lady Huntingdon did, was Dr. Thomas Coke. He was in early life a gentleman commoner of Jesus College, Oxford, and was a man of large private means. But all his social advantages, and all his private means, he devoted to the cause of Methodism. He did not become a Methodist until 1776, by which time the line of demarcation had been drawn between the Methodists proper and the Evangelicals proper; but this distinction only emphasised the contempt with which the Methodists or followers of Wesley were regarded. Southey terms him 'the most efficient of all Wesley's fellow-workers,' and assigns to him the second place in Methodism; but surely this could only be given to him after Fletcher was dead and Charles Wesley had virtually retired from the work. However, without making any invidious comparisons, it is unquestionable that Dr. Coke was a most efficient helper after he joined the move-

Dr. Coke

ment. In the view of Churchmen, a prejudice naturally
attaches to his name as being connected with what they
cannot but think the most false step in Wesley's career,
his taking upon himself to ordain 'superintendents' for
America; but that ought not to blind them to Dr.
Coke's real excellence. He was emphatically a scholar,
a gentleman, and a Christian; not without defects, as
even his greatest admirers have admitted, but a real
honour to the cause which he espoused. Wesley, in
later life, regarded him as his right-hand man, and
looked to him as his successor, so far as there could be
a successor to the unique position which Wesley held
among his societies. Missionary work was the speciality
of Dr. Coke. He crossed the Atlantic eighteen times at
his own expense, and was practically the founder of the
Wesleyan Missions which have since attained such great
proportions. He died on one of his voyages, and was
buried at sea.

One hardly likes to close this sketch of the Methodist
leaders without at least a passing notice of the most
Dr. Adam learned of them all, Dr. Adam Clarke. But
Clarke as he was not born until the year 1760 or
1762, he can hardly be termed a leader of the band.
He joined the movement about the same time as Dr.
Coke, and was very active as a preacher and helper
generally. But, of course, it is as an author that he is
best known, and his *magnum opus* belongs to the nineteenth, not the eighteenth, century.

Among the lesser luminaries of Methodism in the
last century were Thomas Walsh, John Wesley's most
honoured friend; Mr. Perronet, the excellent vicar of
Shoreham, to whom both the brothers Wesley had

recourse in every important crisis, and who was called by Charles Wesley the 'Archbishop of Methodism;' Sir Lesser luminaries of Methodism John Thorold, a pious Lincolnshire baronet; Mr. Brackenbury of Raithby Hall in the same county; John Nelson, the worthy stonemason of Birstal, who was pressed as a soldier simply because he was a Methodist; Sampson Stainforth, Mark Bond, John Haine, the Methodist soldiers who infused a spirit of Methodism into the British army; Thomas Olivers, the converted reprobate, John Pawson, Alexander Mather, and other worthy men, who would, of course, have a niche in any professed history of Methodism, but need not be described at length in a short sketch like the present. Enough has now been said to give the reader a fair idea of the *personnel* of the Methodists of the eighteenth century.

CHAPTER IV.

METHODISM AND EVANGELICALISM.

METHODISM and Evangelicalism (the necessity for using this very clumsy word needs an apology) were both Two depart-ments of the Revival parts of one great religious movement; and it is perhaps only by reading events of the eighteenth century in the light which the nineteenth throws upon them that the two can be separated by any very strong line of demarcation. They both aimed at reviving spiritual religion; they both so far resembled the Puritanism of the seventeenth century in that they contended for the immediate and particular influence of the Holy Spirit, for the total degeneracy

of man, for the vicarious nature of the Atonement,
for the absolute unlawfulness of certain kinds of amusement, for the strict observance of the Lord's Day or
Sabbath, for they used the terms indiscriminately; and
they both agreed in differing from Puritanism, by taking
either no side in politics at all, or else taking the opposite side from that which the Puritans would have
taken, by disclaiming sympathy with Dissenters or
Nonconformists, by glorying in the fact that they were
members of the Church of England (Methodists no less
than Evangelicals), by the most staunch loyalty to the
throne. Even the terms by which they are now distinguished can hardly be called distinguishing terms in the
eighteenth century. For all Methodists would have
wished to be called Evangelical, and all Evangelicals,
whether they wished it or no, were called Methodists.
There was a sharp enough distinction drawn between
Calvinists and Arminians, and a less marked but still
sufficient distinction between those who confined their
ministrations within parochial limits and those who
preferred the system of itinerancy; and, in each case,
broadly speaking, the former may be termed Evangelicals, and the latter Methodists; but the outer world
persisted in confounding the two, in spite of the remonstrance of the Evangelicals, who strongly objected to
being identified with the irregularities of Methodism.
Thomas Scott published his 'Force of Truth' in 1778,
forty years after the date which Wesley gives for the
commencement of the Revival, and it is interesting to
observe what were his sentiments on the point. 'Methodist,' he writes, 'as a stigma of reproach, was first applied
to Mr. Wesley, Mr. Whitefield, and their followers; and

to those who, professing an attachment to our Established Church, and disclaiming the name of Dissenters, were not conformists in point of parochial order, but had separate seasons, places, and assemblies for worship. The term has since been extended by many to all persons, whether clergy or laity, who preach or profess the doctrines of the Reformation, as expressed in the articles and liturgy of our Church. For this fault they must all submit to bear the reproachful name of Methodists, especially the ministers; nor will the most regular and peaceable compliance with the injunctions of the rubric exempt them from it, if they avow the authorised, but in a great measure exploded, doctrines to which they have subscribed. My acquaintance hitherto has been solely with Methodists of the latter description, and I have them alone in view when I use the term!' These are Scott's views after he became a decided Evangelical. His description of his feelings on the subject before he became one, may perhaps account for the perverse confusion of ideas in the public mind of which he justly complains. 'Being situated,' he says, 'in the neighbourhood of those whom the world calls Methodists' [he alludes especially to Mr. Newton] 'I joined in the prevailing sentiment; held them in sovereign contempt, spoke of them with derision, declaimed against them from the pulpit as persons full of bigotry, enthusiasm, and spiritual pride; laid heavy things to their charge, and endeavoured to prove the doctrines which I supposed them to hold (for I had never read their books) to be dishonourable to God, and destructive to morality. And, though in some companies I chose to conceal part of my sentiments, and in all affected to speak as a friend to universal toleration, yet scarcely any person can be more proudly and violently prejudiced against both their persons and principles than I then was.'[1]

What Scott felt in 1778 was also felt at least twenty years earlier by two other famous Evangelicals, Mr. Walker of Truro and Mr. Adam of Winteringham. ' They were,' writes Mr. Richardson of York (another Evangelical who obviously sympathised with their position), in the ' Christian Observer' in 1802, ' both true sons of the Church, and beheld with great anxiety those deviations of the Methodists, from which they both suffered unde- served reproach, as we all do this day, however regularly we conduct ourselves.' There is a curious illustration of the truth of Mr. Richardson's complaint in a ruthless exposure of the weaknesses of the Methodists in articles in the ' Edinburgh Review' written so late as 1808, the writer of which is now known to be Mr. Sidney Smith. He groups together ' Arminian and Calvinistic Method- ists and the *Evangelical* [the italics are his] clergymen of the Church of England ;' and adds : ' We shall use the general term of Methodism to designate those three classes of fanatics, not troubling ourselves to point out the finer shades and nicer discriminations of lunacy, but treating them all as in one general conspiracy against common sense and rational orthodox Christianity.'[2] The point is so important that, at the risk of wearying the reader, one more instance must be quoted to show how Methodists and Evangelicals were confounded, and how grieved the latter were at the confusion. ' I never,' writes Mr. Richardson, in a vindicatory letter to his

[1] *Force of Truth,* Part I. *sub finem.*
[2] *Edinburgh Review,* No. XXII., Art. V. ' Ingram on Methodism.

friend, Mr. Comber, in 1772, 'had any connection with the Methodists, either at Kirkby Moorside or York, more than with my other parishioners. I think of them as i do of other Protestants who differ from myself in opinion, *with charity*. As far as I think their opinions agree with the Word of God and the doctrines of the Church of England I follow them, without regarding common prejudices. At the same time, I dislike the manner in which they speak of the influences of the Holy Spirit, and their unscriptural notions of perfection. As to the persons you call *Methodisers*, they are the most valuable part of my acquaintance, being those whom a malicious world has branded with that name on account of their superior piety and regularity of manners. As soon as a person begins to show any symptoms of seriousness and strictness more than the fashion of the age allows he is called a Methodist, though he may happen to have no sort of connection with them; and when once this stigma is fixed upon him, he becomes like a deer whom the sportsmen have marked out for a chase; he is driven away by the rest of the herd and avoided like an infection. Ridiculed and discouraged in his spiritual progress he is often reduced to this alternative—either to square his conscience by the customs of the world or throw himself into the arms of a party. Those who have the interests of true religion at heart would do well to consider the mischievous consequences of branding strict professors with the odious name of Methodists. It is a stumbling-block to young minds in particular. It discourages the serious, and emboldens the careless and irreligious. With these sentiments I shall never, I hope, renounce a truly pious friend because the world chooses to call him a Methodist, nor avoid a duty which the Gospel of Christ enjoins, for fear of getting the same appellation myself.'[1] An amusing instance of the vague way in which the term Methodist was applied is given in Mr. Vaughan's Life of Robinson, of Leicester. Robinson's tutor and friend, Mr. Postlethwaite, 'hearing that he was bent on turning Methodist, from the kindest motives took him seriously to task, exhorting him to beware, to consider what mischief the Methodists were doing, and at what a vast rate they were increasing. "Sir," said Robinson, " what do you mean by a Methodist? Explain, and I will ingenuously tell you whether I am one or not." This caused a puzzle and a pause. At last, Mr. Postlethwaite said : " Come then, I'll tell you! I hear that in the pulpit you impress on the minds of your hearers that they are to attend to your doctrine from the consideration that you will have to give an account of them, and of your treatment of them, at the Day of Judgment." "I am surprised," rejoined Robinson, " to hear this objected. It is true." Robinson got no further explanation from the tutor, but that the increase of Methodism was an alarming thing.'

It was not solely on the question of parochial order that the Evangelicals differed from the Method-ists, though that was undoubtedly the main crux. They strongly objected to some of Wesley's

Differences of doctrine

---

[1] Quoted in the *Christian Observer* for 1877. Let me once for all express my obligation to the writer of this admirable series of biographical sketches scattered throughout the *Christian Observer* in 1877. It would be a most seasonable work if these sketches were published together in one small volume.

C. H.   E opinions, and still more to his light estimate of the value of all opinions. His favourite doctrine of 'Christian Perfection' was an abomination to them; and, though they were very moderate Calvinists, still they *were* Calvinists, and Wesley's pronounced anti-Calvinism was naturally unpalatable to them. On this point the Whitefield section of the Methodists would be more in harmony with them; and, as a matter of fact, they reverenced the memory of Whitefield—they can scarcely be said to have become a compact body during his life-time—far more than the name of Wesley. But then, Whitefield's followers soon drifted away into other communities; and if Whitefield offended the Evangelicals less by his theological opinions, he offended them more by his vehement abuse of his own order.

If, on the one hand, the Evangelicals objected to being confounded with the Methodists, no less did the Wesley and Methodists object to identifying themselves parochial work with the Evangelicals. It was not only that John Wesley claimed the world for his parish, and made no exception to this all-embracing rule, carrying it out even at Huddersfield where there was a Venn, and at Truro where there was a Walker; but he did not believe in the efficacy of the parish clergyman's ministration, even when he agreed with him. 'We know,' he writes, 'several regular clergymen who do preach the genuine Gospel, but to no effect at all. There is one exception in England—Mr. Walker, at Truro.' But even Mr. Walker in vain attempted to dissuade him from keeping up his societies in those parishes (Truro included) where the Gospel was preached. 'I do not know,' wrote Wesley, in reply to a remonstrance from

Walker, on his not leaving the people of St. Agnes to their Evangelical clergyman, Mr. Vowler, 'that every one who preaches the truth has wisdom and experience to guide and govern a flock. I do not know whether Mr. Vowler would or could give that flock all the advantages for holiness which they now enjoy.' Shortly afterwards, Mr. Walker writes to his friend, Mr. Adam, about this same Mr. Vowler—'His patience and prudence will, I believe, overcome the strange opposition made against him by the Methodists. In their eye both he and I are well-meaning legalists.'

If Wesley, with all his deep attachment to the Church, still felt more than justified in carrying on his Evangelical separate work in parishes which were filled clergy and Methodists by Evangelical clergymen, it is hardly necessary to say that his followers, who had no such attachment, were perfectly ready to follow his lead. In fact, the Evangelicals often found less difficulty in preserving amicable relations with avowed Dissenters than with the Methodists. And one can quite see why. They foresaw the inevitable break which must occur at Wesley's death, if not before, between the Methodists and the Church, and they strongly objected to being thought to be in any way mixed up with a movement which was leading to a separation which they would sincerely deplore. One finds strong traces of this in the 'Church History' of Milner, who never loses an opportunity of dealing a side blow at the Methodist irregularities.

And as years rolled on, the general tone of mind and habits of thought of the Evangelicals differed more and more widely from those of the earlier Revivalists.

A dignified self-restraint, a calmness both of preaching and of action, took the place of the restless activity and Later impulsiveness of many of the first Methodists. Evangelicals As a rule, too, the Evangelicals affected quite a different class of society from that which Methodism influenced. The converts to Methodism proper were mostly drawn from the lower and lower-middle classes. The backbone of Evangelicalism was the upper and upper-middle classes.

It must also be remembered that religious revivals of the Evangelical type had been going on quite inde-pendently of the Methodist movement. In Revivals apart from Wales, for instance, the work of Griffith the Method-ist move-ment Jones, which, in a much more limited area, closely resembled that of Wesley, began at the time when John Wesley was a child, just rescued from the burning rectory of Epworth. Jones' successor, Howell Harris, commenced his career as a Revivalist two years before the first Methodist society was formed. Daniel Rowlands, another Evangelical reformer, was the spiritual son of Harris, rather than of the Wesleys. That remarkable movement in West Cornwall, of which Mr. Walker was the recognised leader, owed neither its commencement nor its course to Methodism, with which, indeed, it was subsequently brought into somewhat sharp collision.

But that which, above all things, distinguished Methodism (that is, Wesleyan Methodism) from Evan-Methodist gelicalism, was that elaborate organisation of Societies the societies, which rendered the term 'Me-thodism,' though given in derision and long before the organisation had taken place, so singularly appropriate to Wesley's system. The world called the Methodists mad, but at any rate there was method in their madness.

This is as convenient a place as any for giving a short outline of the system which is such a marked Methodist feature in the history of the Revival. The system system seems to have grown from special exigencies rather than to have been elaborated as a whole; and the fact that it did so, instead of detracting from, rather adds to, our appreciation of the orderly mind— one may almost say the legislative wisdom—of Wesley, who so skilfully and effectively adapted special and temporary requirements that they became the occasion for general and permanent institutions. Take, for instance, the very name *society*. It was an old and very familiar term to Wesley; the Religious Societies, the Societies for the Reformation of Manners, the Society for Promoting Christian Knowledge, the Society for the Propagation of the Gospel in Foreign Parts, were known to him from his childhood, for they had all found a warm supporter in the Rector of Epworth. John Wesley simply took up the old name, considering probably that if such societies were good for other purposes, why not for binding together in a holy bond his newly-awakened disciples? The older societies, too, suggested what he wanted in another respect. They were essentially, at least with one doubtful exception,[1] organisations

---

[1] The doubtful exception is, of course, the Societies for the Reformation of Manners, in which Churchmen and Dissenters were sometimes, though not always, joined together, and which were discountenanced, or at least coldly regarded, by some Churchmen; they, however, found a strong adherent in John Wesley's father, who was, perhaps, influenced by his friend Robert Nelson, a High Churchman, but a staunch friend of the Societies.

within, not *outside*, the Church of England—helps, not hindrances, to it; and that was what Wesley desired his societies to be.   Take again the *class-meeting*.   This arose simply from the necessity of finding money to pay for what Wesley himself would have called a 'preach-ing-house' at Bristol.   It was suggested by someone : 'Let every member of the Society give a penny a week till all is paid.'   'But,' it was replied, 'many of them are poor, and cannot afford to do it.'   'Then,' said the suggestor, 'put eleven of the poorest with me, and if they can give anything, well : I will call on them weekly ; and if they can give nothing, I will give for them as well as for myself.   And each of you call on eleven of your neighbours weekly ; receive what they give, and make up what is wanting.'   The plan answered in more ways than one.   Some who went round found members living inconsistent lives, and reported it to Wesley, who at once saw an opening for further organisation.   'It struck me,' he says, 'immediately, this is the thing, the very thing, we have wanted so long.'   He assembled the leaders and charged them to look into the conduct of those whom they visited weekly, as well as receive their pence ; then, instead of going round to every house, the 'class-leader,' as he now began to be called, gathered the class, which consisted of about a dozen, more or less, into a room ; and hence that essential feature of Methodism, the class-meeting.   It answered quite as well finan-cially.   'A penny a week and a shilling a quarter,' the class rule, has been the backbone of Methodism from a financial point of view.   Let the precedent be com-

mended to those Churchmen who are anxious to estab-
lish the weekly offertory.

> Via prima salutis,
> Quod minime reris, Graiâ pandetur ab urbe.

Whether the plan of this weekly collection commended itself to Wesley from its resemblance to the
practice of the primitive Church (1 Cor. xvi. 2) is not
known; but it *is* known from his own words that this
was the case with many of the most distinctive features
of his system.   It was so, for instance, with regard to
the *Love Feasts*.   'In order to increase in them a
grateful sense of all the mercies of the Lord, I desired
that one evening in a quarter they should all come
together, that we might eat bread (as the ancient
Christians did) with gladness and with singleness of
heart.   At these Love Feasts—so we term them, retaining the name as well as the thing, which was in
use from the beginning, Jude 12—our food is only a
little plain cake and water; but we seldom return from
them without being fed, not only with the meat that
perisheth, but with that which endureth to everlasting
life.'   It was so with regard to the *Watch Nights*.   'I
was informed that several persons in Kingswood frequently met together in the school and, when they could
spare the time, spent the greater part of the night in
prayer and praise and thanksgiving.   Some advised
me to put an end to this; but, upon weighing the
thing thoroughly, and comparing it with the practice of
the ancient Christians, I could see no cause to forbid it;
rather I believed it might be made of more general use.'
And then he proceeded at once to make it of more
general use by forming some rules with his usual

practical sagacity. It was so with regard to the *Quarterly Tickets*, which, trifles as they may seem, have played no small part in the career of Methodism. ' To each of those, of whose seriousness and good conversation I found no reason to doubt, I gave a testimony under my own hand, by writing their name on a ticket prepared for that purpose; every ticket implying as strong a recommendation of the person to whom it was given as if I had wrote at length, " I believe the bearer hereof to be one that fears God and works righteousness." Those who bore these tickets (these *Tesseræ*, as the ancients termed them, being of just the same force with the commendatory letters mentioned by the apostle) wherever they came were acknowledged by their brethren, and received with all cheerfulness.' It was so probably with regard to the *Band Meetings*, which form, as it were, the inner circle of Methodism. Many met with ' temptations of such a kind that they knew not how to speak of in a class in which persons of every sort, young and old, men and women, met together. These, therefore, wanted some means of closer union ; they wanted to pour out their hearts without reserve, particularly with regard to the sin which did still easily beset them, and the temptations which were most apt to prevail over them ; and they were desirous of this when they observed it was the express advice of an inspired writer, " Confess your faults one to another, and pray one for another that ye may be healed " (James v. 16).' This precept, which, on the presumption that it was obeyed, implied a custom of the primitive Church, appears to have induced Wesley to grant their wish. ' In compliance

with their desire, I divided them into smaller companies, putting the married or single men, and married
or single women together ; ' and then he specifies 'the
chief rules of these bands (i.e. little companies, so that
old English word signifies).' . In fact, one point of difference between Wesley, at least, if not his followers,
and the Evangelicals was that the model of the former
was chiefly the primitive Church, that of the latter
chiefly the reformation of the sixteenth century.

Most of the other institutions of Methodism rose
from the exigencies of the case. Thus, the arrangement
of *circuits* became a necessity in order to bind together
the various little societies grouped round one common
centre. The circuits necessarily required the appoint-
ment of *superintendents*, for Wesley had no idea of a
democracy or an oligarchy in religion any more than
he had in politics. The *circuit-stewards* (that is, two
principal members in the circuit nominated yearly by
the superintendent, and chosen by the quarterly meeting) were a necessity, if the funds were to be managed
in the orderly way which alone would satisfy so business-
like a man as Wesley. And, finally, the *Conference*
grew from a mere informal meeting of preachers summoned by Wesley to help him chiefly in the appoint-
ment of preachers for the various circuits, into a sort
of senate, whose Minutes are the statutory laws of
Methodism, and to whom is the ultimate appeal in
every disputed case. The *President*, elected annually by
the ' Legal Hundred '—who, properly speaking, constitute the Conference, though other preachers are admitted
—is a kind of temporary archbishop of Methodism.

This is only a very inadequate sketch of that minute

and elaborate network which embraces the whole of the complicated and ingenious system established by John Wesley; but it is sufficient to show one point of distinction between the Methodists and the Evangelicals. The latter were quite outside the whole machinery, the former by the mere fact of becoming Methodists became part of it. On the other hand, the latter accepted the parochial system, while the former generally looked upon it, as their founder had looked upon it, as a mere rope of sand; the latter felt themselves more closely bound by the articles and other formularies of the Church, which, though they were never disputed, no doubt sat more lightly upon the former. And, finally, the latter worked less within a groove than the former, who were necessarily tied down very closely within the limits of the system originated by one who was a heaven-born statesman, and who applied his statesmanship to the regulation of his societies.

And yet, after all that has been said, it is not surprising that Methodism and Evangelicalism should have been confused by those who were outside the pale of both. For when we pass from the consideration of general principles to the application of them to particular individuals, we find at once the difficulty of ticketing this one as a Methodist, that one as an Evangelical. It would be easy enough to do so after the eighteenth century closed, and when a new generation arose; but during the first generation of the Evangelical Revival, and indeed to the very close of the eighteenth century, Methodists and Evangelicals were in many respects so inextricably mixed up that it is impossible entirely to separate the one class from the

Methodists and Evangelicals confused

other. It is only, therefore, with many modifications and exceptions·that the group of good men who will come before us in the next chapter can be said to have lived and worked in a different plane from those described in the preceding chapter.

CHAPTER V.

THE EVANGELICAL CLERGY.

THE difficulty touched upon at the close of the last chapter meets us at once when we endeavour to trace James Hervey the course of the earlier members of the Evangelical school. We will begin with James Hervey (1714–58), who was undoubtedly an Evangelical of Evangelicals. In every point on which the Methodists differed from the Evangelicals he decidedly agreed with the latter. He was perfectly content to work within the limits of his own little parish, or rather parishes—for, in a very small way, he was a pluralist, being vicar of Weston Favell and Collingtree, the combined incomes of which were only 180l. a year. Indeed he not only held aloof from the work of itinerancy himself, but had the hardihood to remonstrate with John Wesley on the subject. He was a very decided though moderate Calvinist; his 'Theron and Aspasio' was one of the most popular expositions of Calvinism which the Evangelical school produced; indeed, all his writings were very text-books of devotion with the Evangelicals, not only of his own day, but of a later generation, while they were never valued highly by the Methodists proper. And yet Hervey was actually one

of the original Methodists. He was the college pupil
and also the spiritual son of John Wesley, who never
ceased to regard him with a paternal eye. After having
graduated at Lincoln College, Oxford, he lived a blameless, useful, but uneventful, life at Weston Favell in
Northamptonshire, attending closely to the duties of
his parish, and nobly devoting a large proportion of his
modest income, including all the profits of his literary
work, which must have been considerable, to works of
Christian charity and benevolence.

The same difficulty of classification occurs in the
cases of William Grimshaw (1708–1763) and John

William
Grimshaw
of Haworth Berridge (1716–1793), names which one naturally couples together on account of the
many points of resemblance between the two men.
Both are very justly claimed by the Evangelicals as
their own, and yet both were inextricably mixed up with
Methodism proper. William Grimshaw was to the end
of his career a parochial clergyman, and there is no
doubt that he did a vast amount of good in the wild
and desolate region in which his lot was cast—wild and
desolate even now, and still more so in the eighteenth
century. The name of Haworth has been immortalised
since his time, by the genius of that remarkable family
which after some generations succeeded him at the
vicarage of this secluded spot, the Brontës; but Grimshaw did quite enough to make Haworth a noted name.
He was eccentric to the very verge of insanity; but his
eccentricity helped rather than hindered his work as an
evangelist. Complaints of the decay of discipline are
frequent during the eighteenth century; but Grimshaw
managed to enforce it at Haworth, not by having
recourse to the old-fashioned plan of church censures,

but by a summary method of his own. While the hymn was being sung before sermon, he would go out of church, it is said, armed with a horsewhip, and drive all the loiterers about the village into church. How he pretended to be a mischievous boy and teased a blind woman with a stick to ascertain whether she had really attained a Christian command over her temper; how he dressed himself up as a beggar and appeared at a rich parishioner's door to test whether he was really as charitable as he pretended to be; how he walked in disguise through the fields in order to find out who were breaking the Sabbath—need not be told at length. By these and other means he acquired such an ascendency at Haworth that the village blacksmith positively refused to shoe the horse of a rider who was travelling on an urgent mission of charity on a Sunday, until he had gained the vicar's leave; and drinkers at the public-house would take flight out of the window when the formidable clergyman threatened a visit. It is not surprising that he should have been called 'the mad parson;' but he might also have been called 'the good parson.' It is much easier to laugh at Grimshaw's eccentricities than to follow his nobly self-denying life, spent altogether in the service of his Divine Master, and in endeavouring, according to his light, to better the wild people who lived on and about his rugged Yorkshire moor. Grimshaw was one of the few parochial clergymen who thoroughly sympathised with John Wesley and all his doings. He carried his sympathy so far as actually to build a Methodist 'preaching-house' (that was the name by which Wesley especially desired that such buildings should be called) in his own parish, and almost within a stone's throw of the parish

church. He was not only no enemy to itinerancy,
but itinerated himself, travelling through Lancashire,
Cheshire, and Derbyshire, as well as Yorkshire, preaching sometimes as often as thirty times a week, and
never less than twelve. In fact, if Wesley was the
centre of the Revival throughout the kingdom, Grimshaw was the centre of the Revival within no slight
area about his own home. He was a decided, though
moderate, Calvinist. Death carried him off seven years
before the Calvinistic controversy burst out in all its
fury; and considering his temperament, and considering
the part which Berridge, who so very closely resembled
him, took in that wretched dispute, we may say
that in this respect he was *felix opportunitate mortis*.
However, as he never seems to have come into collision
with Wesley, though he frequently met him at the very
time when the dispute with Whitefield was at its height,
perhaps if he had lived he would have had the good
sense to hold aloof from the fray.

Unhappily, John Berridge, much as he resembled
Grimshaw on other points, did not resemble him in
this. His effusions on the Calvinistic controversy form a painfully conspicuous feature in
his life. From a literary point of view they are beneath
contempt; but they are quite unworthy of the man,
intellectually as well as morally.[1] For John Berridge

John Ber-
ridge of
Everton

---

[1] See, as a specimen, 'The Serpent and the Fox, or an Interview
between Old Nick and Old John,' published in *The Gospel* (!) *Magazine*, with the signature of 'Old Everton,' which, after many pages
of abusive doggerel, concludes :—

'The Priest with a simpering face
Shook his hair-locks, and paused for a space ;
Then sat down to forge lies with his usual grimace.

was not only a most earnest and self-denying man, but also one of very considerable culture. He was a Fellow of Clare Hall, Cambridge, and before his 'conversion' was much sought after as a witty and amusing companion in university circles. The moral courage which enabled such a man avowedly to 'turn Methodist' must have been exceptionally great. When Wesley sacrificed a similar position at Oxford, the name 'Methodist' had not, of course, become a general term of reproach; when Isaac Milner did the same at Cambridge, Methodism, including in that term Evangelicalism, had become a distinct power. But in the interval, during which Berridge cast in his lot with the Methodists, the obloquy was at its height and the power had hardly yet asserted itself. Berridge's eccentricities were at least equal to those of Grimshaw; but so also was his devotedness to his Master's cause and to the good of souls. He was born, he said, with a fool's cap on his head; and he does not seem to have been particularly anxious to take it off. But if he could have said with St. Paul (though in rather a different sense), 'I speak as a fool,' he might also have said in perfect truth, with the same apostle, 'In labours more abundant.' He was at one time a sort of connecting link between Lady Huntingdon and John Wesley, being a firm and faithful friend, but no flatterer of the former, while, like Grimshaw, he was one of the few parochial clergymen who cordially welcomed the latter into his parish. Everton Church, of which he was minister, became one of the most frequent scenes of those physical manifestations which accompanied the preaching of the Revivalists in the earliest stage of the movement; and our excitable vicar was ever ready to

fan the flame of the excitement. Like Grimshaw, he
touched Methodism proper with one hand, and Evangelicalism proper with the other. For he continued to
the end vicar of Everton, as Grimshaw continued
vicar of Haworth, and was equally attentive to the
spiritual wants of his parishioners. But, as Grimshaw
wandered far beyond the limits of Haworth, among the
wolds and moors of Yorkshire, and in other counties,
so Berridge itinerated among the midlands, defying the
opposition of the clergymen into whose parishes he in-
truded, and whose hostility he not unnaturally aroused.
But his motives were always good. A more single-
minded, devoted man never lived ; and the Revival in
Bedfordshire and the neighbouring counties was as
much due to Berridge as that in more northern climes
was due to Grimshaw. His epitaph in Everton Churchyard may still be read, and it is very characteristic of
the man.

Excellent men as both Grimshaw and Berridge were,
it is a little relief to turn from such eccentric beings to
William some more orderly and decorous types of Evan-
Romaine gelical leaders. To make the contrast complete let us first take the gravest of them all. William
Romaine (1714–1795) was, as his name implies, French
by extraction. His father was a Protestant refugee
who had taken refuge in England after the revocation
of the Edict of Nantes. This may account for two
points in his history. The French Huguenots had, of
course, many points in common with the English
Evangelicals; so it is not surprising that Romaine
should have identified himself with the movement without having passed through any of those changes which

are found in the careers of most of the Evangelical leaders. Perhaps, also, his foreign origin may have prevented Romaine from thoroughly understanding English ways, and may in part account for the unpopularity which he met with. He had certainly none of the boisterous *bonhomie* of Grimshaw or Berridge, and not the thoroughly English feeling of Venn or Newton. But he was a thoroughly good, self-denying man, and perhaps the most learned of all the Evangelical leaders. He was at Oxford all through the rise of the Methodist movement, but was in no way connected with it. He was a member of Hertford College; and it is said that ' while there his intense application to study made him so regardless of dress that one day, being observed to pass by rather negligently attired, a visitor asked the Master of the College, ' Who is that slovenly fellow with his stockings down ?' The Master replied, ' That slovenly person, as you call him, is one of the greatest geniuses of the age, and is likely to become one of the greatest men in the kingdom.' [1] Without exactly fulfilling the Master's prediction, he certainly achieved a very considerable reputation for learning. He published a new edition of Calasio's Hebrew Lexicon and Concordance —a work which employed his leisure for seven years, and was deservedly held in esteem. He was so well thought of as an astronomer that he was considered worthy to fill the post which Sir Isaac Newton and Isaac Barrow had held before him—that of Gresham Professor of Astronomy. It cannot be said that he rivalled either of these great men in that capacity. On

[1] Memoir of the Author prefixed to *The Life, Walk, and Triumph of Faith*, edition in 1 vol., 1824.

C. H. F

the contrary he made himself rather ridiculous by in-
dulging in that foolish depreciation of secular studies
which provokes us in the utterances of several of the
Evangelicals. 'Were dying sinners,' he asks with more
wit than wisdom, 'ever converted by the spots on the
moon ? Was ever miser reclaimed from avarice by
Jupiter's Belt? or did Saturn's Ring ever make a
lascivious female chaste ? The modern divinity brings
you no nearer than 121,000,000 of miles short of
heaven.' This effusion is on a par with his famous
university sermon in which he implies that men's preference of hymns—such as Charles Wesley's, for instance
—to Tate and Brady's psalms was a preference of human
compositions to those of the Holy Ghost. But it is an
ungracious and ungrateful task to dwell on a good
man's weaknesses. It is more profitable and more
pleasant to turn to the real good which he did. His appropriate sphere of action was the Metropolis and its
neighbourhood. He spent some years as curate of S.
Olave's, Southwark ; it sounds strange to modern ears
to hear this described as ' a delightful retreat,' ' a curacy
in Surrey, where he enjoyed a quiet time for study,' but
the Southwark of 120 years ago was very different from
the Southwark of to-day. The greater part, however,
of his ministerial life was spent in London proper. He
was ' assistant morning preacher ' at S. George's, Han-
over Square, which was then, even more than it is now,
a central church for the aristocracy ; then lecturer at S.
Dunstan's in the West ; and, finally, rector of S. Andrew
Wardrobe and S. Ann, Blackfriars, still retaining, at
least for a time, his lectureship at S. Dunstan's. Like
the early Methodists, Romaine met with considerable

opposition in his ministrations. Only instead of taking the form of rotten eggs and turnip-tops, it took a less gross, but scarcely less scandalous, shape. He was dismissed from his preachership at S. George's because the parishioners found their pews occupied by the strangers who crowded to hear him. At S. Dunstan's, the churchwardens, failing to procure his legal dismissal, had recourse to the petty annoyance of closing the church doors until the moment when the lecture began, and refusing to light the church when it *was* opened. By this means they probably defeated their own ends: for it must certainly have added greatly to the solemnity and effectiveness of the sermon, when the preacher stood in the midst of a perfectly dark and crowded church, preaching by the light of a single taper which he held in his own hand. Though he was the confidential adviser and senior chaplain of Lady Huntingdon, he showed not a trace of that adulation which is so painful a feature in poor Whitefield's intercourse with the Countess; and it is greatly to the credit of that good lady that, so far from resenting his dignified independence, she helped to procure for him the only piece of real preferment which he ever enjoyed. Romaine withdrew from her 'Connexion' altogether when she virtually separated herself from the Church. Although Romaine was a more extreme Calvinist than most of the Evangelical leaders, he wisely kept himself quite aloof from the wretched Calvinistic controversy. In fact John Wesley makes an honourable exception of William Romaine when he complains of the hard usage he received from the Evangelical Calvinists. The hubbub of that distracting controversy would have been alien to his tastes, for he was a reserved man. 'He lived,' as his biographer touchingly expresses it, 'more with God than with men; and in order to know his real history, or the best part of it, it would be requisite to know what passed between God and his own soul.' But this we do know, as the same writer truly says in reference to what may be called his sacred Trilogy: 'Their author knew by experience what it was to live by faith, to walk by faith, and to triumph in faith.' Take him for all in all, William Romaine was the strongest man connected with the Evangelical branch of the Revival.

There was a certain outward resemblance between William Romaine and Henry Venn (1724–1797). Venn, like Romaine, was a man of very decided

Henry Venn

culture, of great dignity and reserve, and of a blameless and most devoted life. Like Romaine, he was attached to Lady Huntingdon as her chaplain, but thoroughly maintained his independence and self-respect in his relations to her ladyship, and withdrew from the 'Connexion' after the separation of 1781. But he seems to have been a man of less austere and more attractive character than Romaine, and a less extreme Calvinist. The most active part of his life was spent at Huddersfield. Though he was there only eleven years (for he was obliged to retire at the early age of forty-seven, worn out with overwork in his large parish), he made an indelible mark, both as a preacher and a parish priest. It is interesting to observe that one result of his parochial experience was a modification of his views as to Church order. 'Induced,' writes his son and biographer, 'by the hope of doing good, my father

in certain instances preached in unconsecrated places.
But, having acknowledged this, it becomes my pleasing
duty to state that he was no advocate for irregularity
in others; that when he afterwards considered it in its
different bearings and connexions, he lamented that he
had given way to it, and restrained several other persons
from such acts by the most cogent arguments.' Perhaps
it was the same practical experience in pastoral work—
for it was as a pastor even more than as a preacher
that he won his reputation at Huddersfield—which prevented him from rushing into the fray when the Calvinistic controversy broke out. In fact, he discouraged
such disputes, and once administered a judicious snub
' when asked about a young minister, whether he was a
Calvinist or Arminian.' 'I really do not know,' he
replied; 'he is a sincere disciple of the Lord Jesus
Christ, and that is of infinitely more importance than
his being a disciple of Calvin or Arminius.' The
last twenty-six years of Henry Venn's life were spent
in the secluded village of Yelling; there he trained
up a family, which have made the name of Venn an
honoured household word, not only among Evangelicals,
but among all who value true Christianity. One of
this family, John Venn, rector of Clapham, an Evangelical of the second generation, amply repaid the obligations he was under to his excellent father, by writing
his biography, which is as conspicuous for its interesting style and the good taste which preserved it from
degenerating into a mere panegyric, as for the filial
piety of which it is a fitting monument.

But, interesting as Venn's life and character are,
they do not equal in interest those of John Newton

(1725–1807). Most of the other Evangelical leaders
had always led at least outwardly respectable lives; but
John   Newton had sunk into the lowest depths of
Newton   depravity, and passed through terrible experiences, such as fall to the lot of few. How he went as
a common sailor in a merchant vessel, how he was
impressed on board a man-of-war, how he became the
menial servant of a slave-trader on the coast of Africa,
where he was half-starved and scarcely half-clothed,
how he took part in the horrible slave-traffic, need
not here be told at length. His own account of his
state of mind and course of life during this period
is perfectly awful. 'I well remember,' he says, 'that
while I was passing from one ship to the other [in
which he was among strangers, and therefore under no
restraint] I rejoiced in the exchange, with this reflection, that I might now be as abandoned as I pleased,
without any controul; and, from this time, I was
exceedingly vile; indeed little, if anything, short of that
animated description of an almost irrecoverable state,
which we have in 2 Peter ii. 14. I not only sinned
with a high hand myself, but made it my study to
tempt and seduce others upon every occasion; nay, I
eagerly sought occasion, sometimes to my own hazard
and hurt.'[1]   'My whole life, when awake, was a course of
most horrid impiety and profaneness. I know not that
I have ever since met so daring a blasphemer. Not
content with common oaths and imprecations, I daily
invented new ones; so that I was often seriously
reproved by the captain, who was himself a very

[1] See Cecil's *Life of Newton*, prefixed to his edition of Newton's
Works, p. 13.

passionate man, and not at all circumspect in his expressions. From the relation I at times made of my past adventures, and what he saw of my conduct, and especially towards the close of the voyage, when we met with many disasters, he would often tell me that, to his great grief, he had a Jonah on board; that a curse attended me wherever I went; and that all the troubles he met with in the voyage were owing to his having taken me into the vessel.'[1] 'In a word, I seemed to have every mark of final impenitence and rejection; neither judgments nor mercies made the least impression upon me.'[2] Men of Newton's later opinions have been charged with exaggerating their former depravity, but Newton's account of himself is too circumstantial, and too obviously bears on the face of it traces of its reality, to admit of such a suspicion in his case.

But all this while there were some traces of a better self. He had been piously brought up in his very early years; and while quite a boy he had conceived a romantic attachment to a child of thirteen, Mary Catlett, whom he afterwards married. His pure love for her was the one bright spot in those dreary days of darkness. 'My love to Mrs. N. was the only restraint I had left; though I neither feared God nor regarded man, I could not bear that *she* should think meanly of me when I was dead.' The account of his gradual change is almost too sacred, and certainly too long, to be transferred to these pages. But one point ought to be noted, because it has been said that

Counter-influence even in his worst days

---

[1] See Cecil's *Life of Newton*, prefixed to his edition of Newton's Works, pp. 22, 23.
[2] *Ib.* p. 24.

the Evangelicals unduly depreciated intellectual culture. This certainly was not the case with Newton. Simultaneously with his awakening to a sense of religion arose a desire to improve his mind; and it is perfectly marvellous, considering his antecedents, to what an extent he succeeded. He employed his leisure hours in one of his voyages in reading Horace, and 'I began,' he says, 'to relish the beauties of the composition; acquired a spice of what Mr. Law calls *classical enthusiasm*; and indeed, by this means, I had Horace more *ad unguem* than some who are masters of the Latin tongue; for my helps were so few that I generally had the passage fixed in my memory before I could fully understand its meaning.' He then made himself well acquainted with other Latin poets, taught himself as much Greek as would enable him to read the New Testament, acquired enough Hebrew to 'read the Historical books and Psalms with tolerable ease,' and actually began Syriac, 'having surmised some advantages from the Syriac version.' He moreover picked up the French language, and made considerable progress in mathematics.

When the blaspheming slave-dealer became the earnest and devoted Christian, he found that his expe-
His past riences in that fearful past stood him in good
experiences stood him stead. He could sympathise, as none but a
in stead man who had passed through such an ordeal could, with the temptations of others; and he could lead the fallen to restoration by the very ways which he himself had trod. In fact, it was this which led him to seek Holy Orders. 'I thought,' he says, 'I was, above most living, a fit person to proclaim that faithful saying, that *Jesus Christ came into the world to save the*

chief of sinners; and, as my life had been full of remarkable turns, and I seemed selected to show what
the Lord could do, I was in some hopes that perhaps,
sooner or later, He might call me into His service.'
For sixteen years he was curate of Olney, and was then
presented by Mr. John Thornton to the living of
S. Mary Woolnoth, in London. At Olney he was the
spiritual director of William Cowper: opinions differ
as to the judiciousness, or otherwise, of his treatment
of that delicate case; but as to the excellence of his
intentions there can be no doubt whatever. His
ministry was not altogether successful at Olney; he
was more in his element in London, though here too he
met with much disappointment. It is rather as a
friend or director of other leaders of the Evangelical
Revival than as a leader himself that Newton made his
mark. One can well understand the reverence and
love with which he was regarded in his later years; for
if his earlier character, as drawn by himself, is about as
repulsive as one can conceive, his later character is
singularly attractive. It is the greatest mistake in the
world to think of him as a rough, hard man; a more
tender and sympathising heart than that which beat
under the rough exterior of John Newton never existed. Witness his wonderful forbearance with Thomas
Scott, as related by Scott himself, his considerate treatment of Hannah More and William Wilberforce—not
to mention the moot point in regard to William Cowper
(the present writer has a very strong opinion, though
not a popular one, on that point too), his enthusiastic
devotion to Mary Catlett, both before and after their
marriage, and to her memory when she was taken from

him, and a thousand other little traits which will only be observed in a minute study of his life and writings. He was also a singularly genial man, full of quiet humour, as the admirable 'ana' preserved by R. Cecil show. There is a pleasing and characteristic picture of his later years drawn by the same accomplished pen : 'Being of the most friendly and communicative disposition, his house was open to Christians of all ranks and denominations. Here, like a father among his children, he used to entertain, encourage, and instruct his friends; especially younger ministers or candidates for the ministry. Here also the poor, the afflicted, and the tempted found an asylum and a sympathy, which they could scarcely find, in an equal degree, anywhere besides.' Then follows one of those delightful anecdotes which illustrate alike his humour and his gentleness: 'Some time after Mr. N. had published his "Omicron," and described the three stages of growth in religion, from the *blade*, the *ear*, and the *full corn in the ear*, distinguishing them by the letters A, B, and C, a conceited young minister wrote to Mr. N. telling him that he read his own character accurately drawn in that of C. Mr. N. wrote in reply that in drawing the character of C, or full maturity, he had forgotten to add, till now, one prominent feature of C's character—namely, that C *never knew his own face.*'

From John Newton we naturally turn to his successor at Olney, and (in some sense) his spiritual son, Thomas Scott (1746–1821). Scott, like Newton, had to pass through severe trials; but they were of an intellectual rather than a moral nature. Socinianism, in some form or other, was again raising its head, after the severe blow it had received from Waterland, at the time when Scott entered the ministry; and Scott, like many other clergymen of that day, became deeply tainted with its influence. His vivid account in the ' Force of Truth ' of the struggles which he passed through, is eminently characteristic both of the man and the times. From these struggles he was delivered, chiefly through the instrumentality of John Newton. He was curate of a neighbouring parish to Olney, and was conscience-stricken on hearing that his neighbour, Mr. Newton, had been to visit two of his own dying parishioners whom he had neglected. But he had to overcome that strong prejudice which he shared with the majority of the clergy against ' those whom the world called Methodists,' before he could give Newton a hearing at all. Newton at last overcame this prejudice, not by argument, but by carefully resisting the temptation to argue with which Scott was perpetu- ally plying him. How any unprejudiced person can read Scott's overtures to Newton, as described in the ' Force of Truth,' and Newton's letters to ' the Rev. T. S.' in his correspondence, and yet continue to think that Newton was a rough, overbearing, injudicious man seems inconceivable. Nothing can exceed the gentle- ness, the tenderness, the judiciousness, the patience, and forbearance—in short, the true Christian charity— with which Newton treats his neighbour and corre- spondent; and, on the other hand, nothing can exceed the generous frankness with which Scott admits his own perverse obstinacy. He continued to regard New- ton as a Methodist, intellectually beneath contempt, until, one by one, his prejudices dropped off, and he was convinced by what he well terms 'the force of truth.' When Scott succeeded Newton in the curacy of Olney the outgoing tenant of the vicarage gave the incoming one a warning which is so characteristic of the relations between the two, and also of the quaint humour, the gentleness, and the humility of the writer, that it is worth quoting: 'Methinks I see you sitting in my old corner in the study. I will warn you of one thing. That room (do not start!) used to be haunted. I cannot say I ever saw or heard anything with my bodily organs, but I have been sure there were evil spirits in it and very near me : a spirit of folly, a spirit of indolence, a spirit of unbelief, and many others— indeed their name is Legion. But why should I say they are in your study, when they followed me to London and still pester me here?'

Scott met with more difficulties at Olney than Newton had done; and his difficulties were increased Chaplain of the Lock Hospital rather than lessened, when he exchanged his curacy for the very disagreeable office of chaplain to the Lock Hospital in London, an office which in that day was generally held by Evangelical clergymen. He had not the elements of a popular man about him, and he knew it. 'Some things,' he writes, 'requisite for popularity, I would not have if I could, and others I could not have if I would.' The particular line which he took up, though a most useful and necessary line, was not calculated to make him popular. His printed sermons show that he felt it his special duty to protest, as a Calvinist, against the perversions of Calvinism, a course ingeniously adapted to arm Calvinistic Methodists, Arminian Methodists, and all anti-Methodists of every kind against him. No wonder the good man has to complain : ' Everything conduced to render me more and more unpopular, not only at the Lock, but in every part of London ; ' and yet he could add with perfect truth, ' My most distinguishing reprehensions of those who perverted the doctrines of the Gospel to Antinomian purposes, and my most awful warnings, were the language of compassionate love, and were accompanied by many tears and prayers.' But, independently of his preaching, Scott was never likely to be so popular as Newton; he was not so genial, so tender, so lovable a man, and one can quite understand the gentle poet Cowper not getting on so well with him. He was, however, a man of fine, noble, Christian character ; and, even apart from his writings, well deserves to be ranked with the Evangelical leaders. Perhaps the fact that all his life long he had to maintain a hard struggle against poverty may have tended to sour him a little; but we find few, if any, complaints on that score, though they would have been more than excusable. For surely it was a hard case for a man of blameless life and a most conscientious worker, a man, too, above the average both in abilities and attainments, to labour until he was past middle age for the miserable stipend of 100l. a year. It was his poverty which forced him to write the ' Commentary ; ' and one is grieved, not to say indignant, to learn that in spite of the almost unprecedented success of the venture, it increased rather than diminished the pecuniary embarrassments of the author. He died, as he had lived, a very poor man. Like Venn he retired in his later years to a country village—Aston Sandford.

Like Venn, his honoured name was transmitted to worthy descendants of the third and fourth generation; and like Venn he was fortunate—it was almost the only respect in which the poor man *was* fortunate—in having his biography written by a son who executed his labour of love in a most graphic and interesting, but not in the least fulsome, fashion.

It is a striking contrast to turn from Newton and Scott to the friend of both, and the biographer of one, Richard Cecil (1748–1810); a delicate, highly-cultured man who had never passed through the school of adversity, as his friends had done, and who met with no rough experience in his ministerial work. He ministered to a congregation which must, in the fitness of things, have consisted of people more or less refined, in Bedford Row. It is chiefly on account of his pure and lofty character, which would have shed a lustre upon any cause, that he has always been rightly placed among the leaders of the Evangelical Revival, for he was not the man to seek prominence in any position of life. The Evangelical cause could ill afford to place in the background one who, perhaps more than any other of the leaders, was the representative of 'sweetness and light.' His point of contact with the Evangelicals was principally his spiritual-mindedness; for, whatever its defects, the Evangelical school in the last century was without doubt the home of the most spiritually-minded. But some of his utterances will sound very strange in the ears of those who regard Evangelicalism as a new form of Puritanism. Let us hear, for instance, what he says about the Puritans themselves: 'The Puritans treated man as though he had nothing of the animal about him. There was among them a total excision of all amusement and recreation. Everything was effort, everything was severe. I have heard a man of this school preach on the distinction between justifying and saving faith. He tried to make his hearers enter into these niceties, whereas faith in its bold and leading features should have been presented to them if any effect was expected. The bulk of mankind are capable of much more than the Papist allows, but are incapable of that which the Puritan supposes. They should be treated in opposition to both, as rational and feeling creatures, but upon a bold and palpable ground.' What, again, would 'real Protestants' (those who have waded through the Calvinistic controversy will be familiar with this expression, to their sorrow) say to the following ?—' Man is a creature of extremes. The middle path is generally the wise path, but there are few wise enough to find it. Because Papists have made too much of some things Protestants have made too little of them. Papists treat man as all sense; therefore, some Protestants would treat him as all spirit. Because one party has exalted the Virgin Mary as a divinity, the other can hardly think of that most highly favoured among women with common respect. The Papist puts the Apocrypha into his canon; the Protestant will scarcely regard it as an ancient record. The Popish heresy of human merit in justification drove Luther on the other side into most unwarrantable and unscriptural statements of that doctrine. Papists consider grace as inseparable from the participation of sacraments; Protestants too often lose sight of them as instituted means of conveying grace.' And, once more, what would the railers at priestly assumption say of the following?—'I never choose to forget that I am a priest, because I would not deprive myself of the right to dictate in my ministerial capacity. I cannot suffer a man, therefore, to come to me merely as a friend on his spiritual affairs, because I should have no authority to say to him, "Sir, you must do so and so." I cannot suffer my best friends to dictate to me in anything which concerns my ministerial duties. I have often had to encounter this spirit, and there would be no end of it, if I did not check and resist it. I plainly tell them that they know nothing of the matter.' [1] The inherent excellence of these remarks, their thoughtful discrimination, their pure and dignified style, the insight they give us into the writer's character, and, above all, their oddity as coming from an Evangelical leader, will be, it is hoped, a sufficient apology for the length at which they have been quoted.

Two more, and only two more, names must be added to make the complete list of the clerical leaders of the Evangelical Revival, of the first rank. These are the two brothers, Joseph and Isaac Milner. The elder of the two—Joseph Milner (1744–1797)—having shown himself both a classical scholar and a mathematician at Cambridge, entered at once the scholastic profession, first in a private school, and then as head-master of the Grammar School, Hull, combining with this the office of Sunday afternoon lectureship at Holy Trinity, or the High, Church. Both these offices gave him scope for inculcating those Evangelical

Joseph Milner

---

[1] These quotations are all from Cecil's *Remains*, arranged by Josiah Pratt.

opinions, which, like most of the leaders of the movement, he did not embrace until after he had been some little time in Holy Orders : and he certainly availed himself of his opportunities. He passed through the usual experience of Evangelical preachers, raising at first much opposition to his preaching on the ground that it tended to Methodism, but soon living this down and becoming a popular favourite. He also served the church of North Ferriby, a village about eight miles from Hull. Just before his death he was appointed to the vicarage of Holy Trinity, chiefly through the active exertions of William Wilberforce. It was partly through Milner that Hull and its neighbourhood became a stronghold of Evangelicalism—as it continues to be, more or less, up to the present day. But it is as a writer that Joseph Milner's name is chiefly connected with the Evangelical Revival. We may, therefore, pass from his personal history to that of his younger brother.

Isaac Milner (1751–1820) was the one exception to the rule that the leaders of the Evangelical Revival attained to no high preferment in the Church. His career at Cambridge was a singularly brilliant one. He was not only the Senior Wrangler of his year, and First Smith's Prizeman, but was so far above the rest in his degree examination that the epithet 'incomparabilis' was attached to his name in the Mathematical Tripos. He resided at Cambridge and became Professor of Mathematics and President of his College (Queen's), and finally Dean of Carlisle. His position at Cambridge gave him a splendid vantage-ground for helping on the cause of Evangelicalism.

Isaac Milner

He used all his influence to indoctrinate with Evangelical views the future clergy who might afterwards spread them throughout the country; and, being a man of a genial manner and of great conversational powers, as well as of high reputation in the university, he was naturally very successful. In fact, it was greatly owing to Isaac Milner that Cambridge was not marked, as Oxford was, by hostility to Evangelicalism, and that so large a proportion of the Evangelical clergy were always Cambridge men.

It may seem an arbitrary line, but one must draw the line somewhere; and among the other Evangelical clergy of the eighteenth century, none appear quite to hold the position which has been assigned to the leaders of the movement noticed above. There were, however, a few others, without some slight notice of whom even a short sketch like the present would be very incomplete. Among these clergy of what one may *Samuel Walker of Truro* call the second rank the chief place must be assigned to Samuel Walker of Truro (1719–1760). Indeed, if he had lived a little later, and if his lot had been cast in a less remote spot, he would almost certainly have been among the foremost of the Evangelical leaders. But it is a far cry to Cornwall; and in those days, when communication with distant parts was not so complete or so rapid as it is now, it was impossible for a Cornish man, whose forte lay in preaching and practical work rather than in writing, to make his influence adequately felt throughout the country. Moreover, he was an Evangelical before Evangelicalism had become a distinct and recognised power, and he did not live long enough to see the day when that happened. In point of date he belonged to the earlier phase of the movement, but so far as opinions, conduct, and general tone of mind were concerned, he clearly belonged to the later phase. It would, however, be quite incorrect to describe Walker as one born out of due time; there were in his day, and had never ceased to be, numbers of clergy who held precisely the same views as the later Evangelicals did, and the only point on which Mr. Walker differed from them was in the fact that he succeeded in producing within a limited sphere a revival based on their views, but conducted scrupulously on the principle of the parochial system. He was, if not the exclusive originator, at any rate the central figure of that remarkable revival in West Cornwall, which went on side by side with the Wesleyan Revival, and was frequently brought into collision with it. Like Wesley, Walker formed a 'society' at Truro; but it was a society which was to be strictly after the model of those earlier 'religious societies,' which began in the seventeenth century, and which not only professed to be, but actually were, real handmaids to the Church.

With the name of Walker is naturally associated that of his most intimate friend and kindred spirit, Thomas Adam of Winteringham (1701–1784).
Thomas Adam of Wintering-ham A Lincolnshire village in the eighteenth century was not much less remote than a Cornish town from the great centres of life; and of this village Adam was the resident incumbent for no less than fifty-eight years, being in vain tempted, first by his uncle, and then by his diocesan (Bishop Thomas) to put himself in the way of further preferment. There can be

obviously little to record about his uneventful, but blameless and useful life, a short sketch of which will be found prefixed to his best known work, 'Private Thoughts,' by his great friend and co-religionist, Mr. Stillingfleet of Hotham. Archdeacon Bassett of Glentworth, a neighbouring village to Winteringham, the incumbency of which is still held by a member of the Bassett family, was another intimate friend both of Adam and Walker, and held precisely the same religious views as both.

But though there were many country clergymen who before the close of the century were pronounced Evangelicals, the centres of the movement were generally large towns. London, Hull, Huddersfield, and Cambridge have been noticed. To these must be added Leicester and York. The leading Evangelical clergyman at Leicester was Thomas Robinson (1749–1813), who left a deep and permanent impression upon that important midland centre by his preaching and by his parochial activity, and upon the country at large by his pen. He took a leading part in schemes for the amelioration, not only of the spiritual, but also of the temporal, condition of Leicester, and affected largely the clergy of the place, one of whom, Mr. Vaughan, a kindred spirit, has given us an interesting biography of his friend. At York the pioneer of Evangelical principles was William Richardson (1745–1821), who lived long enough to see the rise in the ancient city of a younger generation of Evangelical clergy, who looked up to him in his old age as their spiritual father. Before the century closed Charles Simeon had taken up at Cambridge Isaac Milner's work,

[margin note: Thomas Robinson of Leicester; and William Richardson of York]

which he more than carried out among the future
clergy of England; but his history belongs more to the
nineteenth than to the eighteenth century. Richard
Conyers of Helmsley, John King of Hull, Thomas
Dykes of Hull, John Venn of Clapham, Augustus Toplady of Broad Hemsbury, Rowland Hill of the Surrey
Chapel (though in point of position, not of doctrine, he
was almost *sui generis*), and many others, would claim
place in any extended history of the Evangelical movement; but in this sketch it must suffice to say that before
the nineteenth century began the Evangelical clergy had
become a very numerous and influential body within
the Church of England.

CHAPTER VI.

THE EVANGELICAL LAITY.

IT might, perhaps, have been expected that as the
Evangelical Revival was effected by what is now called
Laity played the Low-Church party in the Church (the term
a subordi- had quite a different meaning in the eighteenth
nate part in
the Revival century), the lay element would have been
quite as prominent as the clerical in the work; for Low
Churchmen are, of course, utterly opposed to anything
like sacerdotalism. This, however, was certainly not
the case. The laity helped nobly with their purses,
and, to some extent, with their personal efforts and
with their pens. But all they did was in strict subordination to the clergy. In fact there is hardly a
single layman who can be said to have attained the

position of a leader of the first rank in the Revival.
This may partly be accounted for by the fact that the
great instrument in the Revival was preaching; and as
the chief point which differentiated the Evangelical from
the Methodist movement was the strict observance by
the former of Church order—or rather, let us say, Church
customs, for outdoor lay-preaching is no infringement of
the rules of Church order—the laity were debarred from
using, nor do they seem to have desired to use, the
main instrument by which the effects were produced.
But this was not all. Some of the leading Evangelical
clergy (like Cecil) took a very high view of ministerial
authority, and none of them were by any means disposed to submit to lay dictation. We have seen how
Romaine, Venn, and others declined to be dazzled even
by the glamour of a Countess; and men like Scott,
Newton, and the Milners, were not the men to let the
reins slip out of their own hands. Indeed, they were
not tried in this peculiar way. It is true that Scott,
especially, had to fight a severe battle against Antinomianism; but it was against the doctrine, not against
the wish for personal supremacy on the part of the men
who held it, that he had to fight. The good men who
agreed with the views of their clergy were perfectly
ready to let those clergy have the undisputed rule.
Hence a very short chapter will suffice to sketch the leading laity who took a part in the Evangelical movement.

A striking instance of what has been said above
may be found in the careers of the two Thorntons, John the father, and Henry the son.
They were wealthy merchants, who in very truth looked
upon their riches, not as their own but as talents en-

John
Thornton

trusted to them for their Master's use. John Thornton was the patron of John Newton. He was much impressed by Newton's thrilling 'Narrative,' and paid him a visit at Olney. The result of this visit was that Thornton told Newton to 'be hospitable, and keep an open house for such as were worthy of entertainment; and help the poor and needy.' 'I will statedly allow you,' he added, '200l. a year, and readily send whatever you have occasion to draw for more.' Mr. Newton told Mr. Cecil that he thought he had received from Mr. Thornton upwards of 3,000l. in this way, during the time he resided at Olney.[1] This was only a sample of John Thornton's princely munificence. To quote the words of Newton's biographer: 'He purchased advowsons and presentations, with a view to place in parishes the most enlightened, active, and useful ministers. He employed the extensive commerce in which he was engaged, as a powerful instrument for conveying immense quantities of Bibles, Prayer-books, and the most useful publications, to every place visited by our trade. He printed, at his own sole expense, large editions of the latter for that purpose, and it may be safely affirmed, that there is scarcely a part of the known world, where such books could be introduced, which did not feel the salutary influence of this single individual. He was a philanthropist on the largest scale, the friend of man under all his wants. Instances might be mentioned of it, were it proper to particularise, which would surprise those who did not know Mr. Thornton. They were so much out of ordinary course and expectation, that I know some who felt it their duty to inquire of him whether the sum they

[1] *Life of Newton*, p. 59.

had received was sent by his intention or by mistake. To this may be added, that the manner of presenting his gifts was as delicate and concealed as the measure was large. Besides this constant course of private donations, there was scarcely a public charity, or occasion of relief to the ignorant or necessitous, which did not meet with his distinguished support. His only question was " May the miseries of men in any measure be removed or alleviated ? " Nor was he merely distinguished by stretching out a liberal hand; his benevolent heart was so intent on doing good, that he was ever inventing or promoting places for its diffusion at home or abroad.' [1]

Henry Thornton was the worthy son of a worthy father. He is said to have divided his income into two

Henry Thornton

parts, retaining only one-seventh for his own use, and devoting six-sevenths to charity; after he became the head of a family, he gave two-thirds away, and retained one-third for himself and his family. It appeared, after his death, from his accounts, that the amount he spent in the relief of distress in one of his earlier years considerably exceeded 9,000*l*. His position as a Member of Parliament enabled him to render material assistance to the Evangelical cause, at least in some of its philanthropical schemes. Next to William Wilberforce he was the firmest supporter in Parliament of the abolition of the slave-trade. Lord Brougham, who was in Parliament with him, pronounces him to be ·'the most eminent in every respect' of the Wilberforce coterie, and describes him as 'a man of strong understanding, great powers of reasoning and of investiga-

[1] *Life of Newton*, pp. 56-8.

tion ; an accurate and a curious observer, but who neither
had cultivated oratory at all, nor had received a refined
education, nor had extended his reading beyond the
subjects connected with moral, political, and theological
learning.'[1]

But though the two Thorntons were thus ready to
spend and be spent in the interests of Evangelicalism,
there is no trace of the spirit of Diotrephes in either of
them. They had full confidence in the clergy on whose
ministry they attended, and were quite content to afford
that aid which was particularly essential—because, as we
have seen, the Evangelical clergy were generally strait-
ened for means—without assuming any of the airs of
dictation.

An intimate friend and relative of the two Thorntons, and a member like them of the so-called ' Clapham
sect,' was William Wilberforce (1759–1831).
Like the Thorntons, Wilberforce aided the
Evangelical cause largely with his purse, and, like the
younger of them, he was of immense service to it as a
Member of Parliament. But he did more than this. As
an intimate friend of William Pitt the younger, and
many other leading men in the State, he was a sort of
connecting link between the Church and the world. In
fact, he had so many ties which bound him to those
who were quite outside the Evangelical circle, that it
has been doubted whether he can be called a *bonâ-fide*
Evangelical at all. But surely all his religious impres-
sions were derived from the Evangelical school. Joseph
and Isaac Milner, John Newton, and Thomas Scott
affected him spiritually more than any other men—and

William
Wilberforce

[1] *Statesmen of the Time of George III.*

it need not be said in what direction their influence
would tend—and in his later years he 'sat under' John
Venn. It may be that his Calvinism was not so marked
as any of theirs was (though they were all very moderate Calvinists); but take away Evangelical influence,
and you take away all the human influence which
affected his religion; take away his religion, and you
take away all the influence which stimulated and
directed him in the great philanthropical work of his
life. Nor was it only in the matter of the slave-trade
that Wilberforce deeply affected national sentiment.
'Few members,' we are told, 'attended with more assi-
duity in their places in Parliament. Though his frame
was always weak, and his health indifferent, he rarely
absented himself from public duty; he had, indeed, a
higher motive for its discharge than most men. Though
singularly destitute of self-importance, he was sensible
that he had gradually risen to a peculiar responsibility,
which there were few, if any, to share with him. He
was regarded by the religious world as the protector, in
the Lower House, of public morals and religious rights.
He was justly conscious that this was the highest trust
confided to his care, and he was vigilant in proportion.
He was never to be found sleeping when any question
trenching on public decorum or the interests of religion
came before the Legislature.'[1]

As to the value of the support which he was able to
give, let us take the unexceptionable evidence of one
who was, above most men, competent to judge; one
who had often heard him speak, and knew him well,

[1] *Memoir of William Wilberforce, Esq.*, by Rev. T. Price, prefixed
to the edition of the *Practical View, &c.* of 1834.

but one who certainly did not share his religious views, and would not therefore be prejudiced in his favour on their account. 'His eloquence,' writes Lord Brougham, 'was of the highest order. It was persuasive and pathetic in an eminent degree, but it was occasionally bold and impassioned, animated with the inspiration which deep feeling alone can breathe into spoken thought, chastened by a pure taste, varied by extensive information, enriched by classical allusion, sometimes elevated by the more sublime topics of Holy Writ—the thoughts and the spirit

That touched Isaiah's hallowed lips with fire.'[1]

The same writer calls him 'the head, indeed the founder, of a powerful religious sect.' This, of course, is absurd. Evangelicalism,—which, by the way, cannot properly be termed a sect at all—was firmly established as a power in the country before William Wilberforce gave in his adherence to it. Lord Brougham was a better judge of parliamentary eloquence than of religious parties; but his remark is worth quoting, as showing what an able man of the world thought of Wilberforce's religious position. And, though he was neither the head nor the founder of the Evangelical party, he contributed more than any other man could do to its prestige and influence, especially in circles into which its real heads and founders could not easily find access. Like most of the other Evangelical laymen, Wilberforce was lavishly generous with his purse; he is said to have spent from a third to a fourth part of his large income upon acts of charity.

[1] *Statesmen of the Time of George III.* First Series, vol. ii. Mr. Wilberforce.

From one point of view the greatest name of all among the Evangelical laity is that of William Cowper (1731–1800). Of course the shy recluse of Olney and Weston Underwood took no active part in the work except with his pen, but that, as we shall see in the next chapter, was a very active part indeed. But his name gave credit to the cause. The mere fact that the most elegant writer of the day both in verse and prose (for though he actually published no prose work, his admirable letters fully entitle him to this rank) thoroughly identified himself with Evangelicalism, might fairly be quoted in answer to the very common charge that it was only fitted for. weak and uncultured minds. It is true that his mind was often unstrung; and that, when it *was* unstrung, his mania took the form, as it so often does, of religious melancholy. But it has yet to be proved that the peculiar tenets of Evangelicalism produced, or contributed to produce, his mental derangement; while it is quite certain that, when his mind *was* sound, those tenets were heartily embraced by him; that he guided his pure and blameless life by them, and derived from them the greatest consolation and support.

Two noblemen will complete the list of those laymen who can by any stretch of the term be called leaders of the Evangelical Revival. The first is Lord Dartmouth, to whom Newton addressed his 'Twenty-six letters to a nobleman,' with which his 'Cardiphonia' commences; and who was so polished a gentleman that Richardson is reported to have said that 'he would have realised his own idea of Sir Charles Grandison, if he had not been a Methodist.' He

advocated the cause of Evangelicalism both among the
nobility and at Court; and he used his influence to
gain preferment for the Evangelical clergy. He is immortalised by Cowper in the well-known lines:

> We boast some rich ones, whom the Gospel sways,
> And one who wears a coronet and prays.[1]

Lord Teignmouth was one of the Clapham coterie who
attended the ministry of John Venn; he was the first
president of the Bible Society, and was much looked
up to by the Evangelicals of the second generation.
An interesting narrative of his life and happy death
was published after his decease and widely circulated.

Among the ladies who took a prominent part in the
Revival the first place must, of course, be given to
Susanna Wesley. If 'the mother of the
Wesleys was the mother of Methodism,' she
was, in one sense, the originator of the whole movement. But Mrs. Wesley can scarcely be said to have
taken personally any part in the Revival. Beyond her
memorable advice to her son John, in the matter of
recognising lay-preachers, there is a singular absence of
the name of Mrs. Wesley in connexion with the movement. As she died in 1742, she had probably little
idea of the proportions which her sons' work was about
to assume, particularly as she had already reached an
advanced age when the Revival began. The immense
influence which she maintained over her sons to the very
end of her life is so well known that we may be quite
sure she encouraged rather than discouraged them in
their efforts. Indeed, John Wesley expressly tells us

Susanna Wesley

[1] *Truth.*

that 'when he was between forty and fifty' [he made a little mistake here, for he was only thirty-nine when she died] 'he judged himself full as much obliged to obey his mother in everything lawful as he did when he was in his leading-strings.'[1] So far as moulding the character of her two famous sons, and especially John, went, she may be regarded as a most important factor in the Evangelical Revival, but that is all.

Mrs. Fletcher (*née* Bosanquet) is another lady whose beautiful Christian character sheds a lustre upon the Mrs. Fletcher cause which she heartily embraced, but she again did not take any prominent part in the general work. Her 'tender and judicious care' of her invalid husband helped to prolong his valuable life for a year or two, and during the four years she lived with him she joined cordially in all his good works. Before her marriage, she had devoted both her personal efforts and her fortune (which was large) to the care of the indigent, especially of orphan children; and she is justly reckoned as one of the saints of Methodism. John Wesley said of her, 'she is the only woman in England I judged worthy of Mr. Fletcher;'[2] a remarkable testimony, seeing that he placed Mr. Fletcher first among all the Christians he ever knew.

Less even than Mrs. Wesley and Mrs. Fletcher can Mrs. Newton be regarded as a prominent character in Mrs. Newton the Revival; but as the almost idolised wife of one of the chief leaders she must not be altogether passed over in silence. John Newton very characteristically made the public his confidant in what

[1] Sermon *On Obedience to Parents.*—Sermon XCI.
[2] Sermon CXXXIII., *On the death of Mr. Fletcher.*

he owns to be his inordinate affection for Mary Catlett, years before she became his wife, and years after she had gone to her rest. It was a bold thing to publish his 'Letters to a Wife'—perhaps a questionable thing in point of delicacy—but there is not one word in them that could offend the most fastidious taste; and we can certainly gather from them that whatever influence Newton exercised over the course of the Revival—and it was obviously very great—was shared by Mrs. Newton. 'She was,' he writes in his Preface to the letters, 'my pleasing companion, my most affectionate friend, my judicious counsellor. I seldom or never repented of acting according to her advice. And I seldom acted against it, without being convinced by the event that I was wrong.' And in the Appendix to the same: 'The Bank of England is too poor to compensate for such a loss as mine. I have lost a right hand, which I cannot but miss continually; but the Lord enables me to go on cheerfully without it.'

> 'Forget her ! No. Can four short years
> The deep impression wear away ?
> She still before my mind appears
> Abroad, at home, by night, by day.'

Thus he begins one of the set of verses, more touching than better poetry, which he regularly wrote on each anniversary of her death. It is rather provoking that neither his letters nor his verses give us any definite picture of one who exercised so large an influence over him, and therefore indirectly over those events *quorum pars magna fuit.*

But there is one lady who really may rank among

the very foremost promoters of the Evangelical Revival, Hannah More (1745–1833). It was not only by her

Hannah More writings, which will come before us in the next chapter, nor by her active exertions to raise by education the condition of the labouring population of the West, that Miss More did great service to the Evangelical cause. She also contributed very largely to break down the prejudices against 'Methodists' (which term included, as we have seen, all who were in any way connected with the Evangelical movement). Before she became in any way 'tainted with Methodism' she was on terms of intimacy with Garrick, Johnson, Burke, Reynolds—in fact, the best literary society in London; and her 'Methodism' did not in the least interfere with that intimacy. It is difficult to over-estimate the value of her work in thus helping to bridge over the chasm, which unfortunately never was thoroughly filled up, between the Evangelicals and Methodists and the people of the highest culture of the day; and Miss H. More's services in this respect deserve the most grateful acknowledgment from all friends of the Evangelical movement.

Before concluding this sketch of individuals, a word must be said of some who hung, as it were,

Dr. Johnson on the outskirts of the movement, sympathising with it and helping it on to a certain extent, but not thoroughly identifying themselves with it. One hardly knows whether to place the great Dr. Johnson in this category. It is true that he spoke very contemptuously of his brother-collegian, George Whitefield, and that he perversely justified that very arbitrary expulsion of the six students from

Oxford on account of their Methodism. But he always respected John·Wesley, and enjoyed conversation with him; and he regarded Hannah More with an almost paternal affection. That his well-known fear of death, in spite of his pious life, may have been removed at the last through Evangelical influence seems highly probable, though it has been indignantly denied. But Dr. Johnson was from first to last an old-fashioned High Churchman, and cannot, in the technical sense of the term, be called an Evangelical.

Dr. Beilby Porteus, Bishop of London, was a prelate whom the Evangelicals highly respected. They were glad to welcome the degree of countenance which he ventured to show them; and he undoubtedly sympathised with their many benevolent schemes, and used the power, which his commanding position and high personal character gave him, to favour the Evangelical clergy. The promotion of Sunday schools, the agitation for the abolition of the slave-trade, the newly re-awakened zeal for foreign missions, all found in him a warm and powerful friend. He expressed publicly an almost extravagant admiration of Hannah More and her writings, and made strong efforts to bring about a better observance of the Lord's Day, a favourite project with the Evangelicals; but he never so far committed himself as to incur the reproach of Methodism—and no thorough Evangelical ever escaped that charge.

Bishop Beilby Porteus

Henry Brooke, the well-known author of the 'Fool of Quality,' so warmly recommended by John Wesley, was a sort of half-Methodist, but can scarcely be identified with the cause. Bishop Lowth,

Others who were friendly

again, showed the deepest respect for John Wesley in his old age, and was certainly no foe to the Evangelical cause. Edward Young, the author of 'Night Thoughts,' was obviously influenced by the Revival when he wrote that gloomy but powerful poem. And, finally, King George III. was always regarded—and justly regarded—by Methodists and Evangelicals as their friend, though of course he only viewed the movement from the outside. It is said that in his old age, after having listened to the music of Charles Wesley the younger, he 'laid a hand on one of the shoulders of the musician and said, "To your uncle, Mr. Wesley, and your father, and to George Whitefield, and the Countess of Huntingdon, the Church in this realm is more indebted than to all others."' [1] When Lady Huntingdon complained to him about Archbishop Cornwallis's 'routs' he told her how highly he estimated her character, zeal, and abilities, 'which,' he said, 'could not be consecrated to a more noble purpose ; ' and he would hear no complaints against the Methodists.

CHAPTER VII.

LITERATURE OF THE REVIVAL.

It was far more by the living voice than by the pen that the Evangelical Revival made its influence felt.
Sermons:—
Wesley's
But the leaders were not altogether inactive with their pens, and therefore a chapter must be devoted to the literature which they produced. And

[1] See *Wesley Memorial Volume*, p. 74.

as they laid the greatest stress upon preaching, it will
be appropriate first to touch upon the sermons which
they have bequeathed to us. The most notable are the
sermons of John Wesley. These possess an adventitious
interest, not only from the startling effects which they
undoubtedly produced and from the unique character of
the preacher, whose idiosyncrasies they reflect in every
page, but also because they are more than sermons;
they are a kind of creed to a very large number of
Christian people. The fifty-three discourses published in
1771 constitute, with Mr. Wesley's ' Notes on the New
Testament,' ' the standard doctrines of the Methodist
Connexion,' and are referred to as such in the trust-deeds
of the Methodist chapels. They are admirable sermons
in their way, plain, practical, and earnest, expressed in
that pure, forcible language of which John Wesley was
a master. They are full of good common-sense, without
any tawdry ornament, and without a particle of cant or
of offence against good taste. But it is difficult for anyone who reads them in cold blood, to understand what
there was in them to produce any of that wild excitement which often attended their delivery. The preacher
seems to have carefully eschewed both language and
topics which would have any tendency to excite. And
perhaps nothing shows more strongly the need there
must have been for some sort of revival than the mere
fact that such plain truths so plainly expressed should
have produced the results which they did. But Wesley
knew perfectly well what he was about when he adopted
this style of preaching. He knew the sort of people he
wished to affect and the best way of affecting them—as
the result proved. All this should be carefully kept in

view as we read Wesley's sermons, otherwise a sense of disappointment is inevitable. As specimens of pulpit oratory they cannot for a moment be compared with those of our great classical preachers, such as Jeremy Taylor, Barrow, or South; or with some of Wesley's contemporaries, Bishop Horsley and others. But the very last thing which Wesley desired was to pose as an orator. What he said of all his writings would apply especially to his sermons. ' I dare no more write in a fine style than wear a fine coat. I should purposely decline what many admire, a highly ornamental style.'

As to George Whitefield's sermons, it is unfortunate for his reputation as a preacher that any specimens
Whitefield's　should have been preserved. It is quite un-necessary to spend any time upon them, for they can hardly be said to come under the head of 'literature' at all.

But, in fact, all the sermons, both of the Methodists and of the later Evangelicals, were intended for present
Newton's,　effect, not for future study. It is not, there-
Scott's,
Milner's　fore, surprising that they do not take any place in sacred literature. But the odd point is that none of them seem at all adapted for revival purposes. Take, for instance, those of John Newton. They are full of matter, and not without humour. We can well understand those who heard them going away with a feeling that their souls had been satisfied with good, solid, substantial food; but we cannot understand them going away with a feeling of excitement. The same may be said of the sermons of Joseph Milner, so far as one can judge from the specimens which are extant; the same of the sermons of Thomas Scott. Compare

any of these with the sermons of Richard Baxter in the preceding century, or those of Thomas Chalmers in the following one, and the difference will be apparent.

Next to sermons we might have expected the Evangelical Revival to have been rich in practical and devotional works. But this was not the case. The two works, indeed, which first set the stone rolling—'The Serious Call' and 'Christian Perfection'—will compare favourably, in point of style and intellectual power, with the very best of their kind. But they can hardly be ranked as belonging to the Evangelical school. Their writer was a pronounced High Churchman when he wrote them, and he certainly did not draw nearer to the Evangelicals when he superadded mysticism to his churchmanship. One can readily understand that Hervey's 'Meditations among the Tombs' and his 'Theron and Aspasio' should have superseded the 'Serious Call' as popular favourites with those who held Evangelical views. The preference, indeed, does not say much for the intellectual taste of our ancestors; for, from a literary point of view, the two writers stand almost at the opposite poles. But the sentiments of Hervey would naturally be more acceptable, at least to the Calvinist section of the Revivalists, than those of Law. How anyone could have been edified by the vapid and turgid declamation of Hervey seems inconceivable; but there is no doubt that his two works, and especially the earlier and more florid one, were immensely popular when they first appeared, and that their popularity long survived the death of their author.

Romaine's 'Life, Walk, and Triumph of Faith' is a

Practical and devotional works:—Hervey's

performance of a very different calibre from Hervey's.
It is a really powerful work in its way, and reminds us,
Romaine's   more than any of the Evangelical writings, of
'Life, Walk,
and Tri-   some of the works of the Puritan divines in
umph of
Faith'   the preceding century. Its Calvinism is more
pronounced and unguarded than that of any work of the
Evangelical leaders ; and we can well understand how
it might be perverted into an encouragement of Antinomianism. Wilberforce tells us that Newton in his
old age ' owned that Romaine had made many Anti-
nomians.'[1] This was, indeed, quite contrary to the
author's intention ; but it was, none the less, a very
likely danger to arise from many of Romaine's expressions. In style and language, as well as in matter,
the book reminds one much more of the seventeenth
than of the eighteenth century. But it was a work
which was much admired by Romaine's contemporaries,
and by many in later generations. To the modern
reader it certainly appears rather dreary reading. Calvinism itself is not popular ; and practical and devotional works are now expected to deal with strictly
practical duties. Romaine does not do this, at any
rate in detail ; he deals chiefly with abstract questions,
and deals with them at too great length to please
modern taste. But it must be remembered that though
' The Life, Walk, and Triumph of Faith ' form really
but one work, they were originally three separate
treatises written and published at different times. And
it should be added that the ' Life, Walk, and Triumph
of Faith ' possesses the strength as well as the defects
of the earlier Puritanism. It is, perhaps, on the whole,

[1] See *Life of Wilberforce*, by his sons, vol. ii. p. 137.

the strongest book, as its author was certainly the strongest man who appeared among the Evangelicals.

It was not, however, and was not likely to be, so useful and acceptable a work as Henry Venn's 'Com-

Venn's plete Duty of Man.' No one can complain *'Complete Duty of* that this book tended to Antinomianism, or *Man'* that it did not enter sufficiently into the duties of daily life. It was, in fact, the direct outcome of the writer's great practical experience in dealing with individual souls; for Venn had been much consulted and had been eminently successful as, what would have been called in the preceding century, a 'casuist;' and his work simply put into print the counsel which he had before given orally. Hence, though its opening chapters give us a distinct enough statement of Evangelical doctrine, the greater portion of the book deals with practical duties. Of course Venn would feel that the latter directions would have been quite useless unless based upon the former; but, unlike Romaine, he devotes the larger space to practice, including the most minute rules about the moral virtues and relative duties. Regarded as a literary composition it by no means attains a high rank, for its style is somewhat heavy and its arguments are not very profound. If we would appreciate its excellence we must take it simply as the counsel of a pious and affectionate friend. The title of the book suggests a comparison and a contrast, which were no doubt intended, between 'The Whole Duty of Man' and 'The Complete Duty of Man.' 'The Whole Duty of Man'—the authorship of which has always been an interesting puzzle to the curious—had, after the Restoration, been raised to an elevation only next to that of the Sacred Volume and the Book of Common Prayer. Bishops had recommended it to be used instead of sermons, teachers of charity schools were required to teach Church principles by its help; it was translated with the Bible and the Liturgy into other languages; young clergymen were advised to ' persuade every family in their parishes to read the " Whole Duty of Man " according to the method of the partition therein prescribed,' that is, three times through the year. A violent reaction set in against it with the rise of the Evangelical movement. ' Its author knew no more of Christianity than Mahomet,' said Whitefield. It was a ' repository of self-righteousness and pharisaical lumber,' said Cowper— and so forth. One can as little endorse the extravagant censure as the extravagant praise with which the book was successively labelled. It is certainly not accurate to say that the ' Whole Duty of Man ' fails to base Christian duties on distinctively Christian doctrines; but one can well understand that Venn would think that sufficient prominence was not given to the latter. To remedy the defect he wrote his useful treatise, which was deservedly one of the most popular of all the practical and devotional works of the Evangelical school.

Its popularity, however, was not equal to that of Wilberforce's famous work, which was entitled in full, Wilberforce's ' Practical View ' ' A Practical View of the Prevailing Religious Systems of Professed Christians in the Higher and Middle Classes in this Country, contrasted with Real Christianity.' 'The main object,' to use the author's own language, ' which he had in view was, not to convince the sceptic or to answer the arguments of persons, who avowedly opposed the fundamental doctrines of our religion, but to point out the scanty and erroneous system of the bulk of those who belong to the class of orthodox Christians, and to contrast their defective scheme with a representation of what the author apprehended to be real Christianity.'[1] The work was a singularly seasonable one for this reason : it appeared just when the minds of Englishmen had received a shock from the horrors of the French Revolution ; the abnegation of Divine revelation in France and the setting up of the Goddess of Reason in its place had produced such results that men who had been inclined to toy with scepticism were abruptly checked and driven back to the old religion. A revulsion from rationalism forced them to accept the Christian creeds but not to lead the Christian life, and Wilberforce's work fell like a bombshell among these inconsistent Christians. The Methodist movement had mainly affected the lower and lower-middle classes, and, in spite of good Lady Huntingdon's efforts, the earlier Evangelical or Calvinistic movement had not touched more than the surface of the upper classes. The later Evangelical movement was *beginning*, but only just beginning, to affect them, and the ' Practical View' immensely contributed to the result. Written by a layman who was well known as an accomplished debater in Parliament—a man who was on terms of intimacy with the most eminent statesmen of the day, and an eminent statesman himself, a man of wit and talent who had been a brilliant ornament to society, a

[1] Introduction to the *Practical View*, p. iii.

man of extraordinary philanthropy and benevolence, the parliamentary representative of the largest county in England—it came with a force which no work of any clergyman or of any unknown layman could possibly possess. The writer's parliamentary experience also stood him directly in good stead. He knew exactly the sort of minds which he wished to impress, and the best way of impressing them. He had been accustomed to the task of persuading such minds on other subjects by his tongue; he now essayed to persuade them on the most important subject of all by his pen. Thus the 'Practical View' was written from a vantage-ground: it commended itself apart from its intrinsic merits. These, however, were by no means inconsiderable. No one can read it even now without feeling touched by the simple earnestness of the writer. It was helped, as all such works are, by foolish opposition; not only did that opposition prevent the interest of the new work from flagging, but it directly recommended its arguments. For Englishmen love fair play, and many of the charges brought against the 'Practical View' were so obviously unfair that they created a reaction in its favour. All this must be taken into account in order to explain the absurd miscalculation which was made about its success, and the fears which the writer himself entertained concerning its reception. He was afraid of 'incurring the imputation of officiousness,' 'of deviating from his proper line, and of impertinently interfering in the concerns of a profession to which he did not belong.'[1] The publisher had so little faith in the project that he would only consent to issue five hundred

[1] See Introduction, p. ii.

copies, on the condition that Wilberforce would give his name. But the first edition was sold off in a few days; within half a year the book passed through five editions, and it has now passed through fifty. It was translated into most of the European languages, and the reprints in America are said to have been considerably more numerous than the editions in this country.

The readiness of the upper classes to receive any stirring appeal to their spiritual consciousness is further

Hannah More's works

illustrated by the extraordinary success which attended Hannah More's first effort in the same direction. Her 'Thoughts on the Manners of the Great' was published in the very year of the French Revolution (1788). The work was published anonymously, because 'she hoped it might be attributed to a better person.' The secret of the authorship was, however, soon discovered, and the effect was not spoiled. Seven large editions were sold in a few months, the second in little more than a week, the third in four hours. When she published a similar work two years later, entitled 'An Estimate of the Religion of the Fashionable World,' it was bought up and read as eagerly as its predecessor. In fact all the practical works of Hannah More were immensely popular, and, what was better still, produced great practical results. The 'manners of the great' are said to have been materially improved in consequence of her treatises on the subject; and her 'Village Politics, by Will Chip,' had an equally good effect upon the humbler classes, who were then much inclined to favour French revolutionary principles. As one of the first workers in a field of literature which has since her day been vastly

extended, she did much useful service by her cheap
Repository Tracts. And in her 'Cœlebs in Search of a
Wife,' which was one of the first specimens of the now
popular religious novel, she supplied wholesome food for
the imagination, instead of the very unwholesome food
which was furnished by the coarse romances of the
period. One can hardly endorse the extravagant lauda-
tions which were lavished upon her as a writer by really
competent judges. The generation which still admired
Hervey would naturally admire Hannah More; for, as
became the friend and admirer of Dr. Johnson, she was
given to long words and ornately polished periods; but
works written with the single aim with which this good
woman wrote, must be judged by the effects they produced, not by the canons of literary criticism, and,
regarded in this light, she was a wonderfully successful
writer. She possessed the same advantage which
Wilberforce had in this respect, inasmuch as she preserved an intimate connexion with people outside the
circle of the Evangelical world. 'You have a great
advantage, madam,' wrote Newton to her; 'there is a
circle by which what you write will be read, and which
will hardly read anything of a religious kind that is
not written by you.' Sydney Smith commenced a
review of her works by a long mock apology for not
treating them as exactly on the same level with the inspired writings; and in truth he scarcely exaggerated
the estimation in which her works were held. It was
said that 'her style and manner were confessedly
superior to those of any moral writer of the age;' that
she was 'one of the most illustrious females that ever
was in the world,' 'one of the most truly Evangelical

divines of this whole age, perhaps almost of any age not apostolic.' ·We˙ may smile at such extravagant praise; but let us also be thankful that she always used that marvellous pen of hers to recommend what was good and pure. There are few writers to whom the Evangelical cause was more indebted than to Hannah More.

Two posthumous works, Adam's ' Private Thoughts ' and Cecil's ' Remains,' were both deservedly popular. The former consists of extracts from Adam's ' Private Diary,' ' given to the public by the surviving editor of the posthumous works ' [William Richardson of York] ' in a convenient form,' as being the most interesting part, and therefore the most in demand, of those works. It is, of course, not a systematic treatise, but simply a set of aphorisms and pious reflections, being something of the nature—to compare small things with great—of the ' Confessions of St. Augustine ' or the ' De Imitatione ' of Thomas à Kempis, after the Evangelical pattern. The ' Thoughts ' were objected to by some as being too full of penitential language; but, as the editor quaintly remarks, ' had he suppressed the passages objected to, this Register of the Thoughts of the Heart would resemble a register of the weather, in which no mention was made of storms and fogs, and nothing recorded but genial warmth and a clear blue sky. But what is the use of such a register?' Some of the aphorisms are wonderfully pointed and racy. For instance, ' I see the devil's hook, and yet cannot help nibbling at his bait.' ' O God! give me what Thou knowest to be good, and Thou alone knowest what is good. Give more than I can ask or think. If the reverse of what I ask is what I should ask, give me that; let me not be undone by my prayers.' 'It is much easier to join oneself to a sect than to God.' It is true that this book is of a more melancholy cast than most of the writings of the Evangelicals, who were, as a rule, singularly bright and hopeful.

This certainly is the character of the little work that we have grouped with Adam's, the 'Remains' of

Cecil's
'Remains'

Richard Cecil, which were edited by his friend, Josiah Pratt. They are chiefly a collection of the gifted writer's views on various subjects connected with Christianity. Slight and brief as they are, they give us the idea of a culture, a refinement, a thoughtfulness, a sense of humour, a dignity, which mark the man's character as effectively as the most elaborate biography could have done. They are not so introspective as Adam's 'Private Thoughts,' and they disclose a grasp of principles, and a width of sympathy, with which the Evangelicals are not always credited.

John Newton's 'Cardiphonia' and 'Omicron' were in the first instance merely letters written to individual

Newton's
'Cardi-
phonia' and
'Omicron'

correspondents; but they are evidently adapted, if they were not actually written, for a larger audience, and they well deserve to be ranked among the devotional literature of the Evangelical school. In one sense, indeed, almost all the literature of that school may be termed practical or devotional; for the writers all felt so intensely the importance of practical religion, that they would have deemed the time wasted which was spent on any other kind of writing than that which would affect, directly or indirectly, the spiritual life.

Take, for instance, a form of literature in which they

were unusually successful—that of biography. The
lives were not written simply to give historical facts, but
to furnish examples or warnings to the reader;
and every opportunity of 'improving the occasion' is seized. But this is done very
artistically, and does not interfere with the interest of
the works. Biographies of all the leaders formed, of
course, a leading feature in the Evangelical literature.
To refer to them all would be wearisome; it must, therefore, suffice to select a few specimens. The lives of
Thomas Scott and Henry Venn, by their respective
sons, are models in their way; while they do full justice
to their subjects, and are monuments of filial piety, they
entirely eschew all fulsome adulation and undue exaggeration; and, what is perhaps a rarer virtue still, the
writers resist the temptation to make their fathers'
enemies their own, and to take up the cudgels which,
as it were, descended to them as heirlooms. John
Newton's eventful life was briefly but effectively told by
his accomplished friend, Richard Cecil; a great part of
this biography is drawn from Newton's own harrowing
'Narrative,' but the biographer has shown, as we should
expect, great judgment in his selections from that most
pathetic, but sometimes repulsive, story, and his own
observations are equally judicious and to the point.

A more striking autobiography still, though, of
course, a less eventful one, than Newton's 'Narrative,'
is Thomas Scott's 'Force of Truth,' in which
he describes the gradual process by which he
was changed, chiefly through Newton's influence, from
an almost avowed Socinian (clergyman though he was)
to an orthodox Christian of the Evangelical type. When

Biographies of Scott, Venn, and Newton

Scott's 'Force of Truth'

it is said 'chiefly through Newton's influence,' the influence of a living man as opposed to the influence of
books is meant. Scott was much affected by the latter;
and as his experience was, *mutatis mutandis*, the experience of many others of his school, it is interesting to
note the books which touched him. They were, he tells
us, Law's 'Serious Call' (of course), Hooker's 'Discourse
on Justification,' Burnet's 'Pastoral Care,' Beveridge's
'Sermons,' Henry Venn's 'Essay on the Prophecy of
Zacharias,' Hervey's 'Theron and Aspasio,' and De
Witsius' 'Two Covenants.' The 'Force of Truth' was
revised by Scott's parishioner, William Cowper, whose
exquisite taste contributed much to the polishing of its
style.

John Wesley was so many-sided a man that it was
perhaps impossible for any one biographer to do justice
Biographies of John Wesley to him all round. What may be called an
official biography by his right-hand man, Dr.
Coke, and Mr. More, was published the year after his
death (1792). Of course so hastily arranged a production
could do little more than give facts from the Wesleyan
Methodist point of view. Life after life, sketch after
sketch, and apology after apology, followed, and are still
going on up to the present day. The difficulty in
regard to this great man seems to be, to combine sufficient sympathy with sufficient literary power. From a
literary point of view, no work has superseded that of
Southey; but there surely is some force in the witty
application of the words of Holy Writ to the biographer: 'Thou hast nothing to draw with, and the
well is deep.' As literary productions, Isaac Taylor's
'Wesley and Methodism,' and Miss Julia Wedgwood's

'Evangelical Reaction' are at least worthy to rank with Southey; but these are mere sketches, and sketches from the outside. The real life of Wesley is that which is contained in his 'Journals;' it is from these, and these alone, that we can picture to ourselves the real man in all his various and varying phases.

George Whitefield's 'Journal,' too, gives us the best picture of George Whitefield; it is, of course, less in-teresting than John Wesley's; but the man himself was a less interesting man. 'The Journal' was an almost necessary part of the lives of all Methodists and Evangelicals. In many cases these journals are evidently, though unconsciously, conven-tional productions, and tell us little of the idiosyncrasies of the writers; but it is not so either with Wesley or Whitefield; the journals of both form a real part of Evangelical literature.

Whitefield's 'Journal'

That tendency to edification which has been noticed as running through all the Evangelical literature was certainly not conducive to its value in some departments. It unduly biassed, for instance, those who wrote on the subject of Church History. What is called 'Milner's History of the Church of Christ,' is in reality a curious amalgamation of the works of several writers of the Evangelical school. The first idea was suggested by John Newton, who left a fragment, which Joseph Milner thought of taking up, beginning only where Newton ended. But he deemed it better, on second thoughts, to commence afresh, owning that he had borrowed the idea from Newton. He carried the work on to the middle of the thirteenth century, though even this part was largely revised and

Milner's 'Church History'

corrected by his brother Isaac. The part from the middle of the thirteenth to the middle of the sixteenth century was edited by the Dean from the MSS. left by his brother Joseph. Dean Milner then took up the work on his own account and wrote nine long chapters. Then Scott wrote a 'Continuation of Milner' in three volumes, treating of the Reformation period and reaching to the Synod of Dort, though this was really a separate work, and is not included in the editions of Milner; and, finally, a part of Dr. Haweis's 'History of the Church of Christ,' was tacked on to some editions of Milner, so as to bring the work up to date—that is, the close of the eighteenth century. It was peculiarly cruel to the memory of the Dean to attach this last portion, because he had actually written ' Animadversions on Dr. Haweis's History.' But in spite of its composite character, the work is fairly attributed to Joseph Milner, for the hints he received from Newton were very slight, and those who followed took up his lines.

The project of Joseph Milner was a most laudable and a most seasonable one. It was to be ' an ecclesiastical history on a new plan ; ' that plan being to give the history of *real*, not merely *nominal*, Christians.[1] Religious controversies were to be omitted, except those which 'seemed to bear a relation to the essence of Christ's religion.' Genuine piety was the only thing he intended to celebrate. He thought that ecclesiastical historians gave a much larger proportion to the history of wickedness than to that of piety in general. Mosheim was a particular offender ; and 'the disagreeable inference '

[1] It is fair to add that this idea entirely originated with Newton from whom Milner avowedly borrowed it.

which the reading of Mosheim produced upon his mind
was, that 'real religion appeared scarcely to have had any
existence.' Judging rightly that 'the terms "Church"
and "Christian" do in their most natural and primary
sense respect only good men,' and that 'a succession of
pious men in all ages must have existed,' he determined,
if he could, to prove in his history 'that in every age
there have been *real* followers of Christ.'[1] If the execu-
tion had been equal to the conception, the work would
have been invaluable. But it is obvious that the tendency
to edification which has been spoken of, would be a
dangerous temptation to a man with very strong views
of his own. He strives to be fair and to do justice to the
piety of Christians of all kinds; but he makes extremely
short work of the piety of those who did not agree with
his own peculiar views, and dwells at inordinate length
on those who did. Thus Augustine, Bishop of Hippo,
has one hundred and forty-five pages devoted to him,
while Chrysostom has only sixteen and Jerome only
eleven. But then 'the peculiar work for which Augustine was evidently raised by Providence was to restore
the doctrines of divine grace to the Church.' A more
outrageous instance still is found in that portion of Dr.
Haweis's History which is bound up with Milner's. No less
than one-third of the whole space given to Great Britain in
the eighteenth century is devoted to Lady Huntingdon,
who is introduced in language which George Whitefield
himself might have used: 'The noble and elect Lady
Huntingdon had lived in the highest circle of fashion;
by birth a daughter of the House of Shirley, by marriage united with the Earl of Huntingdon, both bearing

[1] See *Introduction* by the Rev. Joseph Milner.

the Royal Arms of England, as descendants from her ancient monarchs,' &c., &c. Surely this is language more worthy of a Court lackey than of an historian of the Church of Christ. Moreover, the whole history of the eighteenth century is confined to the history of the Methodist and Evangelical movement, while all the really great theologians of the century are entirely ignored.

But to return to Milner. Hannah More was 'much amused at his going whole leagues about to lug in justification by faith.' The Waldenses, as agreeing with Milner's own views, are not only treated at disproportionate length, but also with so obvious a bias and such inaccuracy, that Milner drew upon himself (though he did not live to see it) a scathing criticism from a far more powerful pen than his own. Dr. Maitland had studied deeply the whole history of the 'Dark Ages;' he had the whole story of the Waldenses at his fingers' ends; no wonder, then, that when he brought his keen, well-stored, lawyer-like mind to bear upon poor Milner, who had only worked up the subject as part of his gigantic task, he found numerous inaccuracies; and, having little sympathy with Milner's religious views, he assailed him remorselessly, and, in fact, demolished him. That excellent Evangelical clergyman, Mr. John King of Hull, took up the cudgels in behalf of his deceased friend and neighbour, but he was no match for Dr. Maitland.

Defects of Milner

Milner, all through, is rather too anxious ' to improve the occasion.' On whatever century one of his eyes is fixed the other eye seems always to be steadily fixed upon the latter half of the eighteenth century. He takes every possible and

His desire 'to improve the occasion'

impossible opportunity of dealing a side-blow at the
Arminians and schismatics of his own day ; for Milner,
though he was called a Methodist, was a most uncom-
promising stickler for every point of Church order.
Holding also the strongest opinions about the utter
depravity of human nature, he would allow no virtues
to those who had not received the light of Christian
revelation. He is far too honest to suppress facts, but
his comments upon facts are often tinged with a quite
unconscious unfairness. Thus he handsomely admits
the estimable qualities which Antoninus Pius possessed ; but, 'doubtless,' he adds, 'a more distinct and
explicit detail of his life would lessen our admiration :
something of the supercilious pride of the Grecian, or of
the ridiculous vain-glory of the Roman, might appear.'
In fact, instead of seeing in these great thinkers of antiquity a yearning after the light which Christianity
alone can give, he can see nothing in them but the
deadliest enmity to Christianity. 'The Church of
Christ is abhorrent in its plan and spirit from the
systems of proud philosophers.' 'Moral philosophy
and metaphysics have ever been dangerous to religion,'
—and much more to the same effect.

But, in spite of these defects, really competent
critics have found pleasure and profit in the pages of
Milner. No less a person than Cardinal Newman has borne a warm testimony to his
merits. 'I read,' he says, 'Joseph Milner's "Church
History," and was nothing short of enamoured of the
long extracts from St. Augustine and the other fathers
which I found there. I read them as being the religion
of the primitive Christians.' Dr. Newman is describing

Merits of Milner

the faith of his early days. Probably, even long before
he went over to Rome, he altered his views about
Milner; but his testimony is valuable on one point at
any rate. If Milner had had no other merit, this alone
would have entitled him to gratitude : that he called the
attention of a generation, which had not much knowledge or appreciation of the early fathers, to their writings.
But he *had* other merits ; and we may well bear with
some shortcomings in a Church history which, instead
of perplexing the mind with interminable disputes between professing Christians, makes it its main business
to detect the spirit of Christ wherever it can be found.
It is a real refreshment, no less than a real strengthen-
ing of our faith, to turn from Church histories, which
might be more correctly termed histories of the abuses
and perversions of Christianity, to one which is what it
professes to be—a history of the good which Christianity
has done.   It used to be said that Mosheim wrote the
history of the sinners, and Milner that of the saints, of
Christendom ; and it is more pleasant and profitable to
read about the saints than about the sinners; though
it must be confessed that the historian of the sinners
is fuller and more accurate than the historian of the
saints.

The only other work on Church History which need
be noticed as emanating from the Evangelical school is
Wesley's John Wesley's ' Ecclesiastical History,' which
' Ecclesias- forms four volumes in his ' Christian Library : '
tical
History' but that indefatigable worker had far too
many irons in the fire to find time for original research ;
his work, therefore, is little else than an abbreviation of
Mosheim.

One might perhaps have expected that Biblical exegesis would have been a favourite field of Evangelical
Biblical literature ; but this was not the case. Adam
Comment- Clark's 'Commentary,' though it was com-
aries :— menced some years before the century closed,
Wesley,
Coke was not completed until the present century had run
through a quarter of its course ; it does not, therefore,
come within our purview. Dr. Coke, twenty years earlier
(1805), had published a commentary on the Bible in six
quarto volumes, which was highly valued. It was
rather unfortunate for the fate of the book that it should
be followed so soon (a most unusual case) by another
and much more elaborate commentary written from
precisely the same point of view. John Wesley's ' Notes
on the Old and New Testament,' like all his writings
and all his life, were intended to serve a directly practical purpose. They do not pretend to any depth or
originality of criticism ; but, like everything he wrote,
they are short, plain, pithy, and to the point, full of
good sense, and manly, sterling piety. They were
written for those who had neither the leisure nor the
mental training to enter very deeply into theological
questions, and they are admirably adapted to that end.
Like his fifty-three sermons, his ' Notes on the New
Testament ' have an adventitious interest as forming
part of a creed as well as a commentary.

By far the most elaborate and important of all the
works on Holy Scripture produced by the Evangelical
Scott's school was Thomas Scott's ' Commentary.' Its
'Com- success was enormous ; 12,000 copies of the
mentary'
English edition, and 25,200 of the American, were issued
during the lifetime of the author, and that in spite of the

great costliness of the work. It is essentially a 'Family Bible;' its value is mainly as a practical and devotional, rather than a critical and exegetical, commentary. Scott fully agreed with the sentiment of his poet parishioner:

> God is His own interpreter,
> And He can make it plain;

and applied it to the Book of revelation as well as to the book of nature. He loves to interpret Scripture by Scripture, and hence his commentary is rather too much like a sort of magnified concordance. But it is a vast monument of industry and piety, and was deservedly much valued by the Evangelicals of the day; nor has it yet ceased to preserve a deep interest of its own.

Passing from Biblical and historical to controversial literature, we have, alas! only too large a mass _{Literature of} of writings emanating from the Evangelical _{the Calvinistic contro-} school. For the whole of the literature con-_{versy} nected with the unhappy Calvinistic controversy falls under this head. But though the volume of it was immense, yet after abstracting what was virtually mere personal abuse, the residuum of what can at all be called literature is very small. To withdraw the veil of obscurity which has now happily been drawn over this very unedifying quarrel in print, would be cruel to the memory of good men. The writers on both sides, but especially on the Calvinistic side, seem to have lost all self-restraint, all sense of dignity—to say nothing of Christian charity—and to have descended into mere Billingsgate. The only two writers who deserve a moment's notice are Fletcher on the Arminian, and

Toplady on the Calvinistic, side. Fletcher's 'Checks to
Antinomianism' still retains a high reputation among a
certain class; and, even from a literary point of view,
they are deserving of attention. They are written with
great elegance and vivacity, and show a considerable
sense of humour and satire; and, as one would expect
from the sweet character of the man, they are almost
entirely free from any unworthy abuse. In fact, the most
cruel part of the work is the republishing of the abusive
epithets which Rowland Hill heaped upon the writer.
(Rowland Hill's biographer published, in revenge, a
collection of some of the flowers of rhetoric employed
by the other side.) But, after all, Fletcher's 'Checks'
are rather thin productions. Let anyone read them,
for instance, side by side with Waterland's detached
remarks on the same subject from the same point of
view, and he will see at once the different calibre of the
two men. The one is at best but a slight skirmisher,
the other a mighty warrior wielding a most powerful
weapon. Augustus Toplady was a really able and well-
read man, and his writings on the Calvinistic question
show great logical powers and considerable research;
but they are marred by the most scurrilous abuse of
those who disagreed with him, and have long ceased to
hold any place in literature.

Before quitting this very unedifying subject, one
remark must be made. The exceedingly poor stuff
which the writers on both sides produced
ought to show us how large a debt of gratitude is due to those who have received scant
recognition from many writers about the religious Revival in the last century. It was men like Butler,

*Superiority
of the
evidence-
writers*

Waterland, Warburton, Law, Sherlock, and Charles Leslie, who were the real defenders of Christianity on the intellectual side. It has already been remarked how thoroughly these men prepared the way for the Revival by beating down the opponents of Christianity from all sides. But this was not the end; the snake was only scotched, not killed. Very powerful opponents of Christianity arose when the Revival was in its mid-course; and again it was men of the type of the old ' evidence-writers ' who came to the rescue. Priestley was a formidable antagonist on the Unitarian side; but Horsley was far more than a match for him. Hume was a still more formidable one; and, if Paley can hardly be said to have crushed him, at any rate the Arch-deacon was much more competent to meet him than any Methodist or Evangelical. Whom, again, of the latter class can we compare in point of theological grasp with Bishop Lowth, or Bishop Horne, or Bishop Watson, or Mr. Jones of Nayland, or many others who might be named? Of course the Revivalists had other and, what they deemed, more important work to do; and we can hardly say what they might have done had they given their minds to the intellectual work; but, as a matter of fact, the intellectual work had to be done, and it was not they who did it. It is curious to observe how John Wesley seems to have felt this; for, in the references to the books which he read, in his Journal, there is hardly one allusion to any book that came from the Methodist or Evangelical School, but a great number to those written by old-fashioned Churchmen.[1] No one could write more

---

[1] There is one exception to John Wesley's silence about Evange-lical literature: he thinks Fletcher the finest writer of the age;

forcibly or logically in his way than John Wesley himself. His ' Appeal ' and ' Further Appeal ' ' to men of reason and religion ' are admirably done ; but he would have been the first to own that his writings were not of the calibre of Butler, Law, Waterland, and the rest. Everything he wrote was full of good, practical, common sense ; but Wesley-like, it was mostly written for one definite and limited purpose—viz., to supply such mental pabulum for his followers as they needed. What he says, in his own abrupt, not to say defiant, style of his sermons, might be said of the design of almost all his literary work : ' I design plain truth for plain people ; therefore, of set purpose, I abstain from all nice and philosophical speculations, from all perplexed and intricate reasonings, and, as far as possible, from even the show of learning. Nothing appears here in an elaborate, elegant, or rhetorical dress. I mention this, that curious readers may spare themselves the labour of seeking for what they will not find ' (Preface). The mental activity which enabled him, amidst all his practical labours, to abridge works of all kinds—from ' The Apostolical Fathers ' to ' The Fool of Quality '—to write a ' Treatise on Medicine,' to compile a ' System of Natural Philosophy,' to edit a magazine, to compose ' Notes on the Old and New Testament,' to give to the world his sentiments in the form of pamphlets on such burning questions as the American War, to break a lance (though most unwillingly) with Calvinists, with Socinians, with Mystics, is simply amazing ; but it was quite beside his purpose to elaborate any original

in which opinion the present writer must venture, with all humility, to disagree with him.

work which would be of much permanent literary value.

The most valuable part of the Evangelical literature was its hymns. Regarded merely as literary composi-tions, many of Charles Wesley's hymns attain a very high standard of excellence. They will bear, and indeed require, the closest analysis, in order to discover their hidden beauties. The writer, with a true poet's eye, catches some one leading incident or striking idea, and works it out thoroughly, without any confusion of metaphor, without any fancifulness, without any offence against good taste, in all its details.

Hymn-wri-ters of the Revival:— Charles Wesley

This will be better seen by an illustration or two. Charles Wesley felt, with a true poetic instinct, that the grand and mysterious incident of Jacob's wrestling with the angel was one which would make a fine subject for sacred verse, and so he uses it for the groundwork of two of his finest hymns: ' Come, O thou traveller unknown!' and 'Soldiers of Christ, arise!' It is wonder-ful how, in both these hymns, he works out without any forced interpretation each detail of the wonderful story, and gives a Christian meaning to it. Take again that more popular hymn still, ' Jesu, lover of my soul.' The analogy of the drowning man is admirably carried out in its every part. This characteristic excellence of Charles Wesley's hymns can hardly have been sufficiently appreciated. Otherwise, well-meaning adapters would never have set about the very unpromising task of altering them, even verbally; for the chances are that the alteration, even of a word, will be, so far, a spoiling of the hymn. Let us take two very glaring instances:

> Hark ! how all the welkin rings
> 'Glory to the King of kings !

wrote Charles Wesley ;

> Hark ! the herald-angels sing
> Glory to the new-born King !

wrote the modern reviser, and completely spoilt the couplet. Charles Wesley's ' Glory to the King of kings ! ' beautifully corresponds to the angels' song, ' Glory to God in the Highest'—the modern version does nothing of the sort. Any earthly king that is born might be called 'the new-born king,' but none but the Deity could be called ' the King of kings.' Thus the doctrine of the true Divinity of Our Blessed Lord—a point on which the writer would lay the greatest stress, since Socinianism was rife at the time—is clearly stated in the original, but ingeniously eliminated from the revised, version. Again, 'Hark! how all *the welkin* rings' recalls the beautiful words of the first psalm for Christmas Day, 'The *Heavens* declare the glory of God'—a point which, to a strong Churchman like Charles Wesley, would be no slight one; the reviser contrives both to spoil the poetry and to miss the allusion.

> Come, let us join our friends above
> Who have obtained the prize,
> And on the eagle wings of love
> To joys celestial rise,

wrote Charles Wesley ;

> Let saints on earth in concert sing
> With those whose work is done ;
> For all the servants of our King
> In Heaven and earth are one,

wrote the modern reviser, and spoilt the poetry, the spiritedness, the point, and the Scripturalness of the whole verse. Charles Wesley turns our thoughts to the apostle of love, whose emblem is the eagle, and who, eagle-like, soars through love, the greatest of Christian graces, into regions higher than those into which his fellow-evangelists penetrated. Charles Wesley, by adopting the first person plural, and by the expression 'our friends above,' brings far nearer home to us the article of the creed, 'I believe in the communion of saints'—which is really the subject of the whole hymn—than the bare statement of doctrine in the third person, to which the modern version is reduced, can possibly do. One can only account for these and many other changes in Charles Wesley's hymns by the theory that our hymnologists have been so desperately afraid of the conventionalities that they shrank from retaining every bold expression, and were content to sacrifice sense, taste, doctrine, poetry, anything, so as to keep within the limits of tame, prim propriety.

Many other gems of sacred poetry besides Charles Wesley's we owe to the Evangelical Revival. Toplady's
Toplady   'Rock of Ages,' as beautiful and as popular as
and others   the most beautiful and most popular of Wesley's
hymns, is its direct outcome. So, too, is his hardly less beautiful, though less popular

> When sickness and disease invade
> This trembling house of clay;

which acquires an additional and plaintive significance, when we remember that the writer's own 'trembling house of clay' was constantly invaded by sickness and disease. Olivers' 'The God of Abraham praise!' Perronet's 'All hail the power of Jesu's name!' Cowper's 'Hark! my soul, it is the Lord,' 'O! for a closer walk with God,' 'God moves in a mysterious way,' and many others of his hymns, are really classical compositions.

Indeed, it would be scarcely claiming too much if we set down the whole of Cowper's original poetry (the Cowper's translation of Homer is of course not included) poetry as belonging to the literature of the Evangelical Revival. No doubt the fire of his genius would have burnt brightly, whatever his religious sentiments might have been. In the productions of his elegant pen we should, under any circumstances, have recognised at least the *disjecti membra poetæ*. But, as a matter of fact, his Christian convictions were the mainspring which set the whole machinery of his poetical work in motion. It was this which gave coherence and symmetry and soul to it all. Abstract the religious element from his compositions, and they all fall to pieces; but, in fact, it is impossible to do so. With the exception of one or two lighter pieces, there is an undercurrent of Christian sentiment running through and inseparable from them all. Mr. Abbey, whose marked dislike of the particular form which Cowper's religious sentiments took renders his testimony unexceptionable, fully admits this: 'The best and most characteristic features of Cowper's poetry are very closely related to the strong Christian feeling which actuated him. Without it his writings might not have been deficient in sweetness and pathos, but they would have been deprived of that which conferred upon them those higher qualities which made his poems a turning-point in eighteenth-century literature. His thorough earnestness, his transparent simplicity of moral aim, his devoted love of all goodness, his shrinking aversion from all forms of evil, his lively sense of a divine purpose and significance in all created works—these principles, operating in a sensitive and poetical temperament, were just what was wanted to give his poetry that simplicity, reality, and vigour which contrasts most favourably with the formalities and artificial graces which had been too popular before.' If this be true, as unquestionably it is, then to the Evangelical Revival is due the best poetry of the time, for Cowper's religion was entirely due to Evangelical influence.

Mr. Lecky thinks that the literature of the Evangelical Revival has scarcely obtained an adequate recognition in literary history. This may be true, but it was not written for that purpose. The object for which the Methodists and Evangelicals wrote was simply to rouse men's consciences and to direct their lives; and this object they did to a great extent attain. Their writings must be regarded as a following-up of their preaching; and those who were affected by the preaching found in the writings exactly what they wanted. Those on the other hand who had never been affected by the preaching were not likely to be affected by the writings. Hence, in part at least, the contemptuous tone which outside critics have adopted towards Evangelical literature. When writers and critics view everything from an entirely different point of view there can be no harmony between them. You might as well expect a blind man to enjoy a beautiful landscape, or a deaf man to be charmed with the sound of sweet music, as expect those who were outside the Evangelical circle

General estimate of the litera- ture

to appreciate Evangelical literature. Perhaps some of the writers were rather too apt to assume that all those were blind who did not see with their eyes, and deaf who did not hear with their ears. This is almost the inevitable result of intense earnestness; it is apt to degenerate into narrowness. The man who has no particular opinions can afford to regard all opinions with philosophic impartiality; but what he gains in breadth he loses in depth. At the same time it was a distinct misfortune that the idea should ever have been allowed to prevail that religion was alienated from intellect. 'Every man of the world,' writes Hannah More, 'naturally arrogates to himself the superiority of understanding over every religious man. He, therefore, who has been accustomed to set a high value on his intellectual powers must have made very considerable advance in piety before he can acquire a magnanimous indifference to this usurped superiority of another.'[1] And again, 'It must be owing to a very fortunate combination of circumstances if a man can at once preserve the character of parts and piety, and retain the reputation of a man of sense after he has acquired that of a Christian.'[2] This was the opinion of a sympathiser with the movement; and her opinion is amply borne out by the remarks (far too numerous to quote) of those who stood outside it. It must be owned that the Methodists and Evangelicals had themselves to blame to a great extent that it was so. The forerunner of the Revival, William Law, set the example of depreciating

---

[1] 'Thoughts on the Manners of the Great.'—Hannah More's *Works*, vol. xi. p. 42.

[2] *Works*, vol. xi. p. 157. 'Religion of the Fashionable World.'

'human learning.' He is never weary of dwelling on the unprofitableness of all studies which are not directly concerned with religion. In a man of great intellectual power and wide and varied culture such utterances only provoke a smile; but when men of no intellectual power and no culture at all take up the cry, one is apt to be exasperated. It was a very convenient doctrine for men who had neither the training nor the talents nor the tastes to make any mark in the learned world themselves to hold that such eminence was worthless; but the doctrine is a mischievous one—mischievous to the men themselves, to the men they sneered at, and to the men who were neither learned nor serious. It is absurd to call men like John and Charles Wesley, Fletcher, Coke, Cecil, Romaine, Newton, Venn, Joseph and Isaac Milner, and others that might be named, mere ignorant bigots, for they were all men of culture and attainments; but some of them (not all) were much too apt to depreciate what, after all, is one of God's highest gifts, intellectual power; and when the cry was taken up by lesser men, the result unfortunately was that to the outer world the Evangelical cause became identified with weakness of intellect and deficiency of culture. 'A symbol of the religion of the illiterate,' writes one of the ablest exponents of the movement. 'Philosophers have called them fools,' writes another. 'Its literature has few readers among the highly educated classes,' writes a third.

CHAPTER VIII.

THE RESULTS OF THE REVIVAL.

SOME—and those the most important—of the results of the Revival it is impossible to tabulate under any defi-

Moral and spiritual results

nite formula. Of these it may be said, as John Wesley said of William Law's practical treatises: 'Of how great service these have been in reviving and establishing true, rational, scriptural religion cannot fully be known till the Author of that religion shall descend in the clouds of Heaven.' Of the faith which enabled a man to abandon the cherished habits of a lifetime and to go forth ready to spend and be spent in his Master's service; which nerved him to overcome the natural fear of death, and, indeed, to welcome the last enemy as his best friend who would introduce him to the better land he had long been living for; which made the selfish man self-denying, the discontented happy, the worldling spiritually-minded, the drunkard sober, the sensual chaste, the liar truthful, the thief honest, the proud humble, the godless godly, the thriftless thrifty— we can only judge by the fruits which it bore. That such fruits *were* borne is surely undeniable. But it is obviously impossible to describe such cases in detail. We must be content to indicate those results which may be summed up in a general and definite form.

1. *On the Young.*—John Wesley, with that true practical instinct which was one secret of his power,

Wesley's views on education

saw that in order to make his work effectual, he must begin at the right end of life; and, therefore, from the very commencement of his labours

he laid great stress upon the influence that was to be
brought to bear upon children. In fact, he anticipated
by almost half-a-century the establishment of Sunday
Schools, setting up one, which was held in the church,
in his parish in Georgia. On his return to England
one of his earliest acts after the date which he assigns
to the Revival, was to obtain possession of a school at
Kingswood in 1740; and to provide for the wants of
this school he himself prepared several text-books: ' A
Short Latin Grammar,' ' A Short English Grammar,'
' A Short Roman History,' and ' A Concise History of
England.' It cannot, however, be said that his efforts
either at Kingswood or elsewhere with children were
either judicious or successful. In fact they were very
much the reverse. One would have thought that his
own early training at Epworth rectory under his in-
comparable mother would have taught him better. He
might have remembered that though the strictest discipline was enforced, there was nothing there of those
absurd regulations which entirely prohibited all play;
that he had never learned there that most fallacious
maxim of his, ' He that plays when he is a boy, will
play when he grows to be a man ; ' that there was
nothing there of that unwholesome excitement which
he too much encouraged, of those rigorous fastings
which were calculated permanently to injure the health
of growing children; of that working upon the tender
nature of the young, the accounts of which in his Journal are sometimes positively revolting. But Wesley,
in this as in many other respects, toned down in his
later years; his errors in the treatment of the young
were errors of the judgment, not of the heart. He

always loved little children dearly; and he took a warm interest in the Sunday Schools which were beginning to be established everywhere when he was an old man.

The first establishment of these Sunday Schools cannot be attributed to the Revival, but the Revival

Sunday Schools and the Revival gave an enormous stimulus to the scheme. The Wesleyan Societies took up the Sunday Schools warmly, and the Evangelical clergy were the very life and soul of them in their several parishes. Hannah More, ably assisted by her sister, Patty, was most persistent, in spite of much opposition, in her efforts to promote the education of the young in the neighbourhood of Cheddar; and, in fact, the whole of the Evangelical school paid marked attention to this most important point.

2. *The Abolition of the Slave-trade* is almost entirely due to Evangelical principles. While doing full

The Slave-trade justice to the noble efforts made by the Quakers many years before the work of William Wilberforce, by Thomas Clarkson, by both Pitt and Fox—it was not often that those two great rival statesmen agreed, but they did on this point—by Lord Grenville, by Earl Grey, by Henry Brougham, and by others, we must still admit that the real success of the effort was due to the unwearied energy of Wilberforce; that the energy of Wilberforce was both awakened and sustained by his religious convictions; and that his religious convictions were entirely due to the Evangelical school. His most efficient helper in Parliament was Henry Thornton, also a noted Evangelical; and Zachary Macaulay and all the so-called ' Clapham sect ' took up the cause most warmly. Nor must we forget the indirect but very real aid which was given to the scheme by the Evangelical poet, William Cowper. His writings were read by many who never read a line of directly Evangelical literature, and he thus tended to form public opinion in a way which those who were only known as Evangelicals could not possibly do.

3. *The Religious Tract Society* was the direct result of the Evangelical Revival. It was founded in 1799, Rowland Hill being the chairman of its first committee. This was not, of course, the first attempt to make use of this species of literature to permeate the masses. The Society for Promoting Christian Knowledge was already a century old, and had, from the beginning of its existence, circulated tracts. Indeed, the virtual originator of the Society, Dr. Bray, is said to have 'sent to America upwards of thirty-four thousand books *and tracts*, to be dispersed among the inhabitants.'[1] John Wesley had been a diligent writer and systematic distributor of tracts more than fifty years before the Society was born. In 1745, he says: 'We had within a short time given away some thousands of little tracts among the common people, and it pleased God thereby to provoke others to jealousy; insomuch that the Lord Mayor had ordered a large quantity of papers, dissuading from cursing and swearing, to be printed and distributed among the train-bands.' His preachers 'were furnished with these short, plain messengers of mercy, as part of the equipment with which their saddle-bags

Religious Tract Society

[1] *Publick Spirit illustrated in the Life and Designs of Dr. Bray,* p. 80.

were stored.'[1] Indeed, he had actually established, in conjunction with Dr. Coke, a sort of Tract Society in 1782, which he called 'The Society for the Distribution of Religious Tracts among the Poor.' Hannah More had written a series of tracts which she published periodically until 1798 (the year before the birth of the Society), under the title of the 'Cheap Repository Tracts.' But the Religious Tract Society was the largest and most permanent of the institutions, the *exclusive* function of which was to circulate tracts.

4. *Two Bible Societies* were the results of the interest in the Holy Scriptures awakened by the Revival. The first in date was the Naval and Military Bible Society, which was founded in 1780, and was probably occasioned by the effect produced by Methodism upon the British Army, which has been already noticed. Within twenty years of its foundation it had circulated no less than thirty thousand copies of the Bible.

Bible Societies : Naval and Military

The British and Foreign Bible Society was not founded until 1804, but the circumstances which led to its formation date from 1787, when a London clergyman was applied to by a brother clergyman in Wales for a supply of Bibles in the Welsh tongue. It was found that there was a great scarcity of Welsh Bibles. This led on to the more general plan of supplying Bibles elsewhere, and hence arose the foundation of a society, 'of which the sole object shall be to encourage a wider diffusion of the Holy Scriptures.' The names of those who were most prominent in its

British and Foreign Bible Society

[1] See *The Wesley Memorial Volume*, edited by Dr. J. O. A. Clark (New York), pp. 315, 316—'Wesley and his Literature.'

establishment will be sufficient to show how closely it was connected with the Evangelical Revival. We find among them Lord Teignmouth its first president, Josiah Pratt one of its first secretaries,—both strong, Evangelical Churchmen—William Wilberforce, Charles Grant (afterwards Lord Glenelg), Thomas Charles, a clergyman, who was also a Calvinistic Methodist. It is fair, however, to add that the first person who suggested a *general* circulation of the Scriptures, as opposed to a mere supply of Welsh Bibles, was Joseph Hughes, a Baptist minister, and therefore not of course connected with the Revival. Also among its first vice-presidents were the Bishops of London, Exeter, and St. David's, the two latter of whom can in no way, and the first can only in a very modified way, be reckoned as belonging to the Evangelical school.

5. The work of *Foreign Missions* received an immense stimulus from the Evangelical Revival. The

Foreign Missions:— Wesleyan

Revival itself may be said to have originated in a foreign mission, for the Wesleys' visit to Georgia was intended especially for missionary work, though very little work in that direction was done. In 1786, Dr. Coke, whose speciality was missionary work, issued an ' Address to the Pious and Benevolent, proposing an Annual Subscription for the Support of Missionaries in the Highlands and adjacent Islands of Scotland ; the Isles of Jersey, Guernsey, and Newfoundland; the West Indies, and the Provinces of Nova Scotia and Quebec.' ' A Mission intended to be established in the British Dominions in Asia ' was also projected, but, for a time, postponed. This led to the establishment in 1787 of what were termed ' Missions established by the Methodist Society.' At the Conference of 1790, a committee of nine preachers, of which Dr. Coke was chairman, was appointed to take charge of the matter. Among the first subscribers are found the names of many leading Evangelicals: William Wilberforce, the two Thorntons, Berridge of Everton, the Earl of Dartmouth, and others; but it was not till 1817 that 'The Wesleyan Missionary Society,' under its present title and with its present organisation was founded. It has so thriven that in England the Church Missionary Society alone exceeds it in annual collections for the foreign field—a very creditable fact considering that Methodism has for the most part drawn its converts from the less opulent classes of society. Dr. Coke, it should be said, was himself a missionary. He visited Nova Scotia, and also some of the West India Islands, for the express purpose of instructing the negroes, and in 1804 he published an interesting account of the difficulties he and his fellow-Methodists met with, entitled 'Rise, Progress, and Present State of the Methodist Missions.'

The 'London Missionary Society' was also the outcome of the Evangelical Revival. It was founded in London Missionary Society 1795 on a broad basis, which included Dissenters as well as Churchmen (all Methodists, it should be remembered, whether Wesleyan, Welsh Calvinistic, or English Evangelical, would then fall under the latter head). Henry Venn the younger thus describes its formation :—'In 1795, some of the clergy usually termed Evangelical united with Dissenters in establishing the London Missionary Society upon the principle of an union of all Denominations of Orthodox

Christians. The first meeting for its establishment was held 21st September, but the great body of the Evangelical clergy could not unite in the plan.' The Evangelicals never held other than a friendly attitude towards the London Missionary Society. It became, however, more and more exclusively Dissenting, and is now supported mainly by the Congregationalists, whose special organ for missionary purposes it is.

But, of course, the most characteristic and distinctive product of the Evangelical Revival in the department of Foreign Missions was the Church Missionary Society, founded in 1799. It will not be out of proportion to describe its rise at some length, and in doing so it will be impossible to do better than to borrow largely from the account of one who, of all men in the world, had a right to speak with authority on such a point—Henry Venn, the son of the virtual founder, and himself, for many years, the most indefatigable and efficient clerical secretary of the Society, particularly as his account also gives us incidentally a vivid and interesting picture of the life and mind of the Evangelicals of that day. 'The immediate origination,' he writes, 'of the Church Missionary Society is closely connected with the history of a Society, formed by a few London clergy for religious intercourse and improvement, whose leading object was the investigation of religious truth; in reference to which design they adopted the title of the " Eclectic Society." This society held its first meeting 16th January, 1783, at the Castle and Falcon, Aldersgate Street, and consisted of the Rev. John Newton, Rev. H. Foster, Rev. R. Cecil, and Eli Bates, Esq.' He then gives some interesting rules adopted by the society, one of which was that no visitors were to be admitted unless balloted for at a previous meeting, the single exception being the case of a missionary. The question appointed for discussion on October 30, 1786, was : ' What is the best method of planting and propagating the Gospel in Botany Bay ? '— with a view to the Rev. R. Johnson [a missionary] whose company was desired for the next evening.' Then in 1789, February 16, we have the question discussed : ' What is the best method of propagating the Gospel in the East Indies ?' And in the autumn of 1791, ' What is the best method of propagating the Gospel in Africa ?' The next notice which has been discovered of any united counsel or effort on the part of the Evangelical clergy in this cause is in connection with a clerical meeting held at Rauceby in Lincolnshire [it is, by the way, a curious fact that Lincolnshire played a prominent part in the foundation both of the Society for the Propagation of the Gospel in Foreign Parts, and also of the Church Missionary Society], on May 6 and 7, 1795. The Rev. Mr. Pugh was incumbent of Rauceby ; and the clerical meeting was attended by the Rev. T. Robinson (Leicester), the Rev. S. Knight (Halifax), the Rev. C. Simeon (Cambridge), all leading Evangelicals. At this meeting Mr. Pugh stated that a legacy of 4,000l. had been left ' to be laid out to the best advantage to the interests of true religion.' The matter was laid before the Eclectic Society in London, at which Mr. Simeon proposed the question : ' With what propriety, and in what mode, can a Mission be attempted to the Heathen from the Established Church ?' The difficulty of procuring proper men, the uncertainty of obtaining

the sanction of the heads of the Church, the fear of
interfering with the Society for Promoting Christian
Knowledge and the Society for the Propagation of
the Gospel in Foreign Parts, and other points, were
discussed; but the result was that this conversation
proved the foundation of the Church Missionary Society.
The name was not adopted until 1812. It was at first
called the Missionary Society for Africa and the East.
On February 18, 1799, the subject was again brought
before the Eclectic Society, and John Venn, who was
in the chair, formally proposed the formation of a
Missionary Society, and laid down some excellent
principles for its establishment. He was supported
by Josiah Pratt, Charles Simeon, and others, and at
another meeting, on April 12, under the presidency of
Mr. Venn, the society was established,—with what
success it is unnecessary here to record.

6. Another very real and beneficial result of the
Evangelical Revival was the large share it had in

Revolution-
ary and
sceptical
spirit
checked

checking the growth of the revolutionary and
sceptical spirit which seemed likely to spread
from France into England at the close of the
eighteenth century. The deistical opinions passed over
from England into France, and, having been exploded
in the former country, appeared in a much more aggra-
vated form, and mixed up with social questions as they
had not been here, in the latter. Indeed, they soon
passed beyond the stage of deism altogether, and cul-
minated in the total abnegation of Christianity and
the setting up of the goddess Reason. The influence of
such men as Voltaire, Rousseau, Diderot, Condillac, and
all the Encyclopædists was incomparably greater and

more destructive than that of any of the English deists. They had also grievances and abuses to work upon, such as the latter had not, and their sentiments, having thoroughly revolutionised France, travelled over into this country, and, by the instrumentality of men like Thomas Paine, would undoubtedly have affected the lower and middle classes far more deeply and widely than they did, had it not been for the counter-influences of the Evangelical Revival. It is not pretended that the Revival was the sole cause of their very different reception here and in France. The very excesses which they produced in France caused here a reaction of feeling among many cultured men, who were not in the least touched by the Revival. Coleridge, Southey, Wordsworth, and others at first deeply sympathised with the rising spirit of liberty in France before it degenerated into licence ; and Edmund Burke, though he never showed so marked a sympathy with the French Revolutionists, may be fairly presumed, from his antecedents, to have been so far in accord with them as to regard with a favourable eye the first efforts against oppression and tyranny across the Channel. But all these great men, when they saw the reckless course which things took, experienced a violent revulsion of feeling, for which the Evangelical Revival was assuredly in no degree responsible. The refined writings and feelings, however, of such men as these did not in the least affect the masses. And it was of incalculable benefit to the nation that such a power as Methodism existed just at the time when otherwise the revolutionary torrent would have swept away multitudes in its course. In fact, Methodism was a sort of safety-valve

through which many let off their superfluous steam.
Many a man, who, under different circumstances,
would have been haranguing about the rights of man,
was happily preoccupied with a far more noble subject
—the love of God. But this was not all. Nothing
distinguished more markedly the earlier Puritanism
from the later Methodism than the very different atti-
tudes which they adopted in regard to social and
political questions. John Wesley and John Fletcher
took, as we have seen, a very decided stand on the
Loyalist side, in the matter of the American war. They
did not live long enough to see the far more destructive
effects of the revolutionary spirit in France; but they
fully impressed their loyal and conservative spirit upon
their followers; and none of the Methodists showed the
slightest trace of sympathy with revolutionary principles in England. Their influence, which over the
lower classes was very large and constantly increasing,
was all exercised in a totally different direction. As to
the Evangelicals, they were anti-revolutionary to a
man, and contributed much towards keeping the upper
classes free from the contagion. Few of them, indeed,
meddled directly with the subject at all; but their
whole tone of mind, and the whole tendency of their
teaching, were of a strictly loyal character. Hannah
More, with the strong approbation/ of the whole
Evangelical party, published her 'Village Politics, or
Will Chip,' in 1792, with the express object of checking the growth of French Revolutionary principles
among the lower classes; and so great was the effect of
this work that it was considered to have contributed
largely to prevent a revolution in England. Moreover,

the sale of her poetical works is said to have been 'much promoted by the zeal of some good people, who believed that in the outbreak of the French Revolution her writings were calculated to be of great service.' Cowper's poetry was all of an intensely loyal character. No one who read him would mistake his attitude; and sometimes, as in the pleasing lines 'On the Queen's visit to London, the night of March 17, 1789,' he touches directly upon the subject.

7. The effects of the Evangelical Revival upon the Church of England were very marked. Mr. Lecky goes so far as to say that the Evangelicals 'gradually changed the whole spirit of the English Church. They infused into it a new fire and passion of devotion, kindled a spirit of fervent philanthropy, raised the standard of clerical duty, and completely altered the whole tone and tendency of the preaching of its ministers.' But it must not be forgotten that there was never wanting a large body of quiet, pious, old-fashioned Churchmen, who had no sympathy with the Calvinism of the Evangelicals; but, in their own way, were doing a vast amount of good. The mere fact that such men as Edmund Burke, Samuel Johnson,[1] Robert Southey, men with a deep sense of religion, were perfectly satisfied with the Church as it was, and were in no way touched by the Revival, is a proof of this. The ablest theological writers of the day, such as Bishop Horsley, Bishop Lowth, Bishop Horne, Mr. Jones of Nayland, Archdeacon Paley, were not found

Effects on the Church of England

---

[1] At any rate Dr. Johnson was not affected by the Revival until just before his death; the remark in the text applies to the whole course of his life.

among the Evangelical party. Nevertheless the Revival did largely affect the Church, and that in two ways : first, by adding to its body a number of most earnest, active, self-denying men of blameless lives, who would have been an honour to any religious community, and who were deeply attached to what they considered to be the teaching of the Church ; and secondly, by directing the attention of those who held aloof from the movement to truths which had been too much placed in the background. We have evidence of its influence in this direction, even as early as 1758, when Archbishop Secker in his charge to the Diocese of Canterbury speaks of 'the new sect pretending to the strictest piety,' and urges his clergy 'to emulate what is good in them, avoiding what is bad ; to edify their parishioners with awakening, but rational and scriptural, discourses ; to teach the principles, not only of virtue and natural religion, but of the Gospel, not as almost refined away by the modern refiner, but the truth as it is in Jesus, and as it is taught by the Church.' He then impresses upon them the duty of vindicating such doctrines as those of the Trinity, Christ's Sacrifice, and Sanctification by the Spirit, and adds, ' The truth, I fear, is that many, if not most, of us have dwelt too little on these doctrines in our sermons ; by no means, I believe, as disbelieving or slighting them, but partly from knowing that formerly they had been inculcated beyond their proportion, and even to the disparagement of Christian obedience, partly from fancying them so generally received and remembered that little needs to be said but on social obligations; partly, again, from not having studied theology deeply enough to treat of them ably and beneficially.. God grant it may never have been for want of inwardly experiencing their importance. But, whatever the cause, the effect hath been lamentable. Our people have grown less and less mindful (1) of the distinguishing articles of their creed; (2) as will always be the case, of that one which they hold in common with the heathens; they have forgotten, in effect, their Creator as well as their Redeemer and ✓ Sanctifier; seldom or never worshipping him, or thinking of their souls in relation to him; but flattering themselves that what they are pleased to call a moral and harmless life, though far from being either, is the one thing needful. Our vindication will be to preach fully and frequently these doctrines, yet so as to reserve a due share to the duties of common life, which, it is reported, some of our censurers do not. We must enforce them mainly by Christian motives.'

No apology is, it is hoped, needed for quoting at some length this passage and those which follow. We are far too apt to despise these old eighteenth-century divines as ✓ mere legalists, who did not understand, and therefore, of course, laid no stress upon, the distinctive doctrines of Christianity. Nothing can be more untrue; they *did* understand and appreciate them; and if many of the clergy did not duly enforce them, Archbishop Secker gives us the true causes—in what lucid, dignified, and deeply earnest language, the appreciative reader of the above admirable passage need not be told.

To the same effect Archdeacon Paley in his seventh William charge, many years later, comments upon the Paley preaching of that period: 'We are setting up a kind of philosophical morality, detached from religion,

and independent of its influence, which may be cultivated, it is said, without Christianity, as well as with it,
and which, if cultivated, renders religion and religious
institutions superfluous.   We are in such haste to fly
from enthusiasm and superstition, that we are approach-
ing to an insensibility to all religious influence.   I do
not mean to advise you to bring men back to enthusiasm, but to retard, if you can, the progress towards
an opposite and worse extreme.' [1]

And, once more, Bishop Horsley, in his first
charge to the diocese of S. David's, dwells on the same
Bishop   subject in that pure, clear, and incisive style
Horsley   of which he was so consummate a master :
' A dread of the pernicious tendency of some extravagant
opinions, which persons more to be esteemed for the
warmth of their piety than the soundness of their judgment, have grafted in modern times upon the doctrine
of justification by faith—opinions which seem to emancipate the believer from the authority of all moral law,
hath given credit to another maxim, which I never hear
without extreme regret from the lips of a divine, either
from the pulpit or in familiar conversation, namely,
that practical religion and morality are one and the
same thing, that moral duties constitute the whole or
by far the better part of practical Christianity.   This
reduces practical Christianity to heathen virtue.   These
maxims, as far as they are received, have a pernicious influence on the ministry of the Word, and
have contributed much to divest our sermons of the
genuine spirit and savour of Christianity, and to reduce
them to mere moral essays.   Moral duties enforced

[1] See vol. vii. 'Charge VII.' in Paley's *Works* in 7 vols.

by such argumènts nowhere appear to so much advantage as in the writings of the heathen moralists, and are quite out of place in the pulpit. The system chiefly in request with thoso who seem most in earnest in this strain of preaching is the strict but impracticable and sullen morality of the Stoic. Thus it too often happens that we lose sight of that which is our proper office, to publish the word of reconciliation. We make no other use of the high commission we bear than to come abroad, one day in the seven, dressed in solemn looks and in the garb of holiness, to be the apes of Epictetus. I flatter myself we are in a state of recovery from the delusion. The compositions which are at this day delivered from our pulpits are, I think, in general of a more Christian cast than were often heard thirty years since, when I entered the ministry. Still the dry strain of preaching is too much in use. It has been the fashion to suppose a want of capacity in common people to be carried any great length in religious knowledge. Creation, preservation, and future punishment the vulgar may comprehend; but the Trinity, Incarnation, Expiation, Intercession, and Communion with the Holy Spirit are supposed above their reach.'

Such passages as the above (to which many more of a like tenor might be added) have a direct and most important bearing upon the Evangelical Revival, because they show how that Revival influenced men who had no particular sympathy with it, and how it drew the notice of Churchmen generally to truths which had been, not so much forgotten, as assumed to be universally admitted, and therefore not requiring special enforcement—a most

Effects on men who had no sympathy with the Revival

fallacious notion. If anyone thinks that the fear of
Bishop Horsley expressed in the first clause of the above
extract was uncalled-for, he has only to turn to Thomas
Scott's sermons, not against Calvinism, but against the
prevalent abuses of Calvinism, and he will soon see that
there was cause enough for alarm. Or, let him take
the same writer's account of the spiritual state of Olney:
' There are above two thousand inhabitants in this town,
almost all Calvinists, even the most debauched of them,
the Gospel having been preached among them for a
number of years by a variety of preachers, statedly and
occasionally, sound and unsound, in church and meeting.
The inhabitants are become like David, wiser than their
teachers; that is, they think themselves so, and in an
awful manner have learned to abuse Gospel notions, to
stupefy their consciences, vindicate their sloth and
wickedness, and shield off conviction.' Most assuredly,
however, the general result of Evangelical principles
was not to make men slothful and selfish; on the
contrary, these principles infused a spirit of active
philanthropy into the Church, which had been, since
the time of good Robert Nelson, too dormant. Proofs
of this have been given in the account of the various
societies which were established; but their energetic
charity did not stop there; it embraced a vast range of
subjects. It is said of the good men of Clapham that
' schools, prison discipline, savings' banks, tracts, village
libraries, district visitings, and church buildings, each
for a time rivalled their cosmopolitan projects. Every
human interest had its guardian, every region of the
globe its representative.' And the same spirit of active
benevolence spread among the Evangelicals throughout

the country. In fact, it is undeniable that they aroused within the Church, not only a spirit of fervent piety, but also a practical energy, which extended to good works of all kinds, and not always of an exclusively religious character.

At the same time, it was inevitable that another movement should arise, supplementary rather than

A supplementary movement inevitable

antagonistic to the Evangelical movement, if people honestly desired to be guided by the Church's directions. For, to say the least of it, the Evangelicals only brought into prominence one side of the Church's teaching. No one can enter thoroughly into the Church's meaning, who does not follow out carefully and reverently the course prescribed in the Church's year. Now the Evangelicals obviously did not attach the slightest value to the Church's course. Take any of the numerous volumes of sermons, or any of the devotional works they have left us, and you will find, as a rule, that course simply ignored. We could not have a better illustration than the Olney Hymns. The preface clearly intimates that they were written primarily, though not exclusively, for use in public worship. The compiler (and composer of the majority of them), the excellent John Newton, ' more particularly dedicates them to his dear friends in the parish and neighbourhood of Olney, for whose use the hymns were originally composed.' They may therefore be regarded as a specimen of the way in which a thoroughly representative Evangelical clergyman would train his parishioners to be good Churchpeople. Book I. is filled with hymns on ' Select Passages of Scripture,' that is, hymns on texts from every book in the Bible in turn, from

Genesis to Revelation; of this little need be said, except
what Fuller said of Sternhold and others, that their
'piety was better than their poetry, and they had drank
more of Jordan than of Helicon.' But Book II. begins
with a number of hymns on 'Seasons,'—presumably
Church Seasons, as they are written by a clergyman for
the edification of his parishioners, and to be used by
them in the Church services. The first season then, it
appears, is the 'New Year,' which is markedly omitted
in the Prayer-book, the Church's year beginning at
Advent. After an inordinately large number of hymns
on this season, which is no Church season at all, the
next seasons are winter, spring, summer, hay-time,
harvest. Then it seems to have dawned upon the good
man that the Church, of which he was a minister, says
something about Christmas; so we have three hymns—
only three, while the New Year has at least thirty—
more or less appropriate to Christmas, and then we pass
on to another Church season, 'Saturday evening,' and
then to one more, 'The Close of the Year.' Positively
not one word in the 'Seasons' of Advent, Epiphany,
Lent, Good Friday, Eastertide, Whitsuntide!

We pass from 'Seasons' to 'Ordinances,' and among
these are seven—only seven—'Sacramental Hymns,'
Newton on and most of these have very little to do with
'Ordinances' the Sacraments. One says naturally 'Sacraments,' but it would appear that, according to Newton,
there was only one Sacrament; for not one word is
there about Baptism in any of these 'Sacramental
Hymns.' Indeed, it would seem as if Baptism were
not only no Sacrament, but not even an 'Ordinance,'
for there is nothing about it in the 'Ordinances.' The

present writer will hardly be suspected of prejudice against Newton, whose character he admires and loves; but really, if this is a specimen of Church teaching, something supplementary, at any rate, was required.

Neither Methodists nor Evangelicals expressed themselves in the least degree dissatisfied with the doctrines of the Church of England. They did not wish, like the Puritans of the seventeenth century, to alter either liturgy, articles, or rubrics; but they had no sense whatever of the beauty and symmetry of her system; they made no attempt to carry out that system in all its details; and, above all, they placed, to say the least of it, those two Sacraments, which the Church expressly teaches her little children to regard 'as generally necessary to salvation,' on a far lower level than any unprejudiced student of the Prayer-book could possibly do.

Church system not fully carried out

Oddly enough the one man who *did* show a marked appreciation of the Church's system is also the one man, who, unintentionally it may be, but very really, is responsible for the greatest secession from the Church in modern times, John Wesley. This appreciation is shown by innumerable passages in his Journals—passages, by-the-way, which occur quite as frequently *after* 1738 as before. Here are a few specimens : 'Easter, 1777 — During the Octave I administered the Lord's Supper every morning after the example of the Primitive Church.' 'Christmas, 1773—We had many opportunities of celebrating the Solemn Feast Days' [that is, of course, Christmas Day, S. Stephen's, S. John the Evangelist's, and Holy Innocents'] 'according to the design of their institution.'

John Wesley's appreciation of the Church system

(There is a similar entry in 1774.) 'Nov. 1, 1767—Being All Saints' Day (a festival I dearly love) I could not but observe the admirable propriety with which the Collect, Epistle, and Gospel are suited to each other.' 'Nov. 1, 1766—God, who hath knit together His elect in one communion and fellowship, gave us a solemn season in praising Him for all His Saints.' 'Friday, Oct. 12, 1739—We had a refreshing meeting with many of our Societies, who fail not to observe, as health permits, the weekly fast of our Church, and will do so, by God's help, as long as they call themselves members of it. And would to God all who contend for the rites and ceremonies of the Church, perhaps with more zeal than meekness of wisdom, would first show their own regard for her discipline in this more important branch of it.' And so one might go on quoting, almost *ad infinitum*; but one might search in vain for any such expressions of appreciation in the writings of others connected with the Evangelical Revival, with the exception perhaps of Charles Wesley.

It is hardly necessary to say that in external matters such as the architecture and adornment of churches Want of aesthetic taste   the Evangelical Revival did nothing. Considering the general bad taste in the arts which prevailed during the eighteenth century, it is perhaps as well that the desire to meddle with those grand old Gothic buildings which are the glory of England was not encouraged. One trembles at the very thought of such buildings being hacked about to suit the taste of the last century. The erection of a hideous gallery, in order to accommodate the crowds who flocked to hear their favourite preacher was generally the extent of the defacement which was effected; and happily such defacement could be removed, without having done any serious damage, when a better taste set in. There was no disposition to follow the evil example of the Puritans of the seventeenth century, whose injuries to our parish churches are irreparable. The Methodists proper were content with their own 'preaching-houses,' and the Evangelicals, so long as they had pulpit to preach in, and space to hold the congregation, who came to hear them, were content to leave the buildings alone.

The effects of the Revival upon the Dissenting interest were at least as marked as upon the Church of England. That interest was at a very low ebb when the Revival began. Isaac Taylor asserts with truth that 'it was rapidly in course to be found nowhere but in books;' and what there was of it was in a very unsatisfactory condition. Latitudinarianism and Socinianism had deeply affected most of the sects. Calamy, himself a Dissenter, laments that 'the heats among Dissenting ministers were perfectly scandalous,' and there was an exodus of many of their best men—Secker and Butler, subsequently two of our most distinguished prelates, among the number—to the Church. Both Methodists and Evangelicals largely revived the drooping cause. Much as John Wesley was attached to the Church of his baptism, it is clear that some of his leading principles were more adapted to make men Dissenters than Churchmen. He calls it 'a glorying peculiar to us' that 'there is no other Religious Society under Heaven which requires nothing of men in order to admission to it but a desire to save souls;

Effects on the Dissenting interest

not opinions—we think and let think; nor modes of
worship, &c.'—Whether there were any other society or
not, the Church of England with its creeds and ritual
was certainly not that society. Still more would Whitefield's preaching encourage men at least as much to
become Dissenters as Churchmen. Henry Venn was
at one time in the habit of attending an Independent
meeting. John Newton at first thought of joining
some Dissenting communion; and if his difficulties in
obtaining Holy Orders had not been removed, he would
have done so. William Wilberforce sometimes attended
other places of worship than the Church. William
Grimshaw actually built a Methodist chapel and a
house for the preacher in his own parish, and within
a stone's-throw of the parish church. In short, the
Evangelicals, like the Methodists, regarded the Church
of England simply as one out of many Protestant bodies,
and as this was the Dissenting, not the Church, view
the principles obviously led to the increase of Dissent.

Trevecca

Lady Huntingdon's college at Trevecca can
really be regarded as little else than a training college for Dissenting ministers. It is true that
her object was to have her students trained in such a
way that they might enter any ministry; but it is
obvious that such a vague training would be more
likely to make them Dissenters than Churchmen. And
as a matter of fact it did. Berridge warns her of this
in a very outspoken and characteristic fashion; and he
also implies that his own and kindred clergymen's efforts
would have the same effect. His prophecy soon became
history, and is worth quoting in full: 'You say the
Lord is sending many Gospel labourers into the Church.

True, and with a view of calling His people out of it, because, when such ministers are removed by death or transferred to another vineyard, I see no fresh Gospel labourers succeed them, which obliges the forsaken flocks to fly to a meeting. And what else can they do? If they have tasted of manna and hungered for it they cannot feed on heathen chaff, nor yet on legal crusts, though baked by some starch Pharisee quite up to perfection. What has become of Mr. Venn's Yorkshire flock? What will become of his Yelling flock, or of my flocks at our decease? Or what will become of your students at your removal? They are virtual Dissenters now, and will be settled Dissenters then. And the same will happen to many, perhaps most, of Mr. Wesley's preachers at his death. He rules like a real Alexander, and is now stepping forth with a flaming torch; but we do not read in history of two Alexanders succeeding each other. "But," you reply, "some of my best preachers leave me in my lifetime." Perhaps they may. God did well in sending some preachers from the Methodist mint among the Dissenters to revive a drooping cause. Be glad, my lady! Lift not up your hand against them for the Lord's sake, nor yet for consistency's sake, because your students are as real Dissenting preachers as any in the land, unless a gown and bands can make a clergyman.'[1] 'Our ministers must come,' writes her ladyship in 1781, 'recommended by that neutrality between Church and Dissent—secession.' And again in 1782 :—'Mr. Wills's secession from the Church (for which he is the most highly

---

[1] Quoted in *The Life and Times of Selina Countess of Huntingdon*, by a member of the houses of Shirley and Hastings, vol. ii. p. 423.

favoured of all from the noble and disinterested motives
that engaged his honest and faithful conscience for the
Lord's unlimited service) brings about an ordination of
such students as are alike disposed to labour in the
place and appointed for those congregations. The
method of these appears the best calculated for the
comfort of the students and to serve the congregations
most usefully, and is contrived to prevent any bondage
to the people or minister. The objections to the Dissenters' plan are many, and to the Church more;
that secession means the neutrality between both, and
so materially offensive to neither.'[1]   Her ladyship's
position is really as odd as her style, which is saying
much.   Neutrality was an impossibility, the distinction
which she draws between secession and separation from
the Church being surely a distinction without a difference.
And the result proved it.   Of Wales, where the Countess's college was, the biographer of Whitefield asserts
with perfect truth : 'The History of Methodism is the
History of Dissent.'[2]   It is said that Venn, on leaving
Huddersfield, sanctioned the erection and assisted in
building a meeting-house, 'and when another vicar
came, from whom he would never have wished the
people to secede, few returned to the parish church.'[3]
It is needless to multiply proofs, though it could easily
be done ; but one can well understand how it came
about that, whereas at George I.'s death, the proportion of Dissenters to Churchmen was about one to
twenty-five, by 1800 it was computed to be one to

[1] *Life and Times of Selina Countess of Huntingdon*, vol. ii. p. 467.
[2] Philip's *Life and Times of George Whitefield*, pp. 112 and 128.
[3] *Life of Henry Venn*, p. 163.

four; and how the four Protestant sects had become Legion.

To trace out the history of the Evangelical Revival in its bearing upon the present century would be an *Later his-* interesting, but far more difficult, task than *tory of the movement* that attempted in these pages. Questions would arise which happily do not fall within the province of the present inquiry. Has Methodism drifted away from its old moorings, or is the Methodism of to-day really a carrying out of the work intended by John Wesley? Is there a reasonable probability of its ever 'looking unto the rock from whence it was hewn, and to the hole of the pit whence it was digged,' and returning to the Church of England? Is Evangelicalism within the Church a decaying power? Do the principles of Newton, Romaine, Venn, Scott, and the rest, still flourish, or are they so modified that their earlier exponents would hardly know them? These questions would have to be manfully grappled with by the historian of the Evangelical movement in the nineteenth century; but they do not come within the scope of the eighteenth. For it is no mere arbitrary line which may be said roughly to divide the centuries. The fact that the life of the founder of Methodism was prolonged to the last decade of the eighteenth century makes the close of that century a convenient landmark for dividing the earlier from the later phase of the movement. For John Wesley kept the reins in his hands to the very last; his death, therefore, naturally marks a new point of departure. The first generation of Evangelicals had pretty nearly done their work by the time that the eighteenth century closed. *Exoriare aliquis,* who can and will, calmly and dispassionately, yet with a true sympathy with its good points, describe the work of both sections of this important movement in its later development.

One question must, however, be briefly discussed. What was the strength of the Evangelical party in the Church of England at the close of the eighteenth century? Two great writers of our own day Position of the Evangelicals at the close of the eighteenth century have joined issue on this interesting question. Mr. Lecky boldly asserts that ' by the close of the century the Evangelical party were incontestably the most numerous and the most active party in the English Church.' Whether this be ' incontestable ' or not, it has at any rate been contested; and that by no less a man than Mr. Gladstone, who enters minutely into statistics to show that this was not the case. If instead of the words ' party ' and ' numerous,' one might substitute ' influence ' and ' definite,' the historian's assertion would, perhaps, be nearer the truth. For a vast number of people had been affected by Evangelical influence who would certainly not have ranged themselves with the Evangelical party. And Evangelical influence was certainly more definite than any other religious influence at that time. ' Nothing,' it has been cynically said, ' is more fallacious than facts—except figures.' While we fully admit the accuracy and pertinency of Mr. Gladstone's statistics, while we own that the Evangelical party were in possession of comparatively few important posts in the Church, and that its professed adherents were strong only in proprietary chapels, fashionable watering-places, and exceptional parishes scattered here and there throughout the country, we may certainly demur to the assumption that such statistics were the measure of the influence which they exercised. The truth seems to be that by the close of the century, the Evangelical party were more compact, that they knew their own minds better, that they were more aggressive— or, to use Mr. Lecky's epithet, more active—than any religious school in the Church. Before the Tractarian movement, High Church principles in the spiritual sense, though they never ceased to have many adherents—as they could hardly fail to have, while men had the Prayer-book in their hands and professed to be guided by its rules—exercised very little influence upon the nation at large. The late Bishop Blomfield is said to have remarked that after William Law's Letters to the Bishop of Bangor, no writer asserted the doctrine of Apostolical Succession until the Tractarians arose.[1] This and kindred doctrines were in abeyance rather than lost. On the other hand, Broad Church principles had fallen into discredit since the utter failure of the attempt of Archdeacon Blackburne and others to relax the obligation to the subscription of the Articles. The dominant party, so far as high position was concerned, seem to have had no very distinctive lesson to teach. They might be ranged under what has been irreverently termed 'High and dry,' on the one side, and 'Low and slow ' on the other. The Evangelicals, on the contrary, knew what they were aiming at perfectly well, and had a very definite system to teach. To the popular mind they certainly represented religious earnestness, and

[1] My authority for this statement is the late Bishop of Lincoln, Dr. Wordsworth.

activity in the Church. The very fact that the epithet
'serious' was applied to them, and, in spite of much
sneering, was recognised as belonging to them by those
outside the circle, shows that they were considered *the*
religious party. To be 'serious' and to be 'Evangelical' were only different ways of saying the same thing.
They might dispute among themselves, chiefly on the
knotty points of Calvinism; but they had become
rather ashamed of the melancholy exhibition which had
been made in the great Calvinistic controversy, and
there was little left of the old bitterness which had been
shown thirty years before; and they were quite ready
to sink all minor differences, and present one united
phalanx to the common foe. They influenced enor-
mously, both in direct and in indirect ways, public
opinion generally and the views of individuals who
would by no means identify themselves with the party.
Nor was it a slight advantage to them that they had—it
is difficult to ascertain how, when, and where—gradually got affixed to them the name 'Evangelical.' Every
Christian must own that to be really Evangelical is to
be really Christian. By friend and foe alike they were
recognised as '*the* Evangelicals.' Assuming Christianity
to be true, that really was settling the whole question;
to be opposed to Evangelical religion was to be opposed
to Christianity. Once more, in many religious movements, the leaders are wont to be succeeded by a weaker
generation. It was not so in this case. The second
generation of Evangelicals, which had come to the
front before the century closed, was equal to the first.
Venn the son was worthy of Venn the father: so
were the second Thornton, the second Scott, and others.

The names of King, Knight, Hoare, Stephen, Jowett, Bickersteth, Pratt—where shall we stop?—were great and good names. There was not the slightest trace of the school degenerating or becoming superseded. In short it would be no exaggeration to say that, morally and spiritually, though by no means intellectually, the dominant religious power, both inside and outside the Church of England at the close of the eighteenth century was that which had been evoked by the Evangelical Revival.

CHAPTER IX.

OPPOSITION TO THE REVIVAL.

EVERY religious movement must expect to meet with a certain amount of opposition at its outset; and the Opposition Evangelical Revival was certainly no excep-to 'the Methodists' tion to the rule. Indeed, the opposition to it was so marked, so persistent, and came from so many different sources, that it cannot be dismissed without careful investigation. And though the remarks which follow will apply more directly to the earlier Methodism than to the later Evangelicalism, yet, looking at the matter from an eighteenth-century point of view, the two cannot in this respect be separated; for the obloquy which attached to the former extended equally to the latter. Protest as they would against the confusion, the Evangelicals, to the end of the century and beyond it, were always grouped with the Methodists by those who stood outside the circle of both. Bearing, therefore, in mind that much which will now be said can only properly apply to the earlier phase, though it was as a matter of fact applied to both, let us first consider the evidences of the opposition, and then try to discover the reasons of it.

The grossest and most popular form of opposition was that of mob riots. In the Black Country, espe-

Mob riots   cially at Birstal, Walsall, and Wednesbury, at Hampton, at Devizes, in many parts of Cornwall, and elsewhere, Wesley and the Methodists were positively persecuted; and Charles Wesley and George Whitefield often met with no better treatment. They were sometimes actually in danger of their lives. Sometimes—one blushes to relate it—these riots were instigated by the clergy; they were rarely stopped, as they ought to have been, by the magistrates. The only places where, as a rule, the Methodists could get common justice done to them were the higher secular courts and the Royal Palace. John Wesley, in his 'Loyal Address to the King' in 1744, described the Methodists, with perfect truth, as 'a people scattered and peeled and trodden under foot.' Drums were beaten, horns blown, guns let off, peals of bells rung, hounds let loose, to drown the voices of the preachers. Fire-engines were played upon them, stones and other missiles hurled at them. 'What evil,' asks Wesley in his 'Earnest Appeal to Men of Reason and Religion' (a short piece, but one of the most effective he ever wrote), 'have we done to you, that you should join the common cry against us? Why should you say, "Away with such fellows from the earth! it is not fit that they should live"?' And in his 'Farther Appeal' (a sequel

to the former and quite equal to it), 'Warm men cry
out to the people wherever one of us comes, "A mad
dog! a mad dog!" if haply we might fly for our lives,
as many have done before us.' To attempt to account
for the fury of a mob is an utterly hopeless task.
Probably, as at Ephesus of old, 'the more part of them
knew not wherefore they were come together.' All the
more shame to those who took advantage of the people's
ignorance to instigate them to deeds of violence!

Without then discussing further the conduct of the
mobs who may be incited to create disturbances for
Opposition anything or nothing, it will be better to draw
of moralists attention to the opposition which was raised
by many who at any rate must have known what they
were doing, and can hardly be supposed to have set
themselves against good, knowing that it *was* good.
Take, for example, the case of Hogarth the painter.
His talents were all enlisted on the side of virtue against
vice. A strong moral purpose runs through all his
admirable pictures. The 'Industrious and Idle Appren-
tices' were, in their way, doing the work of the Wesleys
and Whitefield. Yet he more than once attacked both.
His very last work, the picture entitled 'Credulity,
Superstition, and Fanaticism,' was drawn expressly to
caricature and counteract the effects of their preaching.
Dr. Johnson, again, was, it need scarcely be said, the
sworn foe of vice and irreligion. He respected John
Wesley and loved his society, and he was just enough
to own that Colley Cibber's play, the 'Hypocrite,'
was not applicable to the Methodists. But observe
how contemptuously he speaks of his fellow-collegian:
'Whitefield never drew as much attention as a mounte-

bank does; he did not draw attention by doing better
than others, but by doing what was strange. I never
treated Whitefield's ministry with contempt; I believe
he did good; he had devoted himself to the lower
classes of mankind, and among them he was of use.
But when familiarity and noise claim the praise due to
knowledge, art, and elegance, we must beat down such
pretensions.' With what perverse ingenuity, again, he
defends one of the most unjustifiable of all the outrages
perpetrated against the Methodists, the expulsion of the
six students from St. Edmund's Hall, Oxford, in 1768 :
'Sir, that expulsion was extremely just and proper.
What have they to do at a university who are not
willing to be taught, but presume to teach ?   Sir, they
were examined, and found to be ignorant fellows. They
might be good beings, but they were not fit to be at
Oxford. A cow is a very good animal in a field, but we
turn her out of a garden.' Is there any trustworthy
evidence that these young men, who were expelled
from Oxford simply because they would not desist
from praying and exhorting in private rooms, were
unwilling to be taught; or that they were really and
fairly examined and found inferior to the general run
of students ?

   Let us turn from the moralist to the judge.   Lord
Northington, speaking from the judicial bench—a place
Judicial   where, of all others, language ought to be
opposition   calm and measured—said, in pronouncing
judgment against a Methodist preacher: 'Bigotry and
enthusiasm have spread their baneful influence among
us far and wide, and the unhappy objects of the contagion almost daily increase. Of this not only Bedlam,

but most of the private mad-houses are melancholy and
striking proofs.'

The popular historians of the day write in an
equally condemnatory tone. This is the way in which
Popu'ar Tindal in his 'Continuation of Rapin's History
historians up to the Present Time' [1763], speaks of the
new phenomenon : 'This year' [1739] 'was distinguished by the institution of a set of fanatics under the
name of Methodists, of which one Whitefield, a young
clergyman, was the founder.' [Mark here again an
illustration of what has been said in a former chapter,
viz. that Whitefield, not Wesley, was regarded by
contemporaries as the most prominent character among
the Methodists.] 'Striking in with the common fana-
tical jargon and practices of enthusiasm, he soon found
himself at the head of such a number of disciples as
might have been dangerous to the public repose, had
they attempted to disturb it.' After honestly admitting
the loyalty of the Methodists he adds : 'The established clergy, instead of imitating the practice of former
times, were far from persecuting himself and his followers, and wisely treated him at first with reserve, and
afterwards with silent contempt. This moderation had
not the desired effect ; it set the founder to encroach on
parochial churches without the consent of the incum-
bents, to the great danger of the peace of society.'
Another contemporary historian, Smollett, writes in a
similar tone : 'Imposture and fanaticism still hung
upon the skirts of religion. Weak minds were seduced
by the delusion of a superstition styled Methodism,
raised upon the affectation of superior sanctity, and
maintained by pretensions to Divine illumination. Many

thousands in the lower ranks of life were infected with this enthusiasm by the unwearied exertions of a few obscure preachers, such as Whitefield and the Wesleys,' —Whitefield again put first.

Clerical evidence may perhaps be suspected of prejudice. Professional jealousy of the irregular workers Clerical may be thought to account for the hard judg-opposition ment of the clergy upon the Methodists. Still, will anyone seriously contend that men of deep Christian conviction, like Bishop Benson, Bishop Gibson (whom, in spite of his bitter antagonism, John Wesley with a noble generosity described as a ' great man, who is I trust now in a better world,' and 'a man eminent for piety and learning ')—Bishops Horne, Secker, and Horsley, and the great Dr. Waterland, deliberately opposed Methodism, although they knew it to be a work of God ? The hostility of such clergymen as Bishops Lavington, Warburton, and Hurd, and Mr. Polwhele, was of a different character from that mentioned above ; but still no unprejudiced person can think that in opposing Methodism they were consciously fighting against God.

What may be called the religious opposition to the Revival was not confined to the Church. In the journals Opposition of both the Wesleys and of Whitefield we find of Dis-senters constant reference to the opposition of Dissenters. The amiable Doddridge, who was perhaps a little too anxious to please everybody, was evidently embarrassed by the friendship of Whitefield. He had not the heart to exclude him from his house or even from his pulpit at Northampton, but he plainly lets us see that it would have been much more satisfactory to

him if his inconvenient friend had kept at a distance.
But even the half-hearted sanction which Doddridge
accorded to the Methodists drew upon him the severe
displeasure of his Dissenting brethren. Dr. Watts,
though he afterwards became friendly with Lady Huntingdon and the Methodist leaders, strongly disapproved
of Doddridge's conduct, and rebuked him roundly, on
the ground that he was losing caste by his intimacy
with Whitefield. 'I am sorry,' he writes, 'that since
your departure I have had many questions asked me
about your preaching in the Tabernacle, and sinking the
character of a minister, and especially of a tutor, so low
thereby. I find many of our friends entertain this
idea; but I can give no answer, as not knowing how
much you have been engaged there. I pray God to
guard us from every temptation.' Whitefield's biographer thus describes the opposition he met with from
Dissenters: 'Bradbury lampooned him, Barker sneered
at him, Watts was silent, Coward's trustees were inso-
lent to Doddridge because he countenanced him.' They
called him ' honest, crazy, confident Whitefield.' Doddridge was obliged to assure his friends that he 'saw no
danger that any of his pupils would prove Methodists.'
Neal wrote to Doddridge on his commendation of
Whitefield's sermon, saying that he ' could not reconcile it with the low incoherent stuff he used to hear him
utter at Kennington Common.' Doddridge replied that
he must look upon it as an unhappy circumstance that
Whitefield came to Northampton when he did, as he
perceived that, in conjunction with other circumstances,
it had filled town and country with astonishment and
indignation. As to the Wesleys, they were too strict

Churchmen to embarrass the Dissenters with any overtures of friendship; but as we have already seen from
John Wesley's Journal, from which many other extracts
might have been quoted, his relations to the Dissenters
were, as a rule, by no means cordial.

The opposition to the Revival was both reflected in
and encouraged by the standard literature of the day.
Opposition
of literary
men
Pope in his own incisive fashion satirised the
new preachers in general, and Whitefield in
particular, in the 'Dunciad':

> So swells each windpipe ; ass intones to ass,
> Harmonic twang ! of leather, horn, and brass :
> Such as from labouring lungs the enthusiast blows
> High sound, attemper'd to the vocal nose,
> Or such as bellow from the deep divine ;
> There, Webster ! peal'd thy voice, and Whitefield ! thine.

Webster, by the way, was a writer in the ' Weekly Mis-
cellany,' a paper bitterly opposed to the Methodists.
So Pope's blows were impartially administered to both
sides. In Junius' Letters reference is made to the
' whining piety ' of Whitefield. Methodism is ridiculed
by Anstey in ' The New Bath Guide.' The excellent
' Parson Adams ' in ' Joseph Andrews ' is represented
by Fielding as contrasting his own sermons with those
of Whitefield, ' though,' he says, ' I was once his well-
wisher.' ' I am myself,' he adds, ' as great an enemy
to the luxury and splendour of the clergy as he can be.
I do not, more than he, by the flourishing estate of the
church, understand the palaces, equipages, dress, furni-
ture, rich dainties, and vast fortunes of her ministers.
Surely those things which savour so strongly of this
world, become not the servants of One Who professed

His kingdom was not of it. But when he began to call nonsense and enthusiasm to his aid, and set up the doctrine of faith against good works, I was his friend no longer; for surely that doctrine was coined in hell, and none but the devil himself could have the confidence to preach it.' In 'Amelia,' Mr. Booth is robbed by a Methodist in prison, who 'had, as the phrase of the sect is, searched him to the bottom. In fact, he had thoroughly examined every one of Mr. Booth's pockets; from which he had conveyed away a pen-knife and an iron snuff-box, these being all the moveables which were to be found.' Smollett satirises the Methodists in his picture of the Methodist footman in 'Humphrey Clinker.' And to turn to another kind of literature, Foote caricatured Whitefield in his play of the 'Minor.' One is thankful to find Archbishop Secker protesting against the performance of this play. 'Did I tell you,' wrote Horace Walpole to Montagu, 'that the Archbishop tried to hinder the "Minor" from being played at Drury Lane? For once the Duke of Devonshire was firm, and would only let him correct some passages, and even of these the Duke has restored some. Foote says he will take out a licence to preach Tam Cant against Tom Cant.' Secker, however in point of fact, would not correct the 'Minor,' as suggested by the Duke, because he said he had no wish to see an edition announced by the author as corrected and prepared for the press by the Archbishop of Canterbury.

Thus on all sides the Revival met with bitter opposition; but that opposition did not produce one result which has been popularly but most erroneously

attributed to it. It has been said that the Wesleyans
were thrust out of the Church. But what shadow of a
Methodists foundation is there for such a charge? When,
never thrust out of the how, where, was it done? The assertion
Church is a pure figment of the imagination. If in
this, as in so many other particulars, people would but
turn from second-hand accounts to John Wesley's own
Journal they would find that, so far from this being the
case, the relations between Wesley and the Church of
his baptism were far more close and amicable in his
old age than they were at the beginning of his career
as a Revivalist. In fact it will be seen from the above
quotations that the opposition was far more against
Whitefield than against Wesley. And it is this which
brings in the Evangelicals, as opposed to the Wesleyans, for their share of the odium which was attached
to the Revival; because they were universally regarded
as the legitimate offspring of the Whitefield, not the
Wesley, section of the movement. This is, of course, so
far true in that they were Calvinists, not Arminians;
but the points in Whitefield's career, which stirred up
so much opposition against him, were not applicable to
the majority of Evangelicals.

How are we to account for all this opposition to the
Revival? Was it that 'men loved darkness rather
Causes of than light because their deeds were evil?'
the oppo-sition This is the explanation which ·some have
given, but it is not a charitable one, and, what is more
to the point, it is not a true one. The very names of
those who have been already mentioned among the
opponents is sufficient to show this; and, if we look
into the reasons given, we shall surely find that the

opposition was not purely and simply that opposition which must always exist between the world and the Church, between the flesh and the Spirit.

In this, as in so many other cases, men are apt to judge the past by the light of the present; to assume Yearning for rest in the eighteenth century that the people of the eighteenth century could see with the eyes of the people of the nineteenth. In common fairness we are bound to try and put ourselves in the position of those who lived during the time of the Revival, and see how the Revivalists would naturally appear to them. And in doing so we shall at once see one reason why the movement could hardly fail to be regarded with suspicion even by good men. No fact is more patent to the student of Church history in the eighteenth century than the intense yearning for rest which prevailed. After the many changes and turbulent discussions, both in the religious and the political world, during the sixteenth and seventeenth centuries, the nation in the eighteenth century was above all things anxious to be quiet. Hence, in the domain of politics, its placid acceptance of the first two Hanoverian Kings, whose chief merit was that they let the country govern itself; hence its satisfaction with the policy of a Walpole and his feeble successors, who took for their motto ' quieta non movere;' hence its contentment with the somewhat sleepy state of religion both inside and outside the Church of England. ' Our happy establishment in Church and State,' the favourite phrase of the day, truly expressed the national sentiment. Now it is perfectly true that the Evangelical Revival had not the least intention of disturbing the happy establishment;

but it is equally true that 'quiet' was the very last
epithet that could be applied, at least to the early
Methodists. Their incessant bodily restlessness was
but a picture of their mental and spiritual activity. To
'rest and be thankful' was the very last thing that
they desired. Hence, the movement was unpopular for
the very same reason that popery was unpopular and
deism was unpopular; each in its way tended to disturb the prevailing quiet. Bishop Gibson, in one of his
pastorals, very characteristically classes the Methodists
with deists, papists, 'and other disturbers of the kingdom of God.'

But it was not merely a vague suspicion of its
tendency to disturb the prevailing quiet which raised
Hatred of
Puritanism opposition to the Revival. It was also
charged with a definite design to resuscitate
doctrines and practices which were extremely obnoxious
to the majority of the nation. The reaction, for instance, against the hated reign of the Saints, had by
no means spent its force at the time of the Revival;
and there is no commoner charge against the Revival
than that of attempting to restore this reign. One can
easily see how this idea arose; for the points of agree-
ment between Methodism and Puritanism are obvious
enough. Whitefield expressed a strong sympathy with
the old Puritans, whose memory he had learned to love
in America. Wesley's tone of mind, it is true, was in
many respects utterly antagonistic to Puritanism; but
there were not wanting superficial resemblances between his system and theirs. The later Evangelicals
were, most of them, partial to Puritan divinity—Owen,
Howe, Baxter, Flavel, Manton, and the rest were all

favourites with them. All the Methodists were, as a matter of fact, suspected of a wish to revive the Puritanism of the seventeenth century. 'The nonsensical New Light,' wrote Horace Walpole in 1748, 'is extremely in fashion, and I shall not be surprised if we see all the cant and folly of the last age.' 'I have been lately reading,' wrote Bishop Warburton, 'the trials and last behaviour of the Regicides. They were mostly, you know, enthusiasts ; but, what surprised me, of the same kind with the Methodists. . . . Though the Methodists ought not to be persecuted, yet that the clergy are right in giving no encouragement to this spirit appears from the dismal effects it produced among the fanatics in Charles I.'s time, who began with the same meekness and humility with these.' And again : 'I tell you what I think would be the best way of exposing these idle fanatics—the printing of George Fox's journal, and Ignatius Loyola, and Whitefield's journal in parallel columns.' 'What think you of our new set of fanatics called the Methodists? I have seen Whitefield's journal, and he appears to me as mad as ever George Fox the Quaker was.' Archdeacon Balguy, in his charge at Winchester in 1760, speaks of 'the growth of the modern sect of Puritans, who to all the nonsense of a Calvinistical creed have added the chimerical claims to inspiration.' Messrs. Bogue and Bennett, the joint historians of the Dissenters, assert that 'thousands expressed their delight to see Puritanism revived by a minister of the Church of England. Whitefield found himself at home among these descendants of the Puritans.' But it is needless to multiply evidence upon a point which must be clear to all who have even a superficial acquaintance with the histories of Methodism and Puritanism.

Oddly enough the very opposite charge to that of Puritanism was, at least, as frequently brought against the leaders of the Revival. They were inces-
santly accused of verging towards Rome. 'If,' said Whitefield, 'I am Roman Catholic, the Pope must have given me a large dispensation.' And well might he say so—for there was not one point (except such points as those on which all Christians are agreed) in common between him and the Romanists. Against the Wesleys the charge was not perhaps so utterly absurd on the face of it. For, as we have already seen, there were in John Wesley in especial certain proclivities which, even at the present day, would be thought by some (though most unjustly) to savour of Romanism. Southey's account of the matter is curiously illustrative of the disuse into which some of the plain rules of the Church had fallen in his day, and also of the writer's own mind on the subject. 'Wesley,' he says, 'would have revived a practice which had fallen into disuse throughout all the reformed churches, as being little congenial to the spirit of the Reformation. The society at Bristol passed a resolution that all the members should obey the Church to which they belonged by observing all Fridays in the year as days of fasting or abstinence. This probably gave currency to, if it did not occasion, a report that he was a papist, if not a Jesuit.' One is tempted to ask, Had Dr. Southey ever seen a Book of Common Prayer?—because there the rule stands in black and white, whatever may be the practice of 'all the reformed churches' or 'the spirit of

the Reformation.' Bishop Lavington's elaborate comparison between the 'Enthusiasm of Methodists and Papists' proved, in the author's opinion, the tendency of Methodism to demonstration. He was convinced that the 'peregrinations of the Methodists would lead them to Rome, whither they seemed to be setting their faces.' 'Your progress,' he wrote to Wesley, 'is that of a crab, directly backwards. Nor can I discern any perfection but the perfection of Jesuitism.' And again: 'We may see in Mr. Wesley's writings that he was once a strict Churchman, but has gradually relaxed and put on a more Catholic spirit, tending at length to Roman Catholicism. People of every communion are among his disciples, and he rejects with indignation any design to convert others from any communion, and, therefore, not from popery.' Bishop Warburton 'saw the exact resemblance there was between his [Wesley's] saints and those of the Church of Rome at the time of the new birth.' 'This,' he sagaciously remarks, ' might lead reflecting men to conclude that the original of both was the same.' The keen scent of Protestants sniffed Popery in all sorts of Methodist arrangements. ' One of these artful teachers,' wrote Dr. Scott in 1743, ' has ordered the tickets for his people to be impressed with the crucifix ; and this, with their confessions and other customs, intimates a manifest fondness for the institutions of the Church of Rome.' Bishop Smalbroke, in his charge to the clergy at Lichfield in 1746, declares that 'if the false doctrines of the Methodists prevail, they must unavoidably create a general disorder in our Constitution, and, if so, favour the return of popery itself.'

This last expression, 'a general disorder in our Constitution' points to a ground of alarm which was Fear of Jacobitism eminently characteristic of the eighteenth century. It was quite as much a political as a religious scare which made men see traces of Popery in the Revival. 'The Pope and the Pretender' were constantly bracketed together, and the two were not separated in the charge against the Revivalists which we are now considering. In 1744 both Charles and John Wesley were suspected, without the slightest reason, of being engaged in the plot which, as a matter of fact, *was* then brewing. A ridiculous accusation was laid against Charles Wesley of having spoken treasonable words, and witnesses were summoned before the magistrates at Wakefield to depose against him. He had 'prayed the Lord to bring home his banished ones,' and some believed, or pretended to believe, that he referred to the Jacobites. The charge was too absurd to be substantiated even before the most prejudiced tribunal. But the panic did not cease. 'Every Sunday,' says Charles Wesley, 'damnation is denounced against us, for we are papists, Jesuits, seducers, and bringers-in of the Pretender.' In fact, so strong was the feeling on the point that, when a proclamation was issued commanding all Romanists to leave London, John Wesley thought it expedient to postpone a journey and remain in town, lest he should be suspected of having quitted in consequence of the proclamation.

Nor was it only the enemies of the Revival who detected Popery in some of the doings of the Wesleys. The famous Minutes of the Conference of 1770, which were thought to attribute too much to good works, alarmed 'Lady Huntingdon and many other Christian friends (real Protestants).' The Countess felt her duty to be clear. She wrote to Charles Wesley, declaring that the proper explanation of the Minutes was, 'Popery unmasked.' 'Thinking,' she added, 'that those ought to be deemed papists who did not disavow them, I readily complied with a proposal of an open disavowal of them.' In fact, if Wesley was not a Papist, the only reason was because Popery did not go far enough for him. 'The men of the world,' writes Fletcher in his 'Third Check to Antinomianism,' 'hint sometimes that he is a papist and a Jesuit; but good, mistaken men have gone much farther in the present controversy. They have published to the world that they 'do verily believe his principles are too rotten for even a papist to rest upon ; that it may be supposed popery is about the midway between Protestantism and him '—and so forth.

Lady Huntingdon's Protestant alarm

John Wesley had hardly patience to answer all these ridiculous imputations. With natural indignation in his 'Appeal to Men of Reason and Religion' he brushes them aside with the simple argument: 'O! ye fools, whosoever ye are, high or low, Dissenters or Churchmen, clergy or laity, who have advanced this shameless charge, when will ye understand that the preaching of justification by faith alone, the allowing no meritorious cause of justification but the death and righteousness of Christ, and no conditional or instrumental cause but faith, is overturning popery from the foundation?' This sentence had, of course, no reference to Lady Huntingdon and her.

John Wesley's disclaimer

C. II.   N friends, but to much earlier assailants. It is, however, applicable to all. The later Evangelicals do not appear to have been ever suspected of Popery; there is *some* limit to human absurdity.

We have mentioned the Pope and the Pretender as being coupled together, but we must not forget Diabolical agency that there was another member of the Trium-virate, and some people opposed the Revival because they believed in very truth that some of its phenomena were due to his instigation. 'I really think,' writes Mr. Polwhele in his Introduction to Bishop Lavington's famous treatise, ' it would scarcely be uncandid to resort to the sacred text for a definition of a Methodist—τὰς μεθοδείας τοῦ διαβόλου—Methodism of the devil!' The bishop himself is less hesitating; he attributes the origin of many parts of Methodism point-blank, without the slightest circumlocution, to satanic agency; and Bishop Warburton does the same in his 'Doctrine of Grace.'

All the causes of the opposition to the Revival hitherto mentioned, although they were quite sincerely Extrava-gances of Methodists adduced, were absurd on the face of them. But it must be confessed that there were others which were better grounded. When men's feelings are roused to a high pitch of excitement, it is not always easy to keep them within the bounds of prudence and reason. That extravagances accompanied the early spread of Methodism, that results sometimes followed which savoured of the rankest fanaticism, and which were positively noxious both to the souls and bodies of those who were possessed, few except the extremest partisans will deny. Indeed, we need go no farther

than the admissions of the leaders of the Revival themselves for a proof of this. In reference to the wild
extravagances of Maxfield and Bell, which arose from
a perversion of Wesley's favourite doctrine of Christian
perfection, Fletcher of Madeley wrote : ' Allowing that
what is reported is one-half mere exaggeration, one-
tenth of the rest shows that spiritual pride, stubbornness,
presumption, arrogance, party spirit, uncharitableness,
prophetic mistakes, in short that *every sinew* of enthusiasm, is now at work in many of that body.' John
Wesley admits that ' in some nature mixed with grace,'
and that ' Satan mimicked this work of God.' (He is
referring to the physical symptoms in Berridge's church
at Everton.) Whitefield owned that ' many young persons ran out before they were called; others were
guilty of great imprudences.' Now, if the leaders of the
Revival felt this, how must the matter have appeared
to people who were regarding the movement from the
outside with no friendly eye ? Can one not easily conceive how in an age which was morbidly sensitive about
anything which it vaguely called enthusiasm, which was
suspicious of whatever tended to disturb the prevailing
quiet, reports of cases of fanaticism would be made the
worst of, and eagerly spread, and would thus throw discredit upon the whole movement ? People who, if they
had known such men as the Wesleys, Fletcher, and
Whitefield, would have respected them—even if they
could not altogether agree with them—learnt to shrink
from them as pestilent and seditious fellows, who
would turn the world upside down, and who deserved
to be crushed as nuisances to society. And almost lu-
dicrously unjust as such ideas were, still it is doubtful

whether the leaders of Methodism were exactly the
sort of men who were adapted to stay the evil of all
this fanaticism and extravagance. Whitefield, besides
being a rash, impulsive man, without much discrimination or good judgment, was also hardly strong enough
a man to lay the spirit which he had raised, or to keep
it within due bounds. John Wesley, a far stronger
man than Whitefield, could doubtless have more easily
checked the extravagances of his disciples; but unfortunately his very virtues sometimes disqualified him
for estimating the true state of the case. He was always ready to hope for the best of everyone; he had a
strong tendency from his youth upwards to believe too
readily in the intervention of the supernatural. Guileless and truthful as the day himself, he was willing
to believe that others were like him, and hence he
not seldom became the dupe of designing knaves and
plausible hypocrites. ' My brother,' said Charles, 'seems
born for the benefit of knaves.'

But were the leaders themselves quite free from
giving just grounds for opposition to the movement?
After all, Wesley and Whitefield, and Berridge and Grimshaw, *were* ordained ministers
of the Church of England; they had promised
at their ordination to obey those who were set over
them, and this they certainly did not do. It was all
very well for Wesley to say that ' the world was his
parish,' but the simple answer is that it was *not*. To
appreciate the true state of the case, let us conceive the
analogous case of an army. Suppose that certain
soldiers thought that they could manage a battle or
skirmish better than the commanding officer, and set

Insubordi-
nation of
clerical
Methodists

out to fight independently on their own account; would it be very unreasonable if the authorities failed to appreciate this arrangement? Wesley, indeed, explained the anomaly by contending that he had only bound himself to obey the '*godly* admonitions' of his ecclesiastical superiors; but then, was he to constitute himself as the sole authority as to what were godly admonitions or not? It certainly is not to be wondered at that those in whose hands the real authority rested should be provoked at this setting of their authority at defiance. And perhaps it is also not to be wondered at that they should have hinted that the proper course would have been for those priests who would not obey the rulers of the Church to withdraw themselves from the Church. At any rate their remaining in the Church was obviously a further cause of exasperation against them. 'If,' argues Bishop Warburton, 'we show ourselves thus rightly disposed in favour of this divine principle of toleration, when the law hath left offenders against Church government to the justice of its rulers, much more shall we be disposed to suffer the honest sectary, who hath legally qualified himself for the enjoyment of his religious liberty, to possess it without trouble or control.' ' Every prudent society,' wrote another, probably Bishop Gibson, 'must desire that they would withdraw from her bosom who by sheltering themselves in it can wound and sting her more effectually.'

One more objection to the early Methodists must be noted, viz. that they pronounced dogmatically upon deep questions, which had puzzled far more thoughtful and better-read men. ' What wonder,' said Bishop

Horne, in a sermon preached before the University of
Oxford in 1761, 'antinomianism is rampant when men,
instead of having recourse to the catholic doctors of the
ancient Church, extract their theology from the latest
and lowest of our sectaries; if, instead of drawing living
water from the fresh springs of primitive antiquity,
they take such as comes to them at second hand from
Geneva, and Clement and Ignatius pass for moderate
divines compared to the new lights of the Tabernacle
and the Foundry?' The answer was, so far as Wesley
was concerned, that he *did* endeavour to draw water from
the fresh springs of primitive antiquity, and thought as
little of Geneva as did the Bishop himself.

CHAPTER X.

THE DOCTRINES OF THE REVIVAL.

In one sense, if we might take the express and reiterated
assertions of the leaders of all sections of the Revival,

Doctrines, the whole of the subject of this chapter might
those of the
Church of be summed up in one short sentence: 'The
England doctrines of the Revival were the doctrines of
the Church of England.' Methodists and Evangelicals
alike agreed on this point, that they held no tenets
except those which were to be found in the authorised
formulæ of the Church of England. They might be
abused by the clergy, but they appealed from the pulpit
to the prayer-desk, and asked whether these things
were so. John Wesley tells us, in his Journal, 'Sep-

tember 13, 1739:—A serious clergyman desired to
know in what points we differed from the Church of
England. I answered, "To the best of my knowledge
in none." He asked, "In what points, then, do you
differ from the other clergy of the Church of England?"
I answered, "In none from that part of the clergy who
adhere to the doctrines of the Church."' And again,
'October 15, 1739.—From Acts xxviii. 22, I simply
described the plain old religion of the Church of England, which is now almost everywhere spoken against
under the new name of Methodism.' If it be thought
that he modified his intense convictions on this point in
later years (though the extracts quoted, be it observed,
were written *after* his conversion), let us turn to his
striking sermon on the ministerial office, preached only
two years before his death. 'In God's name, stop! . . .
Ye yourselves were at first called in the Church of
England; and though ye have, and will have, a thousand
temptations to leave it, and set up for yourselves, regard
them not; be Church of England men still; do not cast
away the peculiar glory which God hath put upon you,
and frustrate the design of Providence, the very end for
which God raised you up.' This, be it observed, was
some years *after* he had 'set apart' ministers. And
this is the man who is described by a modern historian
as a 'great schismatic who wished to organise a system
capable of rivalling the Established Church' (Buckle)!
If it be thought that he was deceiving himself, let us see
what is said by one of his most intimate and appreciative
friends in his old age, a keen observer and thinker, one
who, if any man was, was capable of judging, and who
was not prejudiced in favour of his views, for he dis-

/ agreed with many of them. 'He was,' wrote Mr. Alexander Knox after Wesley's death, 'a Church of England man even in circumstantials; there was not a service or a ceremony, a gesture or a habit, for which he had not an unfeigned predilection.' In fact he took a conscious pride in contrasting the teaching of that part of the Revival of which he was the recognised leader, with the teaching both of other Revivals and of other sections of this one. Witness the remarkable sermon which he preached on laying the foundation stone of the City Road Chapel. 'One circumstance,' he says, 'attending the present Revival of religion is, I apprehend, quite peculiar to it. It cannot be denied that there have been several revivals of religion in England since the Reformation. But the generality of the English nation were little profited thereby, because they that were the subjects of those revivals, preachers as well as people, soon separated from the Established Church, and formed themselves into a distinct sect. So did the Presbyterians first; afterwards the Independents, the Anabaptists, and the Quakers; and after this was done, they did scarce any good, except to their own little body. But it is not so in the present Revival of religion. The Methodists (so termed) know their calling. Their fixed purpose is—let the clergy or laity use them well or ill by the grace of God—to endure all things, to hold on their even course, and to continue in the Church, maugre men or devils, unless God permits them to be thrust out.' He then contrasts the conduct of his own followers with those of Mr. Ingham, Mr. Whitefield ('who conversed much with Dissenters, and contracted strong prejudices against the Church'), Mr. W. Cudworth, and

Mr. Maxfield, and 'lastly a school set up near Trevecca, where all who were educated (except those that were ordained—and some of them, too), as they disclaimed all connection with the Methodists so they disclaimed the Church also; nay, they spoke of it upon all occasions with exquisite bitterness and contempt.' In contrast with all these, 'none of whom have any manner of connection with the original Methodists,' 'we,' he concludes, 'do not, will not, form any separate sect, but from principle remain, what we have always been, true members of the Church of England.' And that he might put his sentiments into a more permanent form, he distinctly wrote, in his short history of Methodism, 'Those who remain with Mr. Wesley are mostly Church of England men. They love her articles, her homilies, her liturgy, her discipline, and unwillingly vary from it in any instance.'

Even in regard to Whitefield, in spite of his having 'contracted strong prejudices against the Church,' in Whitefield and the Church spite of his foolish raillery against the 'letter-learned clergy,' and 'the fat, downy doctors of the Establishment,' there is no trace of his recommending any variation of *doctrine* from that of the Church.

And as to 'the school near Trevecca' where Lady Huntingdon's ministers were educated, Dr. Haweis Lady Huntingdon's Connexion wrote, after the Countess's death, to one who desired information on the subject of their teaching: 'You ask of what Church we profess ourselves? We desire to be esteemed as members of Christ's Catholic and Apostolic Church, and essentially one with the Church of England, of which we regard ourselves as living members. The doctrines we sub-scribe—for we require subscription, and, what is better, they are always truly preached by us—are those of the Church of England in the literal and grammatical sense. Nor is the liturgy of the Church of England performed more decently in any Church.'

The Evangelicals to a man professed that they taught nothing and desired nothing but the plain doc-

Doctrine of the Evan-gelicals trine of the Church of England. They found the best expression of their wants in her deeply spiritual liturgy; they valued her articles and her homilies as the fullest and most lucid expositions of their own belief; and they were as strongly opposed as the highest of High Churchmen to the attempts made by Archdeacon Blackburne and others to alter or relax the obligation of her ministers to subscribe to all her formularies.

Thus it would seem that in doctrine all were agreed; and that all who took part in the Revival might join

Disagree-ments in doctrine hands not only with one another, but also with all Churchmen, (who, in profession at least, constituted the vast majority of the nation,) over the venerable teaching of their common mother. But in point of fact this was very far from being the case. Not only in matters of order and practice, but also in distinctly doctrinal questions, both the different sections of the Revival violently disagreed with one another, and the 'Orthodox' (as the term was some-times used in distinction to the Revivalists) as violently disagreed with both. This chapter, therefore, instead of being reduced to one brief sentence, will necessarily have to be extended to several pages, in order that it may give at all an adequate idea of the doctrines of the Revival.

The best method will be, first of all to state, as concisely as possible, the points on which all the Revivalists Points on were agreed, and on which the Evangelical which all agreed system laid the greatest stress; some of them were agreed to by all Christians, or at least by all Churchmen, but had been, as it were, held in reserve or at least had little prominence given to them, in the period immediately preceding the Revival; while others were strongly demurred to by many divines of the day. All, then, who were connected with the Evangelical Revival insisted upon (1) the total depravity of human nature. They held that the Image of God in the soul of man was not only *de*faced but *ef*faced by the Fall; that, in the language of the ninth article of the Church of England, 'man is very far' (as far as possible, *quàm longissimè*) 'gone from original righteousness.' (2) The doctrine of the atonement, or the vicarious sacrifice of Christ, which was made not only in *behalf* of, but *instead* of, sinful man, and was the sole *meritorious* cause of man's acceptance with God. (3) The doctrine of grace, or God's free, undeserved mercy, as the sole *originating* cause of man's salvation. (4) The doctrine of justification by faith alone, as the sole *instrumental* cause of man's salvation; faith was the hand stretched forth to accept the proffered mercy. It will be seen that the interpretation of this doctrine was a fruitful source of dispute among the different sections of the Revival, but the doctrine itself, as stated above, would have been accepted by all. (5) The absolute need of a conscious conversion

or regeneration—the words appear to have been used
synonymously—in every man. This was Wesley's
'New Birth,' of which more will be said presently.
(6) The total inability of man to turn to God without
the aid of His Holy Spirit. (7) The sanctification of
man by God's Holy Spirit. (8) The witness of the
Spirit, whereby man has an inner consciousness that
he is in a state of grace. (9) The plenary inspiration
of all the canonical books of Holy Scripture.

These were the main points on which all were agreed;
others might of course be added, such as the obligation
of the Lord's Day or Christian Sabbath, these words being
used synonymously; the obligation of the two Sacraments of the Gospel, though it is necessary to add that
very different views were held about them from those
which were held by the Anglo-Catholic school, and that
they certainly hold no very prominent place in the
Evangelical system.

On other points there were great and acrimonious
differences between the two sections of the Revival;
but, before we consider these, it will be desir-
able to dwell a little more at length upon
that doctrine which produced such striking results
upon the multitudes who listened with breathless excitement to the impassioned utterances of the new
preachers from the commencement of the Revival.
That doctrine is, of course, the doctrine of the 'New
Birth.' This is popularly supposed to be the great
burden of the early Revivalists' preaching,[1] but Wesley

The 'New Birth'

---

[1] See, for instance, Bishop Fitzgerald's essay on 'The Evidences of
Christianity,' in *Aids to Faith*, § 8 : 'Whitefield and the Wesleys
began their work by preaching the NEW BIRTH, &c.'

at any rate put one other doctrine on a par with it.
He begins his famous sermon on the New Birth,
(Sermon XLV.) :—' If any doctrines within the whole
compass of Christianity may be properly termed fundamental, they are doubtless these two, the doctrine of
justification, and that of the new birth; the former relating to that great work which God does *for us* in
forgiving our sins; the latter to the great work which
God does *in us* in renewing our fallen nature. In
order of *time* neither of these is before the other; in
a moment we are justified by the grace of God, through
the redemption that is in Jesus, we are also " born of the
Spirit; " but in order of *thinking*, as it is termed, justification precedes the New Birth. We first conceive His
wrath to be turned away, and then His Spirit to work
in our hearts.' Hence the two cannot in his view be
practically separated; and hence the assertion that the
New Birth was the primary object of his preaching,
though logically incomplete, is practically correct and
adequate. But how did Wesley as a Churchman reconcile this with the plain teaching of the Church on Holy
Baptism as the Sacrament of Regeneration? He did
not evade the question, but manfully grappled with it,
and justified his insistence upon the necessity of the
New Birth for careless sinners, by contending that they
had lost the germ of life which was once kindled in
them. 'I do not,' he says, ' now speak of infants; it is
certain our Church supposes that all who are baptized
in their infancy are at the same time born again; and
it is allowed that the whole Office for the Baptism of
Infants proceeds upon this assumption. Nor is it an
objection of any weight against this that we cannot

comprehend how this work can be wrought in infants. For neither can we comprehend how it is wrought in a person of riper years.' But he appeals to those who having been baptized were living in habitual sins in language so striking and stirring that it is worth quoting : 'Perhaps the sinner himself, to whom in real charity we say, " You must be born again," has been taught to say, " I defy your new doctrine; I need not be born again; I was born again when I was baptized. What! would you have me deny my baptism?" I answer, first, there is nothing under heaven which can excuse a lie ; otherwise I should say to an open sinner, "If you have been baptized do not own it. For how highly does this aggravate your guilt! How will it increase your damnation! Was you devoted to God at eight days old, and have you been all these years devoting yourself to the devil? Was you, even before you had the use of reason, consecrated to God the Father, the Son, and the Holy Ghost? and have you, ever since you had the use of it, been flying in the face of God and consecrating yourself to Satan?"'

Closely connected with this doctrine of the New Birth was that of the direct personal guidance by the Guidance of Holy Spirit of each individual Christian, the Holy Spirit which was held by all alike who took part in the Evangelical Revival. And here again they could appeal from the pulpit to the prayer-desk.' For if we are taught to pray, ' Cleanse the thoughts of our hearts by the inspiration of Thy Holy Spirit,' and hope that our prayers shall be answered, then surely the Christian is not presumptuous in hoping that he will be directly guided by the Holy Spirit, Who will not suffer him to be led into any serious error.

At the same time it is not unreasonable to think that the intense conviction of this truth led, indirectly Calvinistic at least, to the tone in which the unhappy controversy differences between the different sections of the Revival were discussed. For if each combatant felt that he was led by God's Holy Spirit to the conclusion at which he arrived on questions which seemed to him to be of vital importance, he would naturally believe that those who had come to an opposite conclusion were fighting against the Holy Spirit, and that, therefore, no language could be too strong to be used against them. It is needless to repeat here the very strong language that *was* used on both sides, but especially the Calvinistic. It will suffice to note that the so-called Calvinistic controversy embraced most, if not all, of the points on which the disputants were at issue. For it is a great mistake to suppose that the Calvinistic controversy turned wholly or even mainly upon that mysterious subject of predestination and election.

The chief question was: 'Is justification by faith alone, or justification by faith and works—that is, the Justification *evidence* of works, not the merit of them—the by faith truth?' It should be said that long before this famous controversy burst forth in all its fury it had been objected to the doctrine of justification by faith alone, as stated by Whitefield and others, that it might prove injurious to morality; and no less a personage than Dr. Waterland (the ablest controversialist, perhaps, of the eighteenth century) met by anticipation this objection in his 'Summary View of the Doctrine of

Justification,' which was published together with the same writer's sermons on 'Several Important Subjects of Religion and Morality' by Joseph Clarke in 1742, in order to meet the danger: so it will be seen how early in the Evangelical Revival the objection was raised. The editor says in the Preface: 'There hath of late years sprung up among us a sect of men who are reviving the Solifidian doctrine, contending that we are *so* justified by *faith alone* as to *exclude good works* from being *necessary conditions* of *justification*, admitting them to be only necessary *fruits* and *consequences* of it. Bishop Bull's works, being wrote in Latin, and so of no service to unlearned readers from whom this sect of men gather their converts, there seemed to be wanting some treatise in English on this subject, which might set that important point of doctrine in a clear light to common Christians.' Nearly fifty years later (1790), Bishop Horsley insinuates the same charge when he speaks of 'opinions which seem to emancipate the believer from the obligation of all moral law' (Fifteenth charge of the Bishop of S. David's); so does Bishop Tomline in his 'Refutation of Calvinism;' so does William Law in his 'Dialogue between a Methodist and a Churchman,' and so did many other orthodox divines. It was no doubt the intensely practical character of John Wesley's mind which led him to lay so much stress upon the subject, and there certainly *was* some reason to fear the danger complained of. We have only to turn to the sermons of one who was himself a decided Calvinist, Thomas Scott, to be convinced of this, for he felt it to be his special mission to contend against it.

This, however, though the main point, was not by
any means the only point at issue between the Calvinists
Other points ánd the Arminians. Both names, by-the-way,
in dispute were misnomers; for many of the so-called
Calvinists (Whitefield among the number) knew little
or nothing about John Calvin, while all the so-called
Arminians would have strongly disagreed with many
parts of the teaching of Arminius. The dispute included
all the five points of the Quinquarticular controversy
and many other collateral issues. Are a certain number
predestined to eternal life? Are all others destined to
eternal condemnation? [Perhaps a logical result of the
former question being answered in the affirmative, but
not admitted—at any rate, not dwelt upon—by many
of the Calvinists.] Have all a day of grace? Is justification a result of sanctification, or does it precede it,
or are the two identical? Is Christ's righteousness
imputed or imparted to the believer, or both? Is it
possible to attain to a state of sinless perfection on
earth? Is God's grace indefectible, so that one who is
once a believer must always be a believer, and, no
matter what sins of infirmity he may fall into, is his
final perseverance certain? Are there two justifica-
tions—the one by faith at the time of conversion, the
second by the evidence of works at the Day of Judgment? Are we to work *for* life or *from* life? Has the
expression 'a finished salvation' any other meaning than that of 'a finished redemption'? Is the
liberty of the will consistent with the operations of
divine grace? Did Christ die for the whole world, or
practically only for the elect? These are some, and
only some, of the profound doctrinal questions agitated

C. II. O

in the Calvinistic controversy in which Augustus Top-
lady, John Berridge, Sir Richard Hill, and Rowland
Hill, were the most prominent writers on the one side,
John Fletcher, John Wesley (though very sparingly),
Thomas Olivers, and Mr. Sellon on the other.

It is only fair to say that the now almost-forgotten
writings which appeared on both sides of the question—

Calvinists did them-selves in-justice in their writ-ings or rather questions—would give a most unjust
view of the general attitude of the writers.   It
is particularly necessary to bear this in mind
with regard to the Calvinists who have been
blamed (and justly), for outrivalling their antagonists
in abuse.   The fact is that both sides, but especially
the Calvinists, became intoxicated with the excitement
of the dispute, and to do the party anything like justice
we must appeal from Philip drunk to Philip sober.
Let us begin with one who died long before the controversy reached its height—in fact, before it commenced
in its later phase—James Hervey.   He was not only a
Calvinist of the Calvinists, but he wrote a treatise,
'Theron and Aspasio,' which was for many years a
text-book of Calvinism.   And yet observe how modestly
and moderately he writes in his own private letters on
the mysterious subjects involved in the dispute : ' Predestination and reprobation, I think of with fear and
trembling ; and if I should attempt to study them I
would study them on my knees.'   And again : ' As for
points of doubtful disputation, those especially which
relate to *particular* or *universal* redemption, I profess
myself attached neither to the one nor the other.   I
neither think of them myself nor preach of them to
others.   If they happen to be started in conversation.

I always endeavour to divert the discourse to some more edifying topic. I have often observed them to breed animosity and division, but never knew them to be productive of love and unanimity. Therefore I rest satisfied in this general and indisputable truth, that the Judge of all the earth will assuredly do right.' It is fair to say that these letters were written in 1752 and 1747 respectively,[1] and that 'Theron and Aspasio' was written some years later than either, but there is no reason to believe the good man altered his sentiments.

Again, we must not for a moment suppose that the spirit of the Calvinistic controversy was at all the spirit Moderate of what is called 'moderate Calvinism'—the Calvinism Calvinism, that is, of a Venn, a Newton, a Scott, a Cecil, a Milner. This spirit is well described by the accomplished biographer of Henry Venn : ' He [Venn] had hitherto been a zealous Arminian, hostile to Calvinism, which he considered repugnant to Scripture and reason; but the experience he now had of the corruption of his nature, of the frailty and weakness of man, of the insufficiency of his best endeavours, led him to ascribe more to the grace of God, and less to the power and free-will of man. This change gave a tincture to his preaching ; he exalted in higher strains the grace and love of God in Christ, and spoke less of the power and excellence of man. But his Calvinism stopped here. It was not the result of a theory embraced by reading books of that class; he did not attempt to reconcile difficulties which are found in that system ; he did not enforce as necessary upon others those particular views which he had himself imbibed ;

[1] See Tyerman's *Oxford Methodists*, pp. 270 and 254.

he did not break the bond of brotherly love and union
with those of his friends who were still zealous Arminians; and, above all, it did not lead him to relax his
views on the necessity and nature of holiness : ' in short,
he was a ' moderate Calvinist '—a term which was much
cavilled at in the hot days of the Calvinistic controversy,
but which really expressed the form which the Calvinism
of the Evangelical school ultimately assumed.   Let us
see what the term really meant.   By ' moderate Calvinism ' is understood that frame of mind which loved
especially to dwell upon man's utter unworthiness of
the least of God's mercies, upon his entire helplessness
in spiritual things, and his need of God's grace ' pre-
venting him that he may have a good-will, and following him when he has that good-will.'   It is well
expressed in that beautiful old hymn of Toplady
(o, si sic omnia!):

> Nothing in my hand I bring,
> Simply to Thy Cross I cling;
> Naked, come to Thee for dress,
> Helpless, look to Thee for grace;
> Vile, I to the Fountain fly,
> Wash me, Saviour, or I die!

The spiritual pride which extreme Calvinism is apt
to engender, by teaching the elect to regard themselves
as heaven's peculiar favourites, was utterly alien to the
spirit of these moderate Calvinists.   The exclamation,
' Why me, why me?' so frequent among the earlier
Calvinists, is never found in their writings.   They did
not love to write and talk about what Wesley calls
' their dear decrees.'   They never dwelt upon the
awful doctrine of reprobation, nor did they ever deny

that the most hardened had, or might have had, a day of grace. To associate Antinomianism in any shape or form with the teaching of such men is simply ridiculous. Their doctrine was so carefully guarded that it was hardly possible to pervert it to the purposes of licentiousness. 'Venn,' writes his biographer, with pardonable indignation, 'was assailed with the old insinuation that he preached the doctrine of faith alone to the neglect of works, though his whole life was a refutation of such a falsehood; and the lives of those who received his doctrine became so exemplary and strict that they were immediately accused of carrying holiness to an unnecessary length.' The fallacy of supposing that such Calvinism leads to the depreciation of good works is solved by undeniable facts. These so-called Calvinists were, as we have already seen, the originators or supporters of every philanthropic, no less than of every religious, effort which was made. Neither did they dwell on the gloomy and repulsive side of Calvinism. They were most of them bright, genial, cheerful men, with a considerable sense of humour, not the least like the gloomy Puritan of the Balfour of Burleigh type. They did not love to discuss minutely the unfathomable difficulties which the question involves. 'Instead,' wrote Cecil, and he expressed the sentiments of them all, 'of attempting any logical and metaphysical explanation of justification by the imputed righteousness of Christ, all which attempts have human infirmity stamped upon them, I would look at the subject in the great and impressive light in which Scripture places it before me. The thing is declared, not explained. Let us not, therefore, darken a subject which is held forth in prominent light by our idle endeavours to make it better understood.' In short, their system produced a singularly fine type of Christian character, very humble and loving, active and self-denying, so pure and blameless that those who were most opposed to their doctrine have owned that they were personally good men.

We cannot better conclude this sketch of the doctrines of one important section of the Evangelical Revival than by quoting a kind of creed which one of the most lovable of them all, John Newton, wrote in a private letter to a friend: 'I believe that sin is the most hateful thing in the world; that I and all men are by nature in a state of wrath and depravity, utterly unable to sustain the penalty or to fulfil the commands of God's Holy Law ; and that we have no sufficiency of ourselves to think a good thought. I believe that Jesus Christ is the chief among ten thousand; that He came into the world to save the chief of sinners, by making a propitiation for sin by His death, by paying a perfect obedience to the law in our behalf, and that He is now exalted on high to give repentance and remission of sins to all that believe; and that He ever liveth to make intercession for us. I believe that the Holy Spirit (the gift of God through Jesus Christ), is the sure and only guide into all truth, and the common privilege of all believers; and under His influence, I believe the Holy Scriptures are able to make us wise unto salvation, and to furnish us throughly for every good work. I believe that love to God, and to man for God's sake, is the essence of religion and the fulfilling of the law ; that without holiness no man shall see the Lord ; that those who, by

Newton's creed

a patient course of well-doing, seek glory, honour, and immortality, shall receive eternal life ; and I believe that this reward is not of debt, but of grace, even to the praise and glory of that grace whereby He has made us accepted in the Beloved.   Amen !' [Letter to Mr. O. (Okeley ?) in 'Cardiphonia.'] These were his positive tenets.   Let us add his sentiments as to the way in which controversy should be conducted with those who differ from them : ' Of all people who engage in controversy, we who are called Calvinists are most expressly bound by our own principles to the exercise of gentleness and moderation.   If, indeed, they who differ from us have the power of changing themselves, if they would open their own eyes and soften their own hearts, then we might with less inconsistence be offended at their obstinacy ; but if we believe the very contrary to this, our part is, not to strive, but in meekness to instruct those who oppose, " if peradventure God will give them repentance to the acknowledgment of the truth."   If you write with a desire of being an instrument of correcting mistakes, you will, of course, be cautious of laying stumbling-blocks in the way of the blind, or of using any expressions that may exasperate their passions, confirm them in their prejudices, and therefore make their conviction, humanly speaking, more impracticable.' [Letter XIX., ' Omicron.']

How thoroughly Newton acted up to these principles has been already seen in the account of his gentle but most effective treatment of Thomas Scott's case.

CHAPTER XI.

THE EVANGELICAL REVIVAL COMPARED WITH OTHER MOVEMENTS.

WE have already seen how John Wesley contrasted the movement of which he was the chief leader with other **Evangelical Revival unique** movements in England which bore a superficial resemblance to it. And, no doubt, in many points, the Evangelical Revival in the eighteenth century was unique. Attempts at a reformation both of manners and doctrine within the Church had been frequent, but none of them were quite like this one. It was not, for instance, at all analogous to that of Wiclif and the Lollards. These were avowedly dissatisfied with many of the doctrines, or abuses of doctrine, and still more with many parts of the constitution of the Church as it then stood. The Evangelical Revival arose from no dissatisfaction with any of these things.

Still less did it resemble the Reformation of the sixteenth century. For though that Reformation *was* **The Reformation** a *re-formation*, not the erection of a new Church, still the changes it proposed—and effected—were much more fundamental than any at which the Evangelical Revival aimed. In the sixteenth century the secular arm played a conspicuous part; in the eighteenth it did not; or, when it did, it was against, not for, the Revival. No new articles, no change or even improvement of the liturgy, no alterations of government or discipline, were even dreamed of by the Revivalists; they had none of the highest authorities to help them, and few on their side. Indeed, the differences were so great that the two movements hardly admit of a comparison.

In some respects still less did it resemble the great Puritan wave which swept over the country in the seventeenth century, upsetting in its course for a short while—a very short while—the Church of England as a national establishment. The Revivalists, especially the Evangelicals, appealed to the doctrines of the reformers, but they never appealed to those of the Puritans; indeed, they thoroughly disapproved of their whole course, though they might admire some of their devotional writings. To call them the 'new Puritans' as is frequently done is a thorough, though not unnatural, misnomer. For the Revivalists had no quarrel whatever with the *theory* of religion as it was professed by the Established Church. They only sought to reduce that theory into practice. They have been depreciated for not doing what they never attempted or wished to do. The Revival has been described by an able writer of our own day as 'the new Puritanism, excluding all the most powerful intellectual elements, and, therefore, of necessity a faint reflection of the grander Puritanism of the seventeenth century.' It may be admitted that the Evangelical divines by no means reached the intellectual stature of the Puritan divines; it may be admitted also, that the two sets of men had many objects in common, which have been already noted in the third chapter of this work. But the difference of attitude may surely account to some extent for the difference of intellectual power that was displayed. Intellectual power is more conspicuous when the main object is destruction than when it is construction. The object of the Evangelical Revival was wholly constructive, except in the sense that the 'pulling down of the stronghold of sin and Satan' is destructive. They desired to pull down nothing else, either literally or figuratively. They had no desire to pose as iconoclasts; nor to destroy our constitution either in Church or State. But that they did not do what they never proposed to do does not argue want of power. It is certainly true that on matters which were not concerned with the work of destruction, such as Biblical exegesis, devotional literature, &c., the earlier generation showed far greater strength than the later; but, on the other hand, the later were a more lovable set of men. However, comparisons are proverbially odious; let it suffice to note that the points of contrast were at least as marked as the points of resemblance between the Evangelicals and the Puritans.

To find a movement which really resembled the Evangelical Revival we must travel outside the limits of our own land. The Pietist movement in Germany in the beginning of the eighteenth century, of which Spener was the originator, and the University of Halle the centre, really *did* present some remarkable features of resemblance to our Evangelical Revival. The Halle Pietists, like our own Methodists and Evangelicals, aimed chiefly at throwing some life into the dry bones of the prevailing orthodoxy. Religion in Germany had become, to use a favourite German expression, 'ossified.' The Pietists, as their name implied, simply sought to raise the spirit of piety; they were satisfied with the Lutheran doctrines which were taught, and with the ecclesiastical constitution which was established. Their weak side represented in an exaggerated form the weak side of our own Revivalists. They rather discouraged theological studies of the severer kind, they depreciated human arts and sciences, they were very precise about things indifferent, they condemned indiscriminately the most harmless amusements, they showed a tendency to resolve religion too much into a morbid analysis of each man's self-consciousness, and they were certainly not in touch with the higher intellectual elements which were just beginning to develop themselves to such a remarkable extent in Germany. These defects, though not wholly wanting, were less conspicuous in the English movement. Hence, in part at least, the difference between the results. German Pietism soon yielded to the withering blast of nationalism which blew over from England into Germany. English Evangelicalism has held its own for more than a hundred years; and the essential features of its system will be traceable so long as England continues to be a Christian nation.

INDEX.

Printed by BALLANTYNE, HANSON & Co.
Edinburgh & London

HISTORICAL WORKS FOR SCHOOLS.

A HISTORY OF ROME TO THE DEATH OF CÆSAR.
By W. W. How M.A., Fellow and Lecturer of Merton College, Oxford, and H. D. Leigh, M.A., Fellow and Tutor of Corpus Christi College, Oxford. With 9 Lithographed Maps, 12 Maps and Plans in the Text. and numerous Illustrations. Crown 8vo, 7s. 6d.

GENERAL HISTORY OF ROME. From the Foundation
of the City to the Fall of Augustulus, B.C. 753—A.D. 476. By the Very Rev. CHARLES MERIVALE, D.D. With 5 Maps. Crown 8vo, 7s. 6d.

SCHOOL HISTORY OF ROME. Abridged from Dean
MERIVALE's General History of Rome, with the sanction of the Author. By C. PULLER, M.A. With 13 full-page Maps. Fcap. 8vo, 3s. 6d.

A SKELETON OUTLINE OF ROMAN HISTORY.
Chronologically arranged. By P. E. MATHESON, M.A. Fcap. 8vo, 2s. 6d.

A FIRST HISTORY OF ROME. By W. S. ROBINSON,
M.A. With Illustrations and Maps. 18mo, 2s. 6d.

A HISTORY OF THE ROMANS. For the Use of Middle
Forms of Schools. By R. F. HORTON, M.A. Crown 8vo, 3s. 6d.

A GENERAL HISTORY OF GREECE. From the Earliest
Period to the Death of Alexander the Great; with a Sketch of the subsequent History to the Present Time. By the Rev. Sir G. W. Cox, Bart., M.A. With 11 Maps and Plans. Crown 8vo, 7s. 6d.

A SKELETON OUTLINE OF GREEK HISTORY. Chrono-
logically Arranged. By EVELYN ABBOTT, M.A., LL.D. Fcap. 8vo, 2s. 6d.

A HISTORY OF GREECE. For the Use of Upper Forms
of Schools. By EVELYN ABBOTT, M.A., LL D. Crown 8vo.
Part I.—From the Earliest Times to the Ionian Revolt. 10s. 6d. Part II.—From the Ionian Revolt to the Thirty Years' Peace. 500–445 B.C. 10s. 6d. Part III.—From the Thirty Years' Peace to the Fall of the Thirty at Athens. 445–403 B.C. 10s. 6d.

A HISTORY OF GREECE FROM THE EARLIEST
TIMES TO THE MACEDONIAN CONQUEST. For the Use of Middle Forms of Schools. By C. W. C. OMAN, M.A., F.S.A. With Maps and Plans. Crown 8vo, 4s. 6d.

LONGMANS, GREEN, AND CO.
LONDON, NEW YORK, AND BOMBAY.

P

HISTORICAL WORKS FOR SCHOOLS.

OUTLINE OF ENGLISH HISTORY, B.C. 55—A.D. 1886.
By S. R. Gardiner, D.C.L., LL.D., Fellow of Merton College, Oxford. with 67 Woodcuts and 17 Maps. Fcap. 8vo. 2s. 6d.

A STUDENT'S HISTORY OF ENGLAND. From the
Earliest Times to 1885. By Samuel Rawson Gardiner, D.C.L., LL.D. In One Volume. With 378 Illustrations. Crown 8vo, 12s.

Vol. I. (B.C. 55—A.D. 1509). With 173 Illustrations. Crown 8vo. 4s.

Vol. II. (1509-1689). With 96 Illustrations. Crown 8vo. 4s.

Vol. III. (1689-1885). With 109 Illustrations. Crown 8vo. 4s.

PREPARATORY QUESTIONS ON S. R. GARDINER'S STUDENT'S HISTORY OF ENGLAND. By R. Somervell, M.A., Assistant Master of Harrow School. Crown 8vo. 1s.

A CLASS-BOOK HISTORY OF ENGLAND. Designed
for the Use of Students preparing for the University Local Examinations or for the London University Matriculation, and for the Higher Classes of Elementary Schools. By the Rev. D. Morris, B.A. With 4 Historical Maps, 20 Plans of Battles, and 30 other Illustrations. Fcap. 8vo, 3s. 6d.

HISTORY OF ENGLAND. For the Use of Schools. By
F. York Powell, M.A., and T. F. Tout, M.A. With Maps and Plans. Crown 8vo, 7s. 6d. To be had also in Three Parts :—

Part I.—FROM THE EARLIEST TIMES TO THE DEATH OF HENRY VII. By F. York Powell, M.A. Crown 8vo, 2s. 6d.

Part II.—FROM THE ACCESSION OF HENRY VIII. TO THE REVOLUTION OF 1689. By T. F. Tout, M.A. 2s. 6d.

Part III.—WILLIAM AND MARY TO THE PRESENT TIME. By T. F. Tout, M.A. Crown 8vo, 2s. 6d.

A SHORT HISTORY OF ENGLAND FROM THE
EARLIEST TIMES TO THE PRESENT DAY. For the Use of Middle Forms of Schools. With Tables, Plans, Maps, Index, &c. By Cyril Ransome, M.A. Crown 8vo, 3s. 6d.

*** Or, in Two Parts, 2s. each.

THE RISE OF CONSTITUTIONAL GOVERNMENT IN
ENGLAND. Being a Series of Twenty Lectures on the History of the English Constitution delivered to a Popular Audience. By Cyril Ransome, M.A. Crown 8vo, 6s.

THE ELEMENTS OF ENGLISH CONSTITUTIONAL
HISTORY FROM THE EARLIEST TIME TO THE PRESENT DAY (1895). By F. C. Montague, M.A. Crown 8vo, 3s. 6d.

LONGMANS, GREEN, AND CO.
LONDON, NEW YORK, AND BOMBAY.

HISTORICAL WORKS FOR SCHOOLS.

A HISTORY OF ENGLAND. By the Rev. J. FRANCK BRIGHT, D.D., Master of University College, Oxford.

Period I.—MEDIÆVAL MONARCHY: The Departure of the Romans, to Richard III. From A.D. 449 to 1485. 4s. 6d.

Period II.—PERSONAL MONARCHY: Henry VII. to James II. From 1485 to 1688. 5s.

Period III.—CONSTITUTIONAL MONARCHY: William and Mary, to William IV. From 1689 to 1837. 7s. 6d.

Period IV.—THE GROWTH OF DEMOCRACY: Victoria. From 1837 to 1880. 6s.

A HANDBOOK IN OUTLINE OF THE POLITICAL HISTORY OF ENGLAND TO 1894. Chronologically arranged. By the Right Hon. A. H. DYKE ACLAND, and CYRIL RANSOME, M.A. Cr. 8vo, 6s.

A HANDBOOK IN OUTLINE OF ENGLISH POLITICS FOR THE LAST HALF CENTURY. Extracted from "A Handbook of English Political History. With Appendices on the Reform Bills, Disfranchised and Enfranchised Boroughs, &c. By the Right Hon. A. H. DYKE ACLAND, and CYRIL RANSOME, M.A. Crown 8vo, cloth, 1s. 6d. ; sewed, 1s.

A SKELETON OUTLINE OF THE HISTORY OF ENGLAND: being an Abridgment of "A Handbook in Outline of the Political History of England." By the Right Hon. A. H. DYKE ACLAND, and CYRIL RANSOME, M.A. Fcp. 8vo, 1s. 6d.

A SKELETON OUTLINE OF THE HISTORY OF ENGLAND FOR BEGINNERS. With Maps. By the Right Hon. A. H. DYKE ACLAND, and CYRIL RANSOME, M.A. Fcp. 8vo, 9d.

A TEXT-BOOK OF ENGLISH HISTORY. By OSMUND AIRY, M.A., one of H.M. Inspectors of Schools. With 16 Maps. Crown 8vo, 4s. 6d. Or in Three Parts. Part. I. (B.C. 55–A.D. 1307), 2s Part II. (1307–1689), 2s. Part III (1689–1887), 2s.

. Each Part contains an Appendix, including a full Summary of Events, Glossary of Terms, Genealogical Tables, Treaties, &c. &c.

A FIRST HISTORY OF ENGLAND. By LOUISE CREIGHTON. 16mo, 2s. 6d.

STORIES FROM ENGLISH HISTORY. By LOUISE CREIGHTON 16mo, 3s. 6d.

SIMPLE STORIES FROM ENGLISH HISTORY: For Young Readers. With 6 Illustrations in Colours and 55 in Black and White. Crown 8vo, 1s. 6d.

LONGMANS, GREEN, AND CO.

LONDON, NEW YORK, AND BOMBAY.

EPOCHS OF ANCIENT HISTORY.

EDITED BY THE

Rev. Sir G. W. COX, Bart., M.A., and by C. SANKEY, M.A.

10 Volumes, fcp. 8vo., with Maps, price 2s. 6d. each.

GREECE.

THE GREEKS AND THE PERSIANS (B.C. 560-B.C. 478). By the Rev. Sir G. W. Cox, Bart., M.A. 4 Maps.

THE ATHENIAN EMPIRE from the Flight of Xerxes to the Fall of Athens (B.C. 479-B.C. 405). By the Rev. Sir G. W. Cox, Bart., M.A. 5 Maps.

THE SPARTAN AND THEBAN SUPREMACIES (B.C. 404-B.C. 361). By CHARLES SANKEY, M.A. 5 Maps.

THE RISE OF THE MACEDONIAN EMPIRE (B.C. 700-B.C. 323). By ARTHUR M. CURTEIS, M.A. 8 Maps.

ROME.

EARLY ROME TO ITS CAPTURE BY THE GAULS (B.C. 754-B.C. 390). By WILHELM IHNE. With a Map.

ROME AND CARTHAGE, THE PUNIC WARS (B.C. 264-B.C. 140). By R. BOSWORTH SMITH, M.A. With 9 Maps and Plans.

THE GRACCHI, MARIUS AND SULLA (B.C. 133-B.C. 78). By A. H. BEESLY, M.A. With 2 Maps.

THE ROMAN TRIUMVIRATES (B.C. 78-B.C. 31). By

the Very Rev. CHARLES MERIVALE, D.D., late Dean of Ely. With a Map.

THE EARLY ROMAN EMPIRE. From the Assassination of Julius Cæsar to the Assassination of Domitian (B.C. 44-A.D. 96). By Rev. W. WOLFE CAPES, M.A. With 2 Maps.

THE ROMAN EMPIRE OF THE SECOND CENTURY, or the Age of the Antonines (A.D. 96-A.D. 180). By Rev. W. WOLFE CAPES, M.A. 2 Maps.

EPOCHS OF ENGLISH HISTORY.

Edited by MANDELL CREIGHTON, D.D. LL.D.

BISHOP OF LONDON.

EARLY ENGLAND TO THE NORMAN CONQUEST. By F. YORK POWELL, M.A. 1s.

ENGLAND A CONTINENTAL POWER. 1066-1216. By Mrs. MANDELL CREIGHTON. 9d.

THE RISE OF THE PEOPLE AND THE GROWTH OF PARLIAMENT. 1215-1485. By JAMES ROWLEY, M.A. 9d.

THE TUDORS AND THE REFORMATION, 1485-1603. By MANDELL CREIGHTON, D.D. LL.D. 9d.

THE STRUGGLE AGAINST ABSOLUTE MONARCHY, 1603-1688. By Mrs. S. R. GARDINER. 9d.

THE SETTLEMENT OF THE CONSTITUTION. 1689-1784. By JAMES ROWLEY, M.A. 9d.

ENGLAND DURING THE AMERICAN AND EUROPEAN WARS. 1765-1820. By the Rev. O. W. TANCOCK. 9d.

MODERN ENGLAND. 1820-1885. By OSCAR BROWNING. M.A. 9d.

EPOCHS OF ENGLISH HISTORY. Complete in One Volume, with 27 Tables and Pedigrees, and 23 Maps. Fcp. 8vo. 5s.

THE SHILLING HISTORY OF ENGLAND: being an introductory Volume to the Series of *Epochs of English History*. By MANDELL CREIGHTON, D.D. LL.D. Fcp. 8vo. 1s.

LONGMANS, GREEN, AND CO.

LONDON, NEW YORK, AND BOMBAY

A Selection of Works

IN

THEOLOGICAL LITERATURE

PUBLISHED BY

Messrs. LONGMANS, GREEN, & CO.

London : 39 Paternoster Row, E.C.

New York : 91 and 93 Fifth Avenue.

Bombay : 32 Hornby Road.

Abbey and Overton.—THE ENGLISH CHURCH IN THE EIGHTEENTH CENTURY. By Charles J. Abbey, M.A., Rector of Checkendon, Reading, and John H. Overton, D.D., late Canon of Lincoln. *Crown 8vo. 7s. 6d.*

Adams.—SACRED ALLEGORIES. The Shadow of the Cross —The Distant Hills—The Old Man's Home—The King's Messengers. By the Rev. William Adams, M.A. With Illustrations. *16mo. 3s. net.*

The four Allegories may be had separately, 16mo. *1s. each.*

Aids to the Inner Life.

Edited by the Venble. W. H. Hutchings, M.A., Archdeacon of Cleveland, Canon of York, Rector of Kirby Misperton, and Rural Dean of Malton. *Five Vols. 32mo, cloth limp, 6d. each; or cloth extra, 1s. each.*

OF THE IMITATION OF CHRIST. By Thomas à Kempis.

THE CHRISTIAN YEAR.

THE DEVOUT LIFE. By St. Francis de Sales.

THE HIDDEN LIFE OF THE SOUL. By Jean Nicolas Grou.

THE SPIRITUAL COMBAT. By Laurence Scupoli.

Arbuthnot.—SHAKESPEARE SERMONS. Preached in the Collegiate Church of Stratford-on-Avon on the Sundays following the Poet's Birthday, 1894-1900. Collected by the Rev. George Arbuthnot, M.A., Vicar of Stratford-on-Avon. *Crown 8vo. 2s. 6d. net.*

Baily-Browne.—Works by A. B. Baily-Brown.

A HELP TO THE SPIRITUAL INTERPRETATION OF THE PENITENTIAL PSALMS, consisting of Brief Notes from The Fathers, gathered from Neale and Littledale's Commentary. With Preface by the Rev. George Body, D.D., Canon of Durham. *Crown 8vo. 1s. net.*

THE SONGS OF DEGREES ; or, Gradual Psalms. Interleaved with Notes from Neale and Littledale's Commentary on the Psalms. *Crown 8vo. 1s. net.*

Bathe.—Works by the Rev. ANTHONY BATHE, M.A.

A LENT WITH JESUS. A Plain Guide for Churchmen. Containing Readings for Lent and Easter Week, and on the Holy Eucharist. 32*mo*, 1*s.*; *or in paper cover*, 6*d.*

AN ADVENT WITH JESUS. 32*mo*, 1*s.*, *or in paper cover*, 6*d.*

WHAT I SHOULD BELIEVE. A Simple Manual of Self-Instruction for Church People. *Small 8vo, limp*, 1*s.*; *cloth gilt*, 2*s.*

Benson.—Works by the Rev. R. M. BENSON, M.A., Student of Christ Church, Oxford.

THE FOLLOWERS OF THE LAMB : a Series of Meditations, especially intended for Persons living under Religious Vows, and for Seasons of Retreat, etc. *Crown 8vo.* 4*s.* 6*d.*

THE FINAL PASSOVER : A Series of Meditations upon the Passion of our Lord Jesus Christ. *Small 8vo.*

Vol. I.—THE REJECTION. 5*s.*
Vol. II.—THE UPPER CHAMBER.
Part I. 5*s.*
Part II. 5*s.*

Vol. III.—THE DIVINE EXODUS.
Parts I. and II. 5*s.* each.
Vol. IV.—THE LIFE BEYOND THE GRAVE. 5*s.*

THE MAGNIFICAT ; a Series of Meditations upon the Song of the Blessed Virgin Mary. *Small 8vo.* 2*s.*

SPIRITUAL READINGS FOR EVERY DAY. 3 *vols. Small 8vo.* 3*s.* 6*d. each.*
I. ADVENT.   II. CHRISTMAS.   III. EPIPHANY.

BENEDICTUS DOMINUS : A Course of Meditations for Every Day of the Year. Vol. I.—ADVENT TO TRINITY. Vol. II.—TRINITY, SAINTS' DAYS, etc. *Small 8vo.* 3*s.* 6*d. each ; or in One Volume*, 7*s.*

BIBLE TEACHINGS: The Discourse at Capernaum.—St. John vi. *Small 8vo.* 1*s.* ; *or with Notes.* 3*s.* 6*d.*

THE WISDOM OF THE SON OF DAVID: An Exposition of the First Nine Chapters of the Book of Proverbs. *Small 8vo.* 3*s.* 6*d.*

THE MANUAL OF INTERCESSORY PRAYER. *Royal 32mo ; cloth boards*, 1*s.* 3*d.* ; *cloth limp*, 9*d.*

THE EVANGELIST LIBRARY CATECHISM. Part I. *Small 8vo.* 3*s.*

PAROCHIAL MISSIONS. *Small 8vo.* 2*s.* 6*d.*

Bickersteth.—YESTERDAY, TO-DAY, AND FOR EVER a Poem in Twelve Books. By EDWARD HENRY BICKERSTETH, D.D. late Lord Bishop of Exeter. 18*mo.* 1*s. net. With red borders* 16*mo*, 2*s. net.*
The Crown 8vo Edition (5s.) may still be had.

Blunt.—Works by the Rev. JOHN HENRY BLUNT, D.D.

THE ANNOTATED BOOK OF COMMON PRAYER: Being an Historical, Ritual, and Theological Commentary on the Devotional System of the Church of England. *4to.* 21*s.*

THE COMPENDIOUS EDITION OF THE ANNOTATED BOOK OF COMMON PRAYER: Forming a concise Commentary on the Devotional System of the Church of England. *Crown 8vo.* 10*s. 6d.*

DICTIONARY OF DOCTRINAL AND HISTORICAL THEOLOGY. By various Writers. *Imperial 8vo.* 21*s.*

DICTIONARY OF SECTS, HERESIES, ECCLESIASTICAL PARTIES AND SCHOOLS OF RELIGIOUS THOUGHT. By various Writers. *Imperial 8vo.* 21*s.*

THE BOOK OF CHURCH LAW. Being an Exposition of the Legal Rights and Duties of the Parochial Clergy and the Laity of the Church of England. Revised by the Right Hon. Sir WALTER G. F. PHILLIMORE, Bart., D.C.L., and G. EDWARDES JONES, Barrister-at-Law. *Crown 8vo.* 8*s. net.*

A COMPANION TO THE BIBLE: Being a Plain Commentary on Scripture History, to the end of the Apostolic Age. *Two Vols. small 8vo. Sold separately.* OLD TESTAMEMT. 3*s. 6d.* NEW TESTAMENT. 3*s. 6d.*

HOUSEHOLD THEOLOGY: a Handbook of Religious Information respecting the Holy Bible, the Prayer Book, the Church, etc., etc. *16mo. Paper cover,* 1*s. Also the Larger Edition,* 3*s. 6d.*

Body.—Works by the Rev. GEORGE BODY, D.D., Canon of Durham.

THE LIFE OF LOVE. A Course of Lent Lectures. *16mo.* 2*s. net.*

THE SCHOOL OF CALVARY; or, Laws of Christian Life revealed from the Cross. *16mo.* 2*s. net.*

THE LIFE OF JUSTIFICATION. *16mo.* 2*s. net.*

THE LIFE OF TEMPTATION. *16mo.* 2*s. net.*

THE PRESENT STATE OF THE FAITHFUL DEPARTED. *Small 8vo. sewed,* 6*d. 32mo. cloth,* 1*s.*

Book of Private Prayer, The. For use Twice Daily; together with the Order for the Administration of the Lord's Supper or Holy Communion. *18mo. Limp cloth,* 2*s.; Cloth boards,* 2*s. 6d.*

Book of Prayer and Daily Texts for English Churchmen. *32mo.* 1*s. net.*

Boultbee.—A COMMENTARY ON THE THIRTY-NINE ARTICLES OF THE CHURCH OF ENGLAND.   By the Rev. T. P. BOULTBEE. *Crown 8vo.   6s.*

Brett.—Works by the Rev. JESSE BRETT, L.Th., Chaplain of All Saints' Hospital, Eastbourne.

ANIMA CHRISTI : Devotional Addresses. *Crown 8vo.   1s. net.*

THE BLESSED LIFE : Devotional Studies of the Beatitudes. *Crown 8vo.   2s. net.*

Bright.—Works by WILLIAM BRIGHT, D.D., late Regius Professor of Ecclesiastical History in the University of Oxford.

THE AGE OF THE FATHERS. Being Chapters in the History of the Church during the Fourth and Fifth Centuries. *Two Vols.* 8vo. 28s. net.

LESSONS FROM THE LIVES OF THREE GREAT FATHERS. St. Athanasius, St. Chrysostom, and St. Augustine. *Crown 8vo.   6s.*

Bright and Medd.—LIBER PRECUM PUBLICARUM EC- CLESIÆ ANGLICANÆ. A GULIELMO BRIGHT, S.T.P., et PETRO GOLDSMITH MEDD, A.M., Latine redditus. *Small 8vo.   5s. net.*

Browne.—AN EXPOSITION OF THE THIRTY-NINE ARTICLES, Historical and Doctrinal. By E. H. BROWNE, D.D., sometime Bishop of Winchester. 8vo.   16s.

Campion and Beamont.—THE PRAYER BOOK INTER- LEAVED.   With Historical Illustrations and Explanatory Notes arranged parallel to the Text. By W. M. CAMPION, D.D., and W. J. BEAMONT, M.A. *Small 8vo.   7s. 6d.*

Carpenter and Harford-Battersby. — THE HEXATEUCH ACCORDING TO THE REVISED VERSION ARRANGED IN ITS CONSTITUENT DOCUMENTS BY MEMBERS OF THE SOCIETY OF HISTORICAL THEOLOGY, OXFORD. Edited with Introduction, Notes, Marginal References, and Synoptical Tables.   By J. ESTLIN CARPENTER, M.A. (Lond.) and G. HARFORD-BATTERSBY, M.A. (Oxon.).   *Two vols.* 4to.   (*Vol. I. Introduction and Appendices: Vol. II. Text and Notes*).   36s. net.

THE COMPOSITION OF THE HEXATEUCH : An Introduction with Select Lists of Words and Phrases.   With an Appendix on Laws and Institutions. (*Selected from the above.*) 8vo.   18s. net.

Carter.—LIFE AND LETTERS OF THOMAS THELLUS- SON CARTER, Warden of the House of Mercy, Clewer, and Hon. Canon of Christ Church, Oxford.   Edited by the Ven. W. H. HUTCHINGS, M.A., Archdeacon of Cleveland.   With 3 Portraits and 8 other Illustrations. 8vo.   10s. 6d. net.

Carter.—Works by, and edited by, the Rev. T. T. CARTER, M.A.

SPIRITUAL INSTRUCTIONS. *Crown 8vo.*

THE HOLY EUCHARIST. 3*s.* 6*d.*	OUR LORD'S EARLY LIFE. 3s. 6*d.*
THE DIVINE DISPENSATIONS. 3*s.* 6*d.*	OUR LORD'S ENTRANCE ON HIS
THE LIFE OF GRACE. 3*s.* 6*d.*	MINISTRY. 3*s.* 6*d.*
THE RELIGIOUS LIFE. 3*s.* 6*d.*	

A BOOK OF PRIVATE PRAYER FOR MORNING, MID-DAY, AND OTHER TIMES. 18*mo, limp cloth,* 1*s.* ; *cloth, red edges,* 1*s.* 3*d.*

THE DOCTRINE OF CONFESSION IN THE CHURCH OF ENGLAND. *Crown 8vo.* 5*s.*

THE SPIRIT OF WATCHFULNESS AND OTHER SERMONS. *Crown 8vo.* 5*s.*

THE TREASURY OF DEVOTION : a Manual of Prayer for General and Daily Use. Compiled by a Priest.
18*mo.* 2*s.* 6*d.* ; *cloth limp,* 2*s.* Bound with the Book of Common Prayer, 3*s.* 6*d.* Red-Line Edition. *Cloth extra, gilt top.* 18*mo.* 2*s.* 6*d. net.* Large-Type Edition. *Crown 8vo.* 3*s.* 6*d.*

THE WAY OF LIFE : A Book of Prayers and Instruction for the Young at School, with a Preparation for Confirmation. 18*mo.* 1*s.* 6*d.*

THE PATH OF HOLINESS : a First Book of Prayers, with the Service of the Holy Communion, for the Young. Compiled by a Priest. With Illustrations. 16*mo.* 1*s.* 6*d.* ; *cloth limp,* 1*s.*

THE GUIDE TO HEAVEN : a Book of Prayers for every Want. (For the Working Classes.) Compiled by a Priest. 18*mo.* 1*s.* 6*d.*; *cloth limp,* 1*s. Large-Type Edition. Crown 8vo.* 1*s.* 6*d.* ; *cloth limp,* 1*s.*

THE STAR OF CHILDHOOD : a First Book of Prayers and Instruction for Children. Compiled by a Priest. With Illustrations. 16*mo.* 2*s.* 6*d.*

SIMPLE LESSONS; or, Words Easy to be Understood. A Manual of Teaching. I. On the Creed. II. The Ten Commandments. III. The Sacrament. 18*mo.* 3*s.*

MANUAL OF DEVOTION FOR SISTERS OF MERCY. 8 parts in 2 vols. 32mo. 10*s.* Or separately :—Part I. 1*s.* 6*d.* Part II. 1*s.* Part III. 1*s.* Part IV. 2*s.* Part V. 1*s.* Part VI. 1*s.* Part VII. 1*s.* Part VIII. 1*s.* 6*d.*

UNDERCURRENTS OF CHURCH LIFE IN THE EIGHTEENTH CENTURY. *Crown 8vo.* 5*s.*

NICHOLAS FERRAR : his Household and his Friends. *Crown 8vo.* 6*s.*

Carson. —Works by the Rev. W. R. CARSON, Roman Catholic Priest.

AN EUCHARISTIC EIRENICON. With an Introduction by the Right Honourable the VISCOUNT HALIFAX. 8*vo. Sewed.* 1*s.* 6*d. net.*

REUNION ESSAYS. With an Appendix on the non-infallible force of the Bull *Apost. Curæ* in condemnation of the Holy Orders of the Church of England. *Crown 8vo.* 6*s.* 6*d. net.*

Coles.—Works by the Rev. V. S. S. COLES, M.A., Principal of the Pusey House, Oxford.
LENTEN MEDITATIONS. 18mo. 2s. 6d.
ADVENT MEDITATIONS ON ISAIAH I.-XII. : together with Out-lines of Christmas Meditations on St. John i. 1-12. 18mo. 2s.

Company, The, of Heaven : Daily Links with the Household of God. Being Selections in Prose and Verse from various Authors. With Autotype Frontispiece. *Crown 8vo. 2s. 6d. net.*

Conybeare and Howson.—THE LIFE AND EPISTLES OF ST. PAUL. By the Rev. W. J. CONYBEARE, M.A., and the Very Rev. J. S. HOWSON, D.D. With numerous Maps and Illustrations.
LIBRARY EDITION. *Two Vols.* 8vo. 21s. STUDENTS' EDITION. *One Vol. Crown 8vo.* 6s. POPULAR EDITION. *One Vol. Crown 8vo.* 3s. 6d.

Creighton.—Works by MANDELL CREIGHTON, D.D., late Lord Bishop of London.
A HISTORY OF THE PAPACY FROM THE GREAT SCHISM TO THE SACK OF ROME (1378-1527). *Six Volumes. Crown 8vo. 5s. each net.*
THE CHURCH AND THE NATION : Charges and Addresses. *Crown 8vo. 5s. net.*
THOUGHTS ON EDUCATION : Speeches and Sermons. *Crown 8vo. 5s. net.*
UNIVERSITY AND OTHER SERMONS. *Crown 8vo. 5s. net.*

Dallas. — GOSPEL RECORDS, INTERPRETED BY HUMAN EXPERIENCE. By H. A. DALLAS, Author of 'The Victory that Overcometh.' *Crown 8vo. 5s. net.*

Day-Hours of the Church of England, The. Newly Revised according to the Prayer Book and the Authorised Translation of the Bible. *Crown 8vo, sewed,* 3s. ; *cloth,* 3s. 6d.
SUPPLEMENT TO THE DAY-HOURS OF THE CHURCH OF ENGLAND, being the Service for certain Holy Days. *Crown 8vo, sewed,* 3s. ; *cloth,* 3s. 6d.

Edersheim.—Works by ALFRED EDERSHEIM, M.A., D.D., Ph.D.
THE LIFE AND TIMES OF JESUS THE MESSIAH. *Two Vols.* 8vo. 12s. net.
JESUS THE MESSIAH : being an Abridged Edition of 'The Life and Times of Jesus the Messiah.' *Crown 8vo.* 6s. net.

Ellicott.—Works by C. J. ELLICOTT, D.D., Bishop of Gloucester.
A CRITICAL AND GRAMMATICAL COMMENTARY ON ST. PAUL'S EPISTLES. Greek Text, with a Critical and Grammatical Commentary, and a Revised English Translation. 8vo.

GALATIANS. 8s. 6d.	PHILIPPIANS, COLOSSIANS, AND
EPHESIANS. 8s. 6d.	PHILEMON. 10s. 6d.
PASTORAL EPISTLES. 10s. 6d.	THESSALONIANS. 7s. 6d.

HISTORICAL LECTURES ON THE LIFE OF OUR LORD JESUS CHRIST. 8vo. 12s.

English (The) Catholic's Vade Mecum: a Short Manual of General Devotion. Compiled by a PRIEST. 32*mo. limp, 1s.* ; *cloth, 2s.* PRIEST's Edition. 32*mo. 1s. 6d.*

Epochs of Church History.— Edited by MANDELL CREIGHTON, D.D., late Lord Bishop of London. *Small 8vo. 2s. 6d. each.*

THE ENGLISH CHURCH IN OTHER LANDS. By the Rev. H. W. TUCKER, M.A.

THE HISTORY OF THE REFORMATION IN ENGLAND. By the Rev. GEO. G. PERRY, M.A.

THE CHURCH OF THE EARLY FATHERS. By the Rev. ALFRED PLUMMER, D.D.

THE EVANGELICAL REVIVAL IN THE EIGHTEENTH CENTURY. By the Rev. J. H. OVERTON, D.D.

THE UNIVERSITY OF OXFORD. By the Hon. G. C. BRODRICK, D.C.L.

THE UNIVERSITY OF CAMBRIDGE. By J. BASS MULLINGER, M.A.

THE ENGLISH CHURCH IN THE MIDDLE AGES. By the Rev. W. HUNT, M.A.

THE CHURCH AND THE EASTERN EMPIRE. By the Rev. H. F. TOZER, M.A.

THE CHURCH AND THE ROMAN EMPIRE. By the Rev. A. CARR, M.A.

THE CHURCH AND THE PURITANS, 1570-1660. By HENRY OFFLEY WAKEMAN, M.A.

HILDEBRAND AND HIS TIMES. By the Very Rev. W. R. W. STEPHENS, B.D.

THE POPES AND THE HOHENSTAUFEN. By UGO BALZANI.

THE COUNTER REFORMATION. By ADOLPHUS WILLIAM WARD, Litt. D.

WYCLIFFE AND MOVEMENTS FOR REFORM. By REGINALD L. POOLE, M.A.

THE ARIAN CONTROVERSY. By the Rev. Professor H. M. GWATKIN, M.A.

Eucharistic Manual (The). Consisting of Instructions and Devotions for the Holy Sacrament of the Altar. From various sources. 32*mo. cloth gilt, red edges. 1s. Cheap Edition, limp cloth. 9d.*

Farrar.—Works by FREDERIC W. FARRAR, D.D., late Dean of Canterbury.

TEXTS EXPLAINED; or, Helps to Understand the New Testament. *Crown 8vo. 5s. net.*

THE BIBLE: Its Meaning and Supremacy. *8vo. 6s. net.*

ALLEGORIES. With 25 Illustrations by AMELIA BAUERLE. *Crown 8vo. gilt edges. 2s. 6d. net.*

Fosbery.—VOICES OF COMFORT. Edited by the Rev. THOMAS VINCENT FOSBERY, M.A., sometime Vicar of St. Giles's, Reading. *Cheap Edition. Small 8vo. 3s. net. The Larger Edition (7s. 6d.) may still be had.*

Gardner.—A CATECHISM OF CHURCH HISTORY, from the Day of Pentecost until the Present Day. By the Rev. C. E. GARDNER, of the Society of St. John the Evangelist, Cowley. *Crown 8vo, sewed, 1s. ; cloth, 1s. 6d.*

Geikie.—Works by J. CUNNINGHAM GEIKIE, D.D., LL.D., late Vicar of St. Martin-at-Palace, Norwich.

THE VICAR AND HIS FRIENDS. *Crown 8vo. 5s. net.*

HOURS WITH THE BIBLE : the Scriptures in the Light of Modern Discovery and Knowledge. *Complete in Twelve Volumes. Crown 8vo.*

OLD TESTAMENT.

CREATION TO THE PATRIARCHS. *With a Map and Illustrations. 5s.*

MOSES TO JUDGES. *With a Map and Illustrations. 5s.*

SAMSON TO SOLOMON. *With a Map and Illustrations. 5s.*

REHOBOAM TO HEZEKIAH. *With Illustrations. 5s.*

MANASSEH TO ZEDEKIAH. With the Contemporary Prophets. *With a Map and Illustrations. 5s.*

EXILE TO MALACHI. With the Contemporary Prophets. *With Illustrations. 5s.*

NEW TESTAMENT.

THE GOSPELS. *With a Map and Illustrations. 5s.*

LIFE AND WORDS OF CHRIST. *With Map. 2 vols. 10s.*

LIFE AND EPISTLES OF ST. PAUL. *With Maps and Illustrations. 2 vols. 10s.*

ST. PETER TO REVELATION. *With 29 Illustrations. 5s.*

LIFE AND WORDS OF CHRIST.
    Cabinet Edition. With Map. 2 vols. Post 8vo. 10s.
    Cheap Edition, without the Notes. 1 vol. 8vo. 6s.

A SHORT LIFE OF CHRIST. *With 34 Illustrations. Crown 8vo. 3s. 6d. ; gilt edges, 4s. 6d.*

Gold Dust: a Collection of Golden Counsels for the Sanctification of Daily Life.

    Translated and abridged from the French by E.L.E.E. Edited by CHARLOTTE M. YONGE. Parts I. II. III. Small Pocket Volumes. *Cloth, gilt, each 1s.*, or in white cloth, with red edges, the three parts in a box, *2s. 6d. each net.* Parts I. and II. in One Volume. *1s. 6d.* Parts I., II., and III. in One Volume. *2s. net.*

** The two first parts in One Volume, *large type*, 18mo. *cloth, gilt. 2s. net.*

Gore.—Works by the Right Rev. CHARLES GORE, D.D., Lord Bishop of Worcester.

THE CHURCH AND THE MINISTRY. *Crown 8vo. 6s. net.*

ROMAN CATHOLIC CLAIMS. *Crown 8vo. 3s. net.*

Goreh.—THE LIFE OF FATHER GOREH. By C. E. GARDNER, S.S.J.E. With Portrait. *Crown 8vo. 5s.*

Great Truths of the Christian Religion. Edited by the Rev. W. U. RICHARDS. *Small 8vo. 2s.*

Hall.—Works by the Right Rev. A. C. A. HALL, D.D., Bishop of Vermont.

CONFIRMATION. *Crown 8vo.* 5s. (*The Oxford Library of Practical Theology.*)

THE VIRGIN MOTHER: Retreat Addresses on the Life of the Blessed Virgin Mary as told in the Gospels. With an appended Essay on the Virgin Birth of our Lord. *Crown 8vo.* 4s. 6d.

CHRIST'S TEMPTATION AND OURS. *Crown 8vo.* 3s. 6d.

Hallowing of Sorrow. By E. R. With a Preface by H. S. HOLLAND, M.A., Canon and Precentor of St. Paul's. *Small 8vo.* 2s.

Handbooks for the Clergy. Edited by the Rev. ARTHUR W. ROBINSON, B.D., Vicar of Allhallows Barking by the Tower. *Crown 8vo.* 2s. 6d. net each Volume.

THE PERSONAL LIFE OF THE CLERGY. By the Rev. ARTHUR W. ROBINSON, B.D., Vicar of Allhallows Barking by the Tower.

THE MINISTRY OF CONVERSION. By the Rev. A. J. MASON, D.D., Master of Pembroke College, Cambridge, and Canon of Canterbury.

PATRISTIC STUDY. By the Rev. H. B. SWETE, D.D., Regius Professor of Divinity in the University of Cambridge.

FOREIGN MISSIONS. By the Right Rev. H. H. MONTGOMERY, D.D., formerly Bishop of Tasmania, Secretary of the Society for the Propagation of the Gospel in Foreign Parts.

THE·STUDY OF THE GOSPELS. By the Very Rev. J. ARMITAGE ROBINSON, D.D., Dean of Westminster.

A CHRISTIAN APOLOGETIC. By the Very Rev. WILFORD L. ROBINSON, D.D., Dean of the General Theological Seminary, New York.

PASTORAL VISITATION. By the Rev. H. E. SAVAGE, M.A., Vicar of South Shields.

AUTHORITY IN THE CHURCH. By the Very Rev. J. B. STRONG, D.D., Dean of Christ Church, Oxford.

THE STUDY OF ECCLESIASTICAL HISTORY. By the Rev. W. E. COLLINS, M.A., Professor of Ecclesiastical History in King's College, London.

CHURCH MUSIC. By A. MADELEY RICHARDSON, Mus.Doc. Organist of St. Saviour's Collegiate Church, Southwark.

** Other Volumes are in preparation.

Hatch.—THE ORGANIZATION OF THE EARLY CHRISTIAN CHURCHES. Being the Bampton Lectures for 1880. By EDWIN HATCH, M.A., D.D., late Reader in Ecclesiastical History in the University of Oxford. *8vo.* 5s.

Holland.—Works by the Rev. HENRY SCOTT HOLLAND, M.A. Canon and Precentor of St. Paul's.

GOD'S CITY AND THE COMING OF THE KINGDOM. *Crown 8vo.* 3s. 6d.

PLEAS AND CLAIMS FOR CHRIST. *Crown 8vo.* 3s. 6d.

CREED AND CHARACTER : Sermons. *Crown 8vo.* 3s. 6d.

ON BEHALF OF BELIEF. Sermons. *Crown 8vo.* 3s. 6d.

CHRIST OR ECCLESIASTES. Sermons. *Crown 8vo.* 2s. 6d.

LOGIC AND LIFE, with other Sermons. *Crown 8vo.* 3s. 6d.

GOOD FRIDAY. Being Addresses on the Seven Last Words. *Small 8vo.* 2s.

Hollings.—Works by the Rev. G. S. HOLLINGS, Mission Priest of the Society of St. John the Evangelist, Cowley, Oxford.

THE HEAVENLY STAIR ; or, A Ladder of the Love of God for Sinners. *Crown 8vo.* 3s. 6d.

PORTA REGALIS ; or, Considerations on Prayer. *Crown 8vo. limp cloth,* 1s. 6d. *net* ; *cloth boards,* 2s. *net.*

CONSIDERATIONS ON THE WISDOM OF GOD. *Crown 8vo.* 4s.

PARADOXES OF THE LOVE OF GOD, especially as they are seen in the way of the Evangelical Counsels. *Crown 8vo.* 4s.

ONE BORN OF THE SPIRIT ; or, the Unification of our Life in God. *Crown 8vo.* 3s. 6d.

Hutchings.—Works by the Ven. W. H. HUTCHINGS, M.A. Archdeacon of Cleveland, Canon of York, Rector of Kirby Misperton, and Rural Dean of Malton.

SERMON SKETCHES from some of the Sunday Lessons throughout the Church's Year. *Vols. I and II. Crown 8vo.* 5s. *each.*

THE LIFE OF PRAYER : a Course of Lectures delivered in All Saints' Church, Margaret Street, during Lent. *Crown 8vo.* 4s. 6d.

THE PERSON AND WORK OF THE HOLY GHOST : a Doctrinal and Devotional Treatise. *Crown 8vo.* 4s. 6d.

SOME ASPECTS OF THE CROSS. *Crown 8vo.* 4s. 6d.

THE MYSTERY OF THE TEMPTATION. Lent Lectures delivered at St. Mary Magdalene, Paddington. *Crown 8vo.* 4s. 6d.

Hutton.—THE SOUL HERE AND HEREAFTER. By the Rev. R. E. HUTTON, Chaplain of St. Margaret's, East Grinstead. *Crown 8vo.* 6s.

Inheritance of the Saints; or, Thoughts on the Communion of Saints and the Life of the World to come. Collected chiefly from English Writers by L. P. With a Preface by the Rev. HENRY SCOTT HOLLAND, M.A. *Crown 8vo.* 3s. 6d. net.

ILLUSTRATED EDITION. With 8 Pictures in Colour by HAMEL LISTER. *Crown 8vo.* 6s. net.

James.—THE VARIETIES OF RELIGIOUS EXPERIENCE: A Study in Human Nature. Being the Gifford Lectures on Natural Religion delivered at Edinburgh in 1901-1902. By WILLIAM JAMES, LL.D., etc., Professor of Philosophy at Harvard University. 8vo. 12s. net.

Jameson.—Works by Mrs. JAMESON.

SACRED AND LEGENDARY ART, containing Legends of the Angels and Archangels, the Evangelists, the Apostles. With 19 Etchings and 187 Woodcuts. *2 vols.* 8vo. 20s. net.

LEGENDS OF THE MONASTIC ORDERS, as represented in the Fine Arts. With 11 Etchings and 88 Woodcuts. 8vo. 10s. net.

LEGENDS OF THE MADONNA, OR BLESSED VIRGIN MARY. With 27 Etchings and 165 Woodcuts. 8vo. 10s. net.

THE HISTORY OF OUR LORD, as exemplified in Works of Art. Commenced by the late Mrs. JAMESON ; continued and completed by LADY EASTLAKE. With 31 Etchings and 281 Woodcuts. 2 *Vols.* 8vo. 20s. net.

Jones.—ENGLAND AND THE HOLY SEE: An Essay towards Reunion. By SPENCER JONES, M.A., Rector of Moreton-in-Marsh. With a Preface by the Right Hon. VISCOUNT HALIFAX. *Crown 8vo.* 3s. 6s. net.

Jukes.—Works by ANDREW JUKES.

LETTERS OF ANDREW JUKES. Edited, with a Short Biography, by the Rev. HERBERT H. JEAFFERSON, M.A. *Crown 8vo.* 3s. 6d. net.

THE NAMES OF GOD IN HOLY SCRIPTURE : a Revelation of His Nature and Relationships. *Crown 8vo.* 4s. 6d.

THE TYPES OF GENESIS. *Crown 8vo.* 7s. 6d.

THE SECOND DEATH AND THE RESTITUTION OF ALL THINGS. *Crown 8vo.* 3s. 6d.

Kelly.—Works by the Rev. HERBERT H. KELLY, M.A., Director of the Society of the Sacred Mission, Mildenhall, Suffolk.

A HISTORY OF THE CHURCH OF CHRIST. Vol. I. A.D. 29-342. *Crown 8vo.* 3s. 6d. net. Vol. II. A.D. 324-430. *Crown 8vo.* 3s. 6d. net.

ENGLAND AND THE CHURCH : Her Calling and its Fulfilment Considered in Relation to the Increase and Efficiency of Her Ministry. *Crown 8vo.* 4s. net.

Knox.—PASTORS AND TEACHERS : Six Lectures on Pastoral Theology. By the Right Rev. EDMUND ARBUTHNOTT KNOX, D.D., Bishop of Manchester. With an Introduction by the Right Rev. CHARLES GORE, D.D., Bishop of Worcester. *Crown 8vo. 5s. net.*

Knox Little.—Works by W. J. KNOX LITTLE, M.A., Canon Residentiary of Worcester, and Vicar of Hoar Cross.

HOLY MATRIMONY. *Crown 8vo. 5s.* (*The Oxford Library of Practical Theology.*)

THE PERFECT LIFE : Sermons. *Crown 8vo. 7s. 6d.*

THE CHRISTIAN HOME. *Crown 8vo. 3s. 6d.*

THE MYSTERY OF THE PASSION OF OUR MOST HOLY REDEEMER. *Crown 8vo. 2s. 6d.*

THE LIGHT OF LIFE. Sermons preached on Various Occasions. *Crown 8vo. 3s. 6d.*

SUNLIGHT AND SHADOW IN THE CHRISTIAN LIFE. Sermons preached for the most part in America. *Crown 8vo. 3s. 6d.*

Lear.—Works by, and Edited by, H. L. SIDNEY LEAR.

FOR DAYS AND YEARS. A book containing a Text, Short Reading, and Hymn for Every Day in the Church's Year. *16mo. 2s. net. Also a Cheap Edition, 32mo, 1s.; or cloth gilt, 1s. 6d.; or with red borders, 2s. net.*

FIVE MINUTES. Daily Readings of Poetry. *16mo. 3s. 6d. Also a Cheap Edition, 32mo. 1s.; or cloth gilt, 1s. 6d.*

WEARINESS. A Book for the Languid and Lonely. *Large Type. Small 8vo. 5s.*

DEVOTIONAL WORKS. Edited by H. L. SIDNEY LEAR. *New and Uniform Editions. Nine Vols. 16mo. 2s. net each.*

FÉNELON'S SPIRITUAL LETTERS TO MEN.

FÉNELON'S SPIRITUAL LETTERS TO WOMEN.

A SELECTION FROM THE SPIRITUAL LETTERS OF ST. FRANCIS DE SALES. Also *Cheap Edition, 32mo, 6d. cloth limp ; 1s. cloth boards.*

THE SPIRIT OF ST. FRANCIS DE SALES.

THE HIDDEN LIFE OF THE SOUL.

THE LIGHT OF THE CONSCIENCE. Also *Cheap Edition, 32mo, 6d. cloth limp ; 1s. cloth boards.*

SELF-RENUNCIATION. From the French.

ST. FRANCIS DE SALES' OF THE LOVE OF GOD.

SELECTIONS FROM PASCAL'S 'THOUGHTS.'

Lear.—Works by, and Edited by, H. L. SIDNEY LEAR.—
continued.

CHRISTIAN BIOGRAPHIES.   Edited by H. L. SIDNEY LEAR.
Crown 8vo. 3s. 6d. each.

MADAME LOUISE DE FRANCE, Daughter of Louis XV., known also as the Mother Térèse de St. Augustin.

A DOMINICAN ARTIST: a Sketch of the Life of the Rev. Père Besson, of the Order of St. Dominic.

HENRI PERREYVE. By PÈRE GRATRY. With Portrait,

ST. FRANCIS DE SALES, Bishop and Prince of Geneva.

A CHRISTIAN PAINTER OF THE NINETEENTH CENTURY: being the Life of Hippolyte Flandrin.

THE REVIVAL OF PRIESTLY LIFE IN THE SEVENTEENTH CENTURY IN FRANCE.

BOSSUET AND HIS CONTEMPORARIES.

FÉNELON, ARCHBISHOP OF CAMBRAI.

HENRI DOMINIQUE LACORDAIRE.

Liddon.—Works by HENRY PARRY LIDDON, D.D., D.C.L., LL.D.

SERMONS ON SOME WORDS OF ST. PAUL. *Crown 8vo. 5s.*

SERMONS PREACHED ON SPECIAL OCCASIONS, 1860-1889. *Crown 8vo. 5s.*

CLERICAL LIFE AND WORK : Sermons. *Crown 8vo. 5s.*

ESSAYS AND ADDRESSES : Lectures on Buddhism—Lectures on the Life of St. Paul—Papers on Dante. *Crown 8vo. 5s.*

EXPLANATORY ANALYSIS OF PAUL'S EPISTLE TO THE ROMANS. *8vo. 14s.*

EXPLANATORY ANALYSIS OF ST. PAUL'S FIRST EPISTLE TO TIMOTHY. *8vo. 7s. 6d.*

SERMONS ON OLD TESTAMENT SUBJECTS. *Crown 8vo. 5s.*

SERMONS ON SOME WORDS OF CHRIST. *Crown 8vo. 5s.*

THE DIVINITY OF OUR LORD AND SAVIOUR JESUS CHRIST. Being the Bampton Lectures for 1866. *Crown 8vo. 5s.*

ADVENT IN ST. PAUL'S. *Crown 8vo. 5s.*

CHRISTMASTIDE IN ST. PAUL'S. *Crown 8vo. 5s.*

PASSIONTIDE SERMONS. *Crown 8vo. 5s.*

[continued.

Liddon.—Works by HENRY PARRY LIDDON, D.D., D.C.L., LL.D.—*continued.*

EASTER IN ST. PAUL'S. Sermons bearing chiefly on the Resurrection of our Lord. *Two Vols. Crown 8vo. 3s. 6d. each. Cheap Edition in one Volume. Crown 8vo. 5s.*

SERMONS PREACHED BEFORE THE UNIVERSITY OF OXFORD. *Two Vols. Crown 8vo. 3s. 6d. each. Cheap Edition in one Volume. Crown 8vo. 5s.*

THE MAGNIFICAT. Sermons in St. Paul's. *Crown 8vo. 2s. net.*

SOME ELEMENTS OF RELIGION. Lent Lectures. *Small 8vo. 2s. net.* [*The Crown 8vo Edition* (5s.) *may still be had.*]

Luckock.—Works by HERBERT MORTIMER LUCKOCK, D.D., Dean of Lichfield.

THE SPECIAL CHARACTERISTICS OF THE FOUR GOSPELS. *Crown 8vo. 6s.*

AFTER DEATH. An Examination of the Testimony of Primitive Times respecting the State of the Faithful Dead, and their Relationship to the Living. *Crown 8vo. 3s. net.*

THE INTERMEDIATE STATE BETWEEN DEATH AND JUDGMENT. Being a Sequel to *After Death. Crown 8vo. 3s. net.*

FOOTPRINTS OF THE SON OF MAN, as traced by St. Mark. Being Eighty Portions for Private Study, Family Reading, and Instruction in Church. *Crown 8vo. 3s. net.*

FOOTPRINTS OF THE APOSTLES, as traced by St. Luke in the Acts. Being Sixty Portions for Private Study, and Instruction in Church. A Sequel to 'Footprints of the Son of Man, as traced by St. Mark.' *Two Vols. Crown 8vo. 12s.*

THE DIVINE LITURGY. Being the Order for Holy Communion, Historically, Doctrinally, and Devotionally set forth, in Fifty Portions. *Crown 8vo. 3s. net.*

STUDIES IN THE HISTORY OF THE BOOK OF COMMON PRAYER. The Anglican Reform—The Puritan Innovations—The Elizabethan Reaction—The Caroline Settlement. With Appendices. *Crown 8vo. 3s. net.*

Lyra Germanica: Hymns for the Sundays and Chief Festivals of the Christian Year. *Complete Edition. Small 8vo. 5s. First Series. 16mo, with red borders, 2s. net.*

MacColl.—Works by the Rev. MALCOLM MACCOLL, D.D., Canon Residentiary of Ripon.

THE REFORMATION SETTLEMENT: Examined in the Light of History and Law. Tenth Edition, Revised, with a new Preface. *Crown 8vo.* 3*s.* 6*d. net.*

CHRISTIANITY IN RELATION TO SCIENCE AND MORALS. *Crown 8vo.* 6*s.*

LIFE HERE AND HEREAFTER : Sermons. *Crown 8vo.* 7*s.* 6*d.*

Marriage Addresses and Marriage Hymns. By the BISHOP OF LONDON, the BISHOP OF ROCHESTER, the BISHOP OF TRURO, the DEAN OF ROCHESTER, the DEAN OF NORWICH, ARCHDEACON SINCLAIR, CANON DUCKWORTH, CANON NEWBOLT, CANON KNOX LITTLE, CANON RAWNSLEY, the Rev. J. LLEWELLYN DAVIES, D.D., the Rev. W. ALLEN WHITWORTH, etc. Edited by the Rev. O. P. WARDELL-YERBURGH, M.A., Vicar of the Abbey Church of St. Mary, Tewkesbury. *Crown 8vo.* 5*s.*

Mason.—Works by A. J. MASON, D.D., Master of Pembroke College, Cambridge, and Canon of Canterbury.

THE MINISTRY OF CONVERSION. *Crown 8vo.* 2*s.* 6*d. net.* (*Handbooks for the Clergy.*)

PURGATORY; THE STATE OF THE FAITHFUL DEAD; INVOCATION OF SAINTS. Three Lectures. *Crown 8vo.* 3*s.* 6*d. net.*

THE FAITH OF THE GOSPEL. A Manual of Christian Doctrine. *Crown 8vo.* 7*s.* 6*d. Cheap Edition. Crown 8vo.* 3*s. net.*

THE RELATION OF CONFIRMATION TO BAPTISM. As taught in Holy Scripture and the Fathers. *Crown 8vo.* 7*s.* 6*d.*

Maturin.—Works by the Rev. B. W. MATURIN.

SOME PRINCIPLES AND PRACTICES OF THE SPIRITUAL LIFE. *Crown 8vo.* 4*s.* 6*d.*

PRACTICAL STUDIES ON THE PARABLES OF OUR LORD. *Crown 8vo.* 5*s.*

Medd.—THE PRIEST TO THE ALTAR; or, Aids to the Devout Celebration of Holy Communion, chiefly after the Ancient English Use of Sarum. By PETER GOLDSMITH MEDD, M.A., Canon of St. Albans. Fourth Edition, revised and enlarged. *Royal 8vo.* 15*s.*

Meyrick.—THE DOCTRINE OF THE CHURCH OF England on the Holy Communion Restated as a Guide at the Present Time. By the Rev. F. MEYRICK, M.A. *Crown 8vo.* 4*s.* 6*d.*

Monro.—SACRED ALLEGORIES. By Rev. EDWARD MONRO. *Complete Edition in one Volume, with Illustrations. Crown 8vo.* 3*s.* 6*d. net.*

Mortimer.—Works by the Rev. A. G. MORTIMER, D.D., Rector of St. Mark's, Philadelphia.

THE CREEDS: An Historical and Doctrinal Exposition of the Apostles', Nicene and Athanasian Creeds. *Crown 8vo.* 5*s. net.*

THE EUCHARISTIC SACRIFICE: An Historical and Theological Investigation of the Sacrificial Conception of the Holy Eucharist in the Christian Church. *Crown 8vo.* 10*s. 6d.*

CATHOLIC FAITH AND PRACTICE: A Manual of Theology. Two Parts. *Crown 8vo.* Part I. 7*s. 6d.* Part II. 9*s.*

JESUS AND THE RESURRECTION: Thirty Addresses for Good Friday and Easter. *Crown 8vo.* 5*s.*

HELPS TO MEDITATION: Sketches for Every Day in the Year.

Vol. I. ADVENT TO TRINITY. *8vo.* 7*s. 6d.*

Vol. II. TRINITY TO ADVENT. *8vo.* 7*s. 6d.*

STORIES FROM GENESIS: Sermons for Children. *Crown 8vo.* 4*s.*

THE LAWS OF HAPPINESS; or, The Beatitudes as teaching our Duty to God, Self, and our Neighbour. *18mo.* 2*s.*

THE LAWS OF PENITENCE: Addresses on the Words of our Lord from the Cross. *16mo.* 1*s. 6d.*

SERMONS IN MINIATURE FOR EXTEMPORE PREACHERS: Sketches for Every Sunday and Holy Day of the Christian Year. *Crown 8vo.* 6*s.*

NOTES ON THE SEVEN PENITENTIAL PSALMS, chiefly from Patristic Sources. *Small 8vo.* 3*s. 6d.*

MEDITATIONS ON THE PASSION OF OUR MOST HOLY RE-DEEMER. Part I. *Crown 8vo.* 5*s.*

THE SEVEN LAST WORDS OF OUR MOST HOLY REDEEMER: Being Meditations on some Scenes in His Passions (Meditations on the Passions. Part II.) *Crown 8vo.* 5*s.*

LEARN OF JESUS CHRIST TO DIE: Addresses on the Words of our Lord from the Cross, taken as teaching the way of Preparation for Death. *16mo.* 2*s.*

Mozley.—RULING IDEAS IN EARLY AGES AND THEIR RELATION TO OLD TESTAMENT FAITH. By J. B. MOZLEY, D.D., late Canon of Christ Church, and Regius Professor of Divinity at Oxford. *8vo.* 6*s.*

Newbolt.—Works by the Rev. W. C. E. NEWBOLT, M.A., Canon and Chancellor of St. Paul's Cathedral.

APOSTLES OF THE LORD: being Six Lectures on Pastoral Theology. *Crown 8vo.* 3s. 6d. *net.*

RELIGION. *Crown 8vo.* 5s. (*The Oxford Library of Practical Theology.*)

WORDS OF EXHORTATION. Sermons Preached at St. Paul's and elsewhere. *Crown 8vo.* 5s. *net.*

PENITENCE AND PEACE: being Addresses on the 51st and 23rd Psalms. *Crown 8vo.* 2s. *net.*

PRIESTLY IDEALS; being a Course of Practical Lectures delivered in St. Paul's Cathedral to 'Our Society' and other Clergy, in Lent, 1898. *Crown 8vo.* 3s. 6d.

PRIESTLY BLEMISHES; or, Some Secret Hindrances to the Realisation of Priestly Ideals. A Sequel. Being a Second Course of Practical Lectures delivered in St. Paul's Cathedral to 'Our Society' and other Clergy in Lent, 1902. *Crown 8vo.* 3s. 6d.

THE GOSPEL OF EXPERIENCE; or, the Witness of Human Life to the truth of Revelation. Being the Boyle Lectures for 1895. *Crown 8vo.* 5s.

COUNSELS OF FAITH AND PRACTICE: being Sermons preached on various occasions. *Crown 8vo.* 5s.

SPECULUM SACERDOTUM; or, the Divine Model of the Priestly Life. *Crown 8vo.* 7s. 6d.

THE FRUIT OF THE SPIRIT. Being Ten Addresses bearing on the Spiritual Life. *Crown 8vo.* 2s. *net.*

THE PRAYER BOOK: Its Voice and Teaching. *Crown 8vo.* 2s. *net.*

Newman.—Works by JOHN HENRY NEWMAN, B.D., sometime Vicar of St. Mary's, Oxford.

LETTERS AND CORRESPONDENCE OF JOHN HENRY NEWMAN DURING HIS LIFE IN THE ENGLISH CHURCH. With a brief Autobiography. Edited, at Cardinal Newman's request, by ANNE MOZLEY. 2 *vols. Crown 8vo.* 7s.

PAROCHIAL AND PLAIN SERMONS. *Eight Vols. Crown 8vo.* 3s. 6d. *each.*

SELECTION, ADAPTED TO THE SEASONS OF THE ECCLESIASTICAL YEAR, from the 'Parochial and Plain Sermons.' *Crown 8vo.* 3s. 6d.

FIFTEEN SERMONS PREACHED BEFORE THE UNIVERSITY OF OXFORD. *Crown 8vo.* 3s. 6d.

SERMONS BEARING UPON SUBJECTS OF THE DAY. *Crown 8vo.* 3s. 6d.

LECTURES ON THE DOCTRINE OF JUSTIFICATION. *Crown 8vo.* 3s. 6d.

*** *A Complete List of Cardinal Newman's Works can be had on Application.*

Osborne.—Works by EDWARD OSBORNE, Mission Priest of the Society of St. John the Evangelist, Cowley, Oxford.

THE CHILDREN'S SAVIOUR. Instructions to Children on the Life of Our Lord and Saviour Jesus Christ. *Illustrated.* 16mo. 2s. net.

THE SAVIOUR KING. Instructions to Children on Old Testament Types and Illustrations of the Life of Christ. *Illustrated.* 16mo. 2s. net.

THE CHILDREN'S FAITH. Instructions to Children on the Apostles' Creed. *Illustrated.* 16mo. 2s. net.

Ottley.—ASPECTS OF THE OLD TESTAMENT: being the Bampton Lectures for 1897. By ROBERT LAWRENCE OTTLEY, M.A., Canon of Christ Church and Regius Professor of Pastoral Theology in the University of Oxford. 8vo. 7s. 6d.

Oxford (The) Library of Practical Theology.—Edited by the Rev. W. C. E. NEWBOLT, M.A., Canon and Chancellor of St. Paul's, and the Rev. DARWELL STONE, M.A., Librarian of the Pusey House, Oxford. *Crown 8vo.* 5s. each.

RELIGION. By the Rev. W. C. E. NEWBOLT, M.A., Canon and Chancellor of St. Paul's.

HOLY BAPTISM. By the Rev. DARWELL STONE, M.A., Librarian of the Pusey House, Oxford.

CONFIRMATION. By the Right Rev. A. C. A. HALL, D.D., Bishop of Vermont.

THE HISTORY OF THE BOOK OF COMMON PRAYER. By the Rev. LEIGHTON PULLAN, M.A., Fellow of St. John Baptist's Oxford.

HOLY MATRIMONY. By the Rev. W. J. KNOX LITTLE, M.A., Canon of Worcester.

THE INCARNATION. By the Rev. H. V. S. ECK, M.A., St. Andrew's, Bethnal Green.

FOREIGN MISSIONS. By the Right Rev. E. T. CHURTON, D.D., formerly Bishop of Nassau.

PRAYER. By the Rev. ARTHUR JOHN WORLLEDGE, M.A., Canon and Chancellor of Truro.

SUNDAY. By the Rev. W. B. TREVELYAN, M.A., Vicar of St. Matthew's, Westminster.

THE CHRISTIAN TRADITION. By the Rev. LEIGHTON PULLAN, M.A., Fellow of St. John's College, Oxford.

BOOKS OF DEVOTION. By the Rev. CHARLES BODINGTON, Canon and Precentor of Lichfield.

HOLY ORDERS. By the Rev. A. R. WHITHAM, M.A., Principal of Culham College, Abingdon.

THE CHURCH CATECHISM THE CHRISTIAN'S MANUAL. By the Rev. W. C. E. NEWBOLT, M.A., Joint Editor of the Series.

[*continued.*

Oxford (The) Library of Practical Theology.—*continued.*
THE HOLY COMMUNION. By the Rev. DARWELL STONE, M.A.,
Joint Editor of the Series. [*In preparation.*
RELIGIOUS CEREMONIAL. By the Rev. WALTER HOWARD
FRERE, M.A., Superior of the Community of the Resurrection,
Examining Chaplain to the Bishop of Rochester. [*In preparation.*
VISITATION OF THE SICK. By the Rev. E. F. RUSSELL, M.A.,
St. Alban's, Holborn. [*In preparation.*
CHURCH WORK. By the Rev. BERNARD REYNOLDS, M.A.,
Prebendary of St. Paul's. [*In preparation.*
OLD TESTAMENT CRITICISM. By the Rev. HENRY WACE, D.D.,
Dean of Canterbury. [*In preparation.*
NEW TESTAMENT CRITICISM. By the Rev. R. J. KNOWLING,
D.D., Professor of New Testament Exegesis at King's College, London.
[*In preparation.*

Paget.—Works by FRANCIS PAGET, D.D., Bishop of Oxford.
CHRIST THE WAY: Four Addresses given at a Meeting of School-
masters and others at Haileybury. *Crown 8vo.* 1s. 6d. net.
STUDIES IN THE CHRISTIAN CHARACTER: Sermons. With an
Introductory Essay. *Crown 8vo.* 4s. net.
THE SPIRIT OF DISCIPLINE: Sermons. *Crown 8vo.* 4s. net.
FACULTIES AND DIFFICULTIES FOR BELIEF AND DIS-
BELIEF. *Crown 8vo.* 4s. net.
THE HALLOWING OF WORK. Addresses given at Eton, January
16-18, 1888. *Small 8vo.* 2s.
THE REDEMPTION OF WAR: Sermons. *Crown 8vo.* 2s. net.

Passmore.—Works by the Rev. T. H. PASSMORE, M.A.
THE THINGS BEYOND THE TOMB IN A CATHOLIC LIGHT.
Crown 8vo. 2s. 6d. net.
LEISURABLE STUDIES. *Crown 8vo.* 4s. net.
CONTENTS.—The 'Religious Woman'—Preachments—Silly Ritual—The Tyr-
anny of the Word—The Lectern—The Functions of Ceremonial—Homo Creator—
Concerning the Pun—Proverbia.

Percival.—THE INVOCATION OF SAINTS. Treated Theo-
logically and Historically. By HENRY R. PERCIVAL, M.A., D.D.
Crown 8vo. 5s.

Powell.—CHORALIA : a Handy-Book for Parochial Precentors
and Choirmasters. By the Rev. JAMES BADEN POWELL, M.A.,
Precentor of St. Paul's, Knightsbridge. *Crown 8vo.* 4s. 6d. net.

Practical Reflections. By a CLERGYMAN. With Preface by
H. P. LIDDON, D.D., D.C.L., and the LORD BISHOP OF LINCOLN.
Crown 8vo.

THE BOOK OF GENESIS. 4s. 6d.	THE MINOR PROPHETS. 4s. 6d.
THE PSALMS. 5s.	THE HOLY GOSPELS. 4s. 6d.
ISAIAH. 4s. 6d.	ACTS TO REVELATION. 6s.

Praeparatio : HOLY DAYS ; or, Notes of Preparation for Holy Communion, founded on the Collect, Epistle, and Gospel. With Preface by the Rev. GEORGE CONGREVE, of the Society of St. John the Evangelist, Cowley.

> SUNDAYS. *Crown 8vo. 6s. net.*
>
> HOLY DAYS AND SAINTS' DAYS. *Crown 8vo. 6s. net.*

Priest's Prayer Book (The). Containing Private Prayers and Intercessions ; Occasional, School, and Parochial Offices ; Offices for the Visitation of the Sick, with Notes, Readings, Collects, Hymns, Litanies, etc. With a brief Pontifical. By the late Rev. R. F. LITTLEDALE, LL.D., D.C.L., and Rev. J. EDWARD VAUX, M.A., F.S.A. *Post 8vo. 6s. 6d.*

Pullan.—Works by the Rev. LEIGHTON PULLAN, M.A., Fellow of St. John Baptist's College, Oxford.

> LECTURES ON RELIGION. *Crown 8vo. 6s.*
>
> THE HISTORY OF THE BOOK OF COMMON PRAYER. *Crown 8vo. 5s. (The Oxford Library of Practical Theology.)*

Puller.—THE PRIMITIVE SAINTS AND THE SEE OF ROME. By F. W. PULLER, of the Society of St. John the Evangelist, Cowley. *8vo. 16s. net.*

Pusey.—Works by the Rev. E. B. PUSEY, D.D.

> PRIVATE PRAYERS. With Preface by H. P. LIDDON, D.D., late Chancellor and Canon of St. Paul's. *Royal 32mo. 1s.*
>
> SPIRITUAL LETTERS OF EDWARD BOUVERIE PUSEY, D.D. Edited by the Rev. J. O. JOHNSTON, M.A., Principal of the Theological College, Cuddesdon ; and the Rev. W. C. E. NEWBOLT, M.A., Canon and Chancellor of St. Paul's. *Crown 8vo. 5s. net.*

Pusey.—THE STORY OF THE LIFE OF DR. PUSEY. By the Author of 'Charles Lowder.' With Frontispiece. *Crown 8vo. 7s. 6d. net.*

Randolph.—Works by B. W. RANDOLPH, D.D., Principal of the Theological College and Hon. Canon of Ely.

> THE EXAMPLE OF THE PASSION : being Addresses given in St. Paul's Cathedral at the Mid-Day Service on Monday, Tuesday, Wednesday, and Thursday in Holy Week, and at the Three Hours' Service on Good Friday, 1897. *Small 8vo. 2s. net.*
>
> THE LAW OF SINAI : Being Devotional Addresses on the Ten Commandments delivered to Ordinands. *Crown 8vo. 3s. 6d.*
>
> MEDITATIONS ON THE OLD TESTAMENT for Every Day in the Year. *Crown 8vo. 5s. net.*
>
> MEDITATIONS ON THE NEW TESTAMENT for Every Day in the Year. *Crown 8vo. 5s. net.*
>
> THE THRESHOLD OF THE SANCTUARY : being Short Chapters on the Inner Preparation for the Priesthood. *Crown 8vo. 3s. 6d.*
>
> THE VIRGIN BIRTH OF OUR LORD : a Paper read (in Substance) before the Brotherhood of the Holy Trinity of Cambridge. *Crown 8vo. 2s. net.*

RIVINGTON'S DEVOTIONAL SERIES.

16*mo*, *Red Borders and gilt edges.* *Each* 2*s. net.*

BICKERSTETH'S YESTERDAY, TO-DAY, AND FOR EVER. *Gilt edges.*

CHILCOT'S TREATISE ON EVIL THOUGHTS. *Red edges.*

THE CHRISTIAN YEAR. *Gilt edges.*

HERBERT'S POEMS AND PROVERBS. *Gilt edges.*

THOMAS À KEMPIS' OF THE IMITATION OF CHRIST. *Gilt edges.*

LEAR'S (H. L. SIDNEY) FOR DAYS AND YEARS. *Gilt edges.*

LYRA APOSTOLICA. POEMS BY J. W. BOWDEN, R. H. FROUDE, J. KEBLE, J. H. NEWMAN, R. I. WILBERFORCE, AND I. WILLIAMS; and a Preface by CARDINAL NEWMAN. *Gilt edges.*

FRANCIS DE SALES' (ST.) THE DEVOUT LIFE. *Gilt edges.*

WILSON'S THE LORD'S SUPPER. *Red edges.*

*TAYLOR'S (JEREMY) HOLY LIVING. *Red edges.*

*—— —— HOLY DYING. *Red edges.*

SCUDAMORE'S STEPS TO THE ALTAR.. *Gilt edges*

LYRA GERMANICA: HYMNS FOR THE SUNDAYS AND CHIEF FESTIVALS OF THE CHRISTIAN YEAR. *First Series. Gilt edges.*

LAW'S TREATISE ON CHRISTIAN PERFECTION. Edited by L. H. M. SOULSBY. *Gilt edges.*

CHRIST AND HIS CROSS: SELECTIONS FROM SAMUEL RUTHERFORD'S LETTERS. Edited by L. H. M. SOULSBY. *Gilt edges.*

* *These two in one Volume.* 5*s.*

18*mo*, *without Red Borders.* *Each* 1*s. net.*

BICKERSTETH'S YESTERDAY, TO-DAY, AND FOR EVER.

THE CHRISTIAN YEAR.

THOMAS À KEMPIS' OF THE IMITATION OF CHRIST.

HERBERT'S POEMS AND PROVERBS.

SCUDAMORE'S STEPS TO THE ALTAR.

WILSON'S THE LORD'S SUPPER.

FRANCIS DE SALES' (ST.) THE DEVOUT LIFE.

*TAYLOR'S (JEREMY) HOLY LIVING.

*—— —— HOLY DYING.

* *These two in one Volume.* 2*s. 6d.*

Robbins.—Works by WILFORD L. ROBBINS, D.D., Dean of the General Theological Seminary, New York.

AN ESSAY TOWARD FAITH. *Small 8vo.* 3*s. net.*

A CHRISTIAN APOLOGETIC. *Crown 8vo.* 2*s. 6d. net.* (*Handbooks for the Clergy.*)

Robinson.—Works by the Rev. C. H. ROBINSON, M.A., Editorial Secretary to the S.P.G. and Canon of Ripon.

STUDIES IN THE CHARACTER OF CHRIST. *Crown 8vo.* 3*s. 6d.*

HUMAN NATURE A REVELATION OF THE DIVINE: a Sequel to 'Studies in the Character of Christ.' *Crown 8vo.* 6*s. net.*

SOME THOUGHTS ON THE INCARNATION. *Crown 8vo.* 1*s. 6d. net.*

Romanes.—THOUGHTS ON THE COLLECTS FOR THE TRINITY SEASON. By ETHEL ROMANES, Author of 'The Life and Letters of George John Romanes.' With a Preface by the Right Rev. the LORD BISHOP OF LONDON. 18*mo.* 2*s. 6d.* ; *gilt edges.* 3*s. 6d.*

Sanday.—Works by W. SANDAY, D.D., LL.D., Lady Margaret Professor of Divinity and Canon of Christ Church, Oxford.

THE ORACLES OF GOD : Nine Lectures on the Nature and Extent of Biblical Inspiration and the Special Significance of the Old Testament Scriptures at the Present Time. *Crown 8vo.* 4*s.*

DIFFERENT CONCEPTIONS OF PRIESTHOOD AND SACRIFICE : a Report of a Conference held at Oxford, December 13 and 14, 1899. Edited by W. SANDAY, D.D. *8vo.* 7*s.* 6*d.*

INSPIRATION : Eight Lectures on the Early History and Origin of the Doctrine of Biblical Inspiration. Being the Bampton Lectures for 1893. *8vo.* 7*s.* 6*d.*

Sanders.—FÉNELON : HIS FRIENDS AND HIS ENEMIES, 1651-1715. By E. K. SANDERS. With Portrait. *8vo.* 10*s.* 6*d. net.*

Scudamore.—STEPS TO THE ALTAR: a Manual of Devotion for the Blessed Eucharist. By the Rev. W. E. SCUDAMORE, M.A. *Royal 32mo.* 1*s.*

On toned paper, and rubricated, 2*s.: The same, with Collects, Epistles, and Gospels,* 2*s.* 6*d.* ; 18*mo,* 1*s. net*; *Demy* 18*mo, cloth, large type,* 1*s.* 3*d.*; 16*mo, with red borders,* 2*s. net*; *Imperial* 32*mo, limp cloth,* 6*d.*

Skrine.—PASTOR AGNORUM : a Schoolmaster's Afterthoughts. By JOHN HUNTLEY SKRINE, sometime Warden of Glenalmond, Author of 'A Memory of Edward Thring, etc. *Crown 8vo.* 5*s. net.*

Soulsby.—SUGGESTIONS ON PRAYER. By LUCY H. M. SOULSBY. 18*mo, sewed,* 1*s. net.* ; *cloth,* 1*s.* 6*d. net.*

Stone.—Works by the Rev. DARWELL STONE, M.A., Librarian of the Pusey House, Oxford.

THE INVOCATION OF SAINTS: an Article reprinted, with slight additions, from 'The Church Quarterly Review.' *8vo.* 2*s.* 6*d. net.*

OUTLINES OF MEDITATIONS FOR USE IN RETREAT. *Crown 8vo.* 2*s.* 6*d. net.*

CHRIST AND HUMAN LIFE: Lectures delivered in St. Paul's Cathedral in January 1901 ; together with a Sermon on 'The Fatherhood of God.' *Crown 8vo.* 2*s.* 6*d. net.*

OUTLINES OF CHRISTIAN DOGMA. *Crown 8vo.* 7*s.* 6*d.*

THE INVOCATION OF SAINTS. *8vo.* 2*s.* 6*d. net.*

HOLY BAPTISM. *Crown 8vo.* 5*s.* (*The Oxford Library of Practical Theology.*)

Strong.—Works by THOMAS B. STRONG, D.D., Dean of Christ Church, Oxford.

CHRISTIAN ETHICS: being the Bampton Lectures for 1895. *8vo. 7s. 6d.*

GOD AND THE INDIVIDUAL. *Crown 8vo. 2s. 6d. net.*

AUTHORITY IN THE CHURCH. *Crown 8vo. 2s. 6d. net. (Handbooks for the Clergy).*

Stubbs.—ORDINATION ADDRESSES. By the Right Rev. W. STUBBS, D.D., late Lord Bishop of Oxford. Edited by the Rev. E. E. HOLMES, formerly Domestic Chaplain to the Bishop; Hon. Canon of Christ Church, Oxford. With Photogravure Portrait. *Crown 8vo. 6s. net.*

Waggett.—THE AGE OF DECISION. By P. N. WAGGETT, M.A., of the Society of St. John the Evangelist, Cowley St. John, Oxford. *Crown 8vo. 2s. 6d. net.*

Wakeford.—Works by the Rev. JOHN WAKEFORD, B.D., Vicar of St. Margaret, Anfield, Liverpool.

THE GLORY OF THE CROSS: a Brief Consideration of the Force, Effects, and Merits of Christ's Death and Passion. Sermons delivered in Liverpool Cathedral. *Crown 8vo. 2s. 6d. net.*

INTO THE HOLY OF HOLIES THROUGH THE VAIL OF THE FLESH OF THE ETERNAL HIGH PRIEST, JESUS CHRIST: Prayers and Devotions for Private Use at Home and in Church. *18mo, cloth limp, 9d. net; cloth boards, 1s. net.*

Williams.—Works by the Rev. ISAAC WILLIAMS, B.D.

A DEVOTIONAL COMMENTARY ON THE GOSPEL NARRATIVE. *Eight Vols. Crown 8vo. 5s. each.*

THOUGHTS ON THE STUDY OF THE HOLY GOSPELS.	OUR LORD'S MINISTRY(Second Year).
A HARMONY OF THE FOUR EVANGELISTS.	OUR LORD'S MINISTRY(Third Year).
	THE HOLY WEEK.
OUR LORD'S NATIVITY.	OUR LORD'S PASSION.
	OUR LORD'S RESURRECTION.

FEMALE CHARACTERS OF HOLY SCRIPTURE. A Series of Sermons. *Crown 8vo. 5s.*

THE CHARACTERS OF THE OLD TESTAMENT. *Crown 8vo. 5s.*

SERMONS ON THE EPISTLES AND GOSPELS FOR THE SUNDAYS AND HOLY DAYS. *Two Vols. Crown 8vo. 5s. each.*

Wirgman.—THE DOCTRINE OF CONFIRMATION. By A. THEODORE WIRGMAN, D.D., D.C.L., Canon of Grahamstown, and Vice-Provost of St. Mary's Collegiate Church, Port Elizabeth, South Africa. *Crown 8vo. 3s. 6d.*

Wordsworth.—Works by CHRISTOPHER WORDSWORTH, D.D., sometime Bishop of Lincoln.

THE HOLY BIBLE (the Old Testament). With Notes, Introductions, and Index. *Imperial 8vo.*
Vol. I. THE PENTATEUCH. 25*s.* Vol. II. JOSHUA TO SAMUEL. 15*s.*
Vol. III. KINGS to ESTHER. 15*s.* Vol. IV. JOB TO SONG OF SOLOMON. 25*s.* Vol. V. ISAIAH TO EZEKIEL. 25*s.* Vol. VI. DANIEL, MINOR PROPHETS, and Index. 15*s.*
Also supplied in 13 Parts. Sold separately.

THE NEW TESTAMENT, in the Original Greek. With Notes, Introductions, and Indices. *Imperial 8vo.*
Vol. I. GOSPELS AND ACTS OF THE APOSTLES. 23*s.* Vol. II. EPISTLES, APOCALYPSE, and Indices. 37*s.*
Also supplied in 4 Parts. Sold separately.

CHURCH HISTORY TO A.D. 451. *Four Vols. Crown 8vo.*
Vol. I. TO THE COUNCIL OF NICÆA, A.D. 325. 8*s.* 6*d.* Vol. II. FROM THE COUNCIL OF NICÆA TO THAT OF CONSTANTINOPLE. 6*s.* Vol. III. CONTINUATION. 6*s.* Vol. IV. CONCLUSION, TO THE COUNCIL OF CHALCEDON, A.D. 451. 6*s.*

THEOPHILUS ANGLICANUS : a Manual of Instruction on the Church and the Anglican Branch of it. 12*mo.* 2*s.* 6*d.*

ELEMENTS OF INSTRUCTION ON THE CHURCH. 16*mo.* 1*s.* cloth. 6*d.* sewed.

THE HOLY YEAR : Original Hymns. 16*mo.* 2*s.* 6*d.* and 1*s.* *Limp*, 6*d.*
,,   ,,   With Music. Edited by W. H. MONK. *Square 8vo.* 4*s.* 6*d.*

ON THE INTERMEDIATE STATE OF THE SOUL AFTER DEATH. 32*mo.* 1*s.*

Wordsworth.—Works by JOHN WORDSWORTH, D.D., Lord Bishop of Salisbury.

THE MINISTRY OF GRACE : Studies in Early Church History, with reference to Present Problems. *Crown 8vo.* 6*s.* 6*d. net.*

THE HOLY COMMUNION : Four Visitation Addresses. 1891. *Crown 8vo.* 3*s.* 6*d.*

THE ONE RELIGION : Truth, Holiness, and Peace desired by the Nations, and revealed by Jesus Christ. Eight Lectures delivered before the University of Oxford in 1881. *Crown 8vo.* 7*s.* 6*d.*

UNIVERSITY SERMONS ON GOSPEL SUBJECTS. *Sm. 8vo.* 2*s.* 6*d.*

PRAYERS FOR USE IN COLLEGE. 16*mo.* 1*s.*

5000/11/03.

Edinburgh : T. and A. CONSTABLE, Printers to His Majesty.